A Gathering of Gaines

The Man and the Writer

by Anne K. Simpson

Published by The Center for Louisiana Studies
University of Southwestern Louisiana

ISBN Number: 0-940984-69-5

Library of Congress Catalog Number: 91-71686

Published by The Center for Louisiana Studies
University of Southwestern Louisiana
P.O. Box 40831
Lafayette, LA 70504-0831

A Gathering of Gaines

The Man and the Writer

Contents

ACKNOWLEDGMENTS

Writing this book would not have been possible without the encouragement, support and caring of several people who helped me to do my best on a project which I feel is a worthy addition to the existing publications on Ernest J. Gaines.

These special persons are Bruce Turner, Dupré Library archivist; Glenn R. Conrad, director of the Center for Louisiana Studies, and his staff, Ron Bodin, Carl A. Brasseaux, Flossie Montgomery, and Becky Batiste; Richard and Thetis Cusimano, and Christopher Lyons, my treasured family; Joan Landry, my dear friend and intelligent reader who could also write a book; and Ebba Schoonover, professor of German at USL.

Others to be sincerely thanked are Gary Marotta, the staff of Dupré Library, Michael Maher, F. Ray Mouton, Betty Rankin, Thomas A. Tenney, Helen Whitson, Mary Harper, William Decker, Jason Berry, Madeline Caillet, the Freddie Thomas Foundation, the Lafayette Chamber of Commerce, and the Pointe Coupée Chamber of Commerce, who responded so generously to my needs in preparing this book. I am grateful to each of you.

PREFACE

A Gathering of Gaines attempts a chronological, biographical essay, followed by an objective presentation of ana on Gaines' style and works. Some rather lengthy excerpts from Gaines' speeches of the past twenty years are included, for they reflect his thoughts and attitudes about himself and his writing. This gathering has been compiled in large part from material found in Ernest J. Gaines' personal papers which he donated to Dupré Library at the University of Southwestern Louisiana (USL) in Lafayette, Louisiana. Material not otherwise identified has been drawn from the sources.

Personal and business correspondence, notebooks, scrapbooks, reviews of his books, speeches, news clippings, brochures, a "little black book" with phone numbers and addresses, and handwritten and typed manuscripts of his novels and stories are all within these papers which Gaines was wise enough to keep.

Anyone who reads Gaines' works is aware of his meticulous thought processes in molding and shaping his characters and their actions. There is nothing missing in the fabric of his stories. The myriad mosaic-like pieces that have waited to take their places will all be fitted in. A few of these colorful tiles, jotted as notes, either in a notebook, on a sheet of yellow typing paper, must be shared, for they provide some insight into Gaines' life style, working habits, sense of humor, and above all, his humanness.

Unfortunately, many of the entries are not dated. One, titled "Projects in the future," reads: (1) "The Park" a love story between a dying white girl and a Negro writer takes place in Golden Gate Park. (2) "Merikey" [Merchey?] the story about one of the lost beatniks. She wanted to love everyone. She went about it in a most unconventional way. (3) "A Short Biography" a very old Negro woman has just been buried. Three of her closest friends tell her story. (4) "John Henry" the story of a giant Negro who tries to show everyone how to be a man. (5) "Leaves" a Negro boy, an idiot almost, goes to Bayonne with a bucket of __________ and tramples all over the town with the bucket of __________ trying to get waited on by his doctor. The doctor has told him to come with the specimen but now has no time to wait on him. (6) "The Man who Forgot"—man kills his wife, her lover, then sees the light and regrets, and then contemplates on killing himself. Beside numbers 1, 3 and 4 was written "Books." Another fragment must have been a sentence he planned to use: "Like a car running on bad gas, Bea goes on talking after the conversation is over."

Gaines made a note that "Car 54, Where Are You?" was William Faulkner's favorite television show. Another entry made predictions on the Joe Louis vs. Max Schmeling fight. Still another was a hand printed menu: "Breakfast Saturday and Sunday hotcakes. Monday, Tuesday and Wednesday boil [*sic*] eggs and toast. Thursday and Friday grits and eggs. Lunch sandwiches and a can of soup, hot dogs in beans. Dinner meat twice a week."

The copy of a handwritten poem, a Christmas greeting to "Dee," (Dorothea Oppenheimer) Gaines' literary agent, signed "From Eee," reads: "It's 'bout that time/Though we haven't a dime/To wish those we've chose/To be our friend to the very end. A Merry Christmas and Happy New Year."

In one of the small notebooks Gaines noted the months to plant cotton, corn, cane and when to harvest them, and when to cut wood. He made a list of "flowering shrubs and trees—camellias, azallas [*sic*], magnolia." There are notes on "Angola prison (near Baton Rouge);" "Gris-gris;" and more notes for the beginnings of a story. Other fragments were "corn pone" and "pot liquor," defined as "the juice or liquid in which greens have been cooked with a piece of salt meat or ham." "Pool doo," as Gaines spelled it, is no doubt the south Louisiana black diving duck, the poule d'eau.

Gaines made notes for religious customs: "People marching to the cemetery with candlelight. To patch a burnt hole in your clothes means that some one in the family would die. To prevent losing money, people burnt onion peelings." Of superstitions he wrote: "Birds flying in a circle meant bad weather. If horses ran and jumped for no particular reason, bad weather. Bad luck to get a haircut on Friday. Sneezing at the table meant that someone would die." And about death: "all clocks were stopped at the hour of death; mirrors were covered, and black crepe was hung on the front door." He wrote a question concerning graveyards and the moving of graves: "Can this handful of dust be placed in a metal pail, a shoebox, etc.?"

With the input of Gaines' friend, Professor Alvin Aubert, he compiled a list of "10 or 12 of the most significant things that have happened in LA [Louisiana] since turn of century: WW I, WW II, high water of 1912, Huey Long, Pres. Roosevelt, high water of 1927, Joe Louis, Jackie Robinson, desegregation bill, Depression, Relief, Charity Hospital, Jackson Mental Hospital, Angola State Prison, first automobile, electric lights, the screen porch to keep away mosquitoes which caused yellow fever epidemic of 1909." This list laid the groundwork for *Miss Jane Pittman*, as Gaines continued to gather similar ideas from others, weaving them into his extensive library research.

Other notes were taken, perhaps, as Gaines was making a train trip, for he commented on the snow, dryness of the land, and bodies of dirty water along the way. As an example of how he "listens" he wrote: "A drunk on the train punctuates everything with 'I'm right or wrong? ' or 'That's right or wrong? ' " And of a Swede talking he quotes: "Right? Yes. Sure." Another note says, "Goofy looking baby. Goofy looking parents. Hill people."

Another page in the notebook contained a list of food expenses: "pigtail .63, steak and rice .73, veal steaks .63, fried chicken and rice .75, red beans and rice .45, cabbage .41, yams .93, green lima beans, chitlings .93."

A more introspective reflection bears quoting:

> I write because I must. Because there's something out there that's need to be said. If I don't say it, nobody else might not say it either. By this I mean, who else will write about my part of the country? Who will write about the way my people talk, the way they sing, the way they feel about God, the way they work; their superstitions. There are so many things that can be said about this particular area. Money is not the objective, though I want to make money with my writing. But I want to get self-satisfaction.

And in the same vein another fragment reads:

> Deep down inside—*I know* I don't have anything the world can't do without, but I *think* I have something the world can't do without." And perhaps the most insightful of all: "I believe deep in me that what man and woman want most on this earth is to love each other. And I also believe deep in me that unless we begin to love each other we cannot possibly survive. This is my argument against the separationist, this is my argument against the isolationist. Our world is no longer what our world once was.

INTRODUCTION

Geographers have divided the state of Louisiana into three natural regions: the West Gulf Coastal Plain, the Mississippi Flood Plain, and the East Gulf Coastal Plain, each running lengthwise over the state. Oscar, Louisiana, a small plantation community near the Mississippi River and the state of Mississippi, is in the center of the second of these. River Lake Plantation, a part of Oscar, is the place of Ernest James Gaines' birth. Gaines' fictitious Bayonne is in essence New Roads, Louisiana, a larger town near Oscar and some thirty miles northwest of Baton Rouge, the Louisiana state capital. (Bayonne is actually a family last name of Gaines' stepfather).

Gaines descends from five generations of Creole slaves who formerly lived, worked, died and were buried on River Lake Plantation near False River. Because this river, called "Fausse Rivière" by the French and "Falso Rivera" or "Rio Falso" by the Spanish, was the waterway used as a main source of transportation for the cotton growers in the 1800s, several prominent plantation houses were built along its south side. The twenty-two mile long river, actually a lake, was formed when the Mississippi River changed course and circumvented the bend in the riverbed.

The big River Lake plantation house was built around 1780 on a French land grant issued to Isaac Gaillard. Originally the plantation house had wrap-around galleries, or porches, similar to French houses in the Caribbean, with hand-cut and pegged timbers. The main floor, built over a raised brick basement, was constructed of cypress and bousillage, a mixture of mud and Spanish moss daubed between the timbers. By 1823 River Lake Plantation boasted almost 2,000 acres, a cotton gin, a sugarhouse, two pigeon houses, and thirty slave cabins, one of which would later be Gaines' first home.

In 1892 Purvis Major bought the estate, which has remained with his heirs. The two-and-a-half-storied house is of typical Louisiana colonial style with wide center steps leading to the front gallery. The kitchen wing has recently been restored by the present owners, Mr. and Mrs. Gerald Caillet. River Lake is listed on the National Register of Historic Places, as "the birth place of Pointe Coupée's celebrated Ernest Gaines, the author of *Autobiography of Miss Jane Pittman.*" After *Miss Jane*'s publication the owners of River Lake presented Gaines with a framed collection of coupons, coupons his ancestors were given in place of money, spendable for supplies in the plantation store.

Though slavery in the old sense had gradually given way to a modicum of freedom, obvious remnants of a caste system still remained in the late 1930s when Gaines was a child. Black people were treated with little respect by the plantation whites who manipulated them. Life for the blacks continued to be a struggle, not only for basic necessities, but for personal dignity. Gaines himself says:

> By the 30s, conditions were not too much different from the times of slavery. We were attached to the place. You couldn't move around and do whatever you wanted to do. During the time I grew up, I understood much of what has been written in books about slavery and the reconstruction period, farm life and plantation life. I could never have written *The Autobiography of Miss Jane Pittman* or *A Gathering of Old Men* had I not lived it. But I would not wish it on any other child.[1]

Given this inherent oppression, one marvels that a writer who has to say what Gaines *must* say so seldom allows real violence to erupt. Rather, a sensitive nature resembling his own is reflected in many of his stronger characters. Gaines might have written of violence if he had been raised in New Orleans or a similar city and actually seen it. He said:

> I didn't know a thing about urban life. . . . I came from a place where people sat around and chewed sugar cane and roasted sweet potatoes and peanuts in the ashes and sat on ditch banks and told tales and sat on porches and

[1] Baton Rouge *Morning Advocate*, December 4, 1988.

> went into the swamp and went into the fields—that's what I came from.[2]

Gaines' uncanny insight into human behavior is the result of a depth of understanding of his own ethnic family and their humble beginnings.

Author Ernest J. Gaines is presently a professor of creative writing at the University of Southwestern Louisiana (USL) in Lafayette, Louisiana. To date his publications include miscellaneous short stories, five of which are in *Bloodline* (1968), and five novels: *Catherine Carmier* (1964), *Of Love and Dust* (1967), *The Autobiography of Miss Jane Pittman* (1971), *In My Father's House* (1978), and *A Gathering of Old Men* (1983). His springs and summers are spent in San Francisco, where he maintains an apartment and is free to write and accept speaking engagements. A tall, well built man, he is often seen wearing a beret. He has a wonderful smile and a soft, pleasant, cultured voice. In his large brown eyes which shine when he speaks one detects a wisdom and pride. Ernest Gaines knows who he is.

[2] Carl Wooten and Marcia Gaudet, "Talking with Ernest J. Gaines," *Callaloo*, XI (Spring, 1988), 231.

PART I

A NON-CRITICAL BIOGRAPHY

BEGINNINGS

In Gaines' possession are treasured photos which he took of his family's modest plantation cabin ("the sixth house down the road"), the surrounding cotton and cane fields, the River Lake plantation house, and False River, where the five generations of his family fished and drew water. (See Appendix 1.) Both of Gaines' parents worked in the sugarcane fields on River Lake Plantation. Adrian, his mother, was sixteen when she gave him birth in a small cabin, on January 15, 1933. The gray, unpainted wooden shack with its tin roof, sagging porch, garden, and clothesline, was no different from the others in the Quarters. It had no electricity, no running water, no inside plumbing. It has since been razed by tractors. At least one of the old cabins, however, has been restored by the Louisiana State University School of Architecture and moved to a museum site just a few miles northwest of River Lake.

Ernest James Gaines was the first of twelve children, nine boys and three girls, seven of whom were by Gaines' father who left the family when Gaines and his siblings were still very young. Though Gaines does not explain his father's departure, he has said that such a situation was not uncommon at that time. A man who left his family need not have been an irresponsible person, but more often one who could no longer tolerate working in the sharecropper system. Gaines' mother subsequently took a job in New Orleans, and later remarried. Her children stayed on the plantation with a physically crippled great aunt, Miss Augusteen Jefferson, Gaines' mother's father's sister. Miss Augusteen was one of the older people who tended children while the more able ones of the family toiled in the fields.

By the age of eight Gaines himself was working in the fields for fifty cents a day. Though he was a rather withdrawn child, he sometimes played games with the other children, but more often took long walks alone, picking blackberries and other seasonal edibles along the way. At twelve he was sent to the swamps, a dismal area of the plantation too undesirable for the white Cajun sharecroppers to farm. Since these Cajuns had the "forward land," they were the major competitors of the black sharecroppers. Despite this situation which made a deep impression on the young Gaines, in retrospect he has not failed to see a bit of humor in the Cajun versus black situation. In 1969 he said:

> The people you make fun of more are the people who are closer to you. So when my people had to make fun of something, when they had to laugh, they made fun of the whites. You always make fun of your competitors. They are the people very close to you. And we had this relationship all the time.
>
> I saw these people, the Cajuns, every day; we went to the same store, but we could not drink in the same room. They didn't allow that. But we bought our food at the same place, and we talked to each other going to and from the fields. All this was going on. And the Cajuns have this distinct way of speaking, with this French accent, it's a broken accent. Of course, we could not speak English any better than they could speak French, but we thought they sounded very funny. And I suppose when my own people would speak French using the Creole accent, we sounded as foolish and funny to the Cajuns as they did to us. But still we laughed, and I'm sure they laughed at us also.[1]

Gaines elaborated further on this situation in an interview in 1979, published in USL's *Southwestern Review*.

> The same Cajun family who were share cropping there when my uncles were, when I was coming up, they

[1]Gregory Fitzgerald, "An Interview: Ernest J. Gaines," *The New Orleans Review*, I (1969), 333; Copyright © 1970 by Loyola University, New Orleans. Reprinted by permission of the *New Orleans Review*.

> are the people who now are leasing the entire plantation. They made a heck of a lot of money . . . enough money that they could demand and get better machinery. And, of course, blacks started out having the worst of the land, or the land that was not as productive as the Cajuns had, the whites had. Those blacks who had better land than some of the other blacks, produced better crops and lasted longer. It was obvious whenever there was a problem between us the whites had the advantage . . . . 'Damn those Cajuns,' is what is said. . . . You've got to find a scapegoat. And in the case of the people where I come from, if the scapegoat was white, then he was a Cajun. That's all there is to it, whether he *was* Cajun or not. He *was* our competitor. The blacks have been put in the position of being the scapegoat in most of this country and especially in the southern part of the United States.[2]

Gaines says that when he comes back to the plantation area to visit, his people still have some sort of feeling about the Cajuns along the river. He does not try to romanticize anybody, blacks or Cajuns, or any of their situations, but puts down what people feel, what they think. In actuality the Cajuns had to fight the Creole plantation owners. But Gaines thinks that readers would prefer hearing about the Cajuns as a happy, music-making group.

Gaines termed his relationships with the seasoned male swamp workers "tenuous," not as comfortable and relaxed as with the older women and men who visited his Aunt Augusteen's house. The physically crippled Miss Augusteen Jefferson was a remarkable, spirited woman, and one whom Gaines called "the greatest person, the strongest person I ever knew." This precious woman always remained a dear treasure to him. He felt that she loved him as much as anyone ever could have, and the feeling was mutual. As the oldest child Gaines was considered "man of the house," since his stepfather, Mr. Colar, was rarely with the family at Miss Augusteen's.

[2]"An Interview with Ernest J. Gaines, September 22, 1978," *The Southwestern Review,* IV (1979), 37.

The exact cause of Miss Augusteen's ailment was not diagnosed, though one possibility was that as an infant she had been accidentally dropped and thereby irreparably injured. She was paralyzed from the legs down, but her arms, hands, and upper body were very strong. Since she could not walk, she crawled as energetically as would a healthy infant, pulling herself across the house floor and yard. She chose to completely ignore a welfare-donated wheelchair, which soon became a plaything for the Gaines children. She cooked on a wood stove, sewed on a treadle machine, working the pedal with her hands, did the washing with a tin washboard and bar soap, ironed, and even made a garden with a shortened hoe. Gaines loves to write about the earth, probably because Miss Augusteen loved putting her hands in the dirt while gardening. As if there were not enough chores, in the fall Miss Augusteen crawled about under the pecan trees with a keen eye, picking up their nuts for shelling.

The children gave her full support, bringing her the cooking ingredients, the clothes to wash and iron, and the garden tools. When they misbehaved, she was quite capable of whipping them hard with a switch which they cut to the size she ordered, depending on the seriousness of the crime. They would dutifully kneel in dread for her punishment. The discipline which Gaines received was a far cry from that of today's parents. He was taught to respect old people, and never to insult anyone, for fear of getting a beating by that person, and another at home for causing an incident.

Miss Augusteen, born around the turn of the century, lived until 1952. Among other family dedications of *The Autobiography of Miss Jane Pittman* was one to Miss Augusteen "who did not walk a day in her life but who taught me the importance of standing." Gaines says that his older women characters are not based literally on his aunt, though her moral strength appears in many of them. They were the women who got on with what they had to do, with no time for self pity. Because of Miss Augusteen's strength and courage, Gaines expects a great deal of himself. He allows no excuses for failure to make something meaningful of the "twenty-six letters," the tools of his trade with which he works.

Speaking of his aunt, Gaines told an interviewer for *Essence* in 1975,

> I know the kind of burden she carried trying to raise us and I feel any character I write about has to have a burden. The main character has to have a heavy burden, one that can knock the average person down; sometimes it does, but he has to get up. This is the philosophy I have, if I have any at all, because of the struggle of my aunt, the struggle of my race, the struggle of people in general. Any person who's worth a goddamn must really struggle.[3]

In addition to the strong figures of his mother and Miss Augusteen, Gaines grew up near his maternal grandmother, Julia McVay, who worked for over twenty years as a cook at the big River Lake plantation house. Gaines has called this sturdy lady, who was 80 percent white and a master of Creole cooking, "the greatest cook that ever lived." She was careful to keep up her burial insurance in order to be interred on the plantation with her predecessors. Much like Miss Jane, no job was too hard for her. Six days before Mrs. McVay died of cancer in 1971 she tried to walk to the hospital, but became too weak. She had to call a cab to take her there, where she admitted herself. Gaines' paternal grandfather, like Felix in "Bloodline," was the plantation's yard and repair man who cleaned and kept the tools in shape.

EARLY EDUCATION

If Negro children stayed on the plantation long enough, they were almost certain to get schooling through the eighth grade, but for Gaines, a youngster of unusual curiosity and native intelligence, this modest benefit proved haphazardly unsatisfactory and inadequate. School, held five days a week in the plantation's small Negro church, usually began in October

[3]Tom Carter, "Ernest Gaines," *Essence* (July, 1975), 52-53, 71-72.

after most of the crops were in, and continued until time for spring planting in April. Some years there were only five months of elementary classes. All children of sharecroppers were required to work in the fields during planting and harvesting months.

The church/school, which Gaines attended until he was twelve, had no inside toilet, no chairs, no desks, only the pews or benches used for church services. In order to write the students either used their laps, or got down on their knees and wrote on the pews. Drinking water was drawn from the well, and wood was hauled by the students to burn for heat. The student/teacher ratio was abysmal, and black teachers' salaries, paid by the white school board, were only a fraction of those paid the white teachers. Twice a year the white superintendent made a cursory visit to the plantation school. (This church building is still standing.)

* * *

In retrospect Gaines has recognized that a vital part of his education came from oral tradition. Curiously, some of the first words he remembers hearing were church hymns. Perhaps their rhythmic appeal subconsciously caught his attention. Since there was no radio or television in Miss Augusteen's cabin, family and visitors entertained themselves by telling stories. Because Miss Augusteen could not go out, visitors came to her. Gaines listened and remembered as they talked, as they "talked" stories, and stored these tales away in his head to be molded and mixed with his own imagination for future use. The most talking would take place at a gathering following a wedding or funeral, when twenty or more years of events might be rehashed in conversations, some of them obvious repetitions with embellishments.

In a speech at Southern University in Baton Rouge (1971), Gaines elaborated on the conversations at the cabin.

> Then there were the people who used to come to our house, because she [Augusteen] was crippled and could not go to theirs. In summer they would sit out on the

> porch, the gallery—'the garry,' we called it—and they would talk for hours. Sometimes there would be only one other person besides my aunt; other times maybe a half dozen. Sometimes they would sew on quilts and mattresses while they talked; other times they would shell pecans and beans while they talked. Other times they would just sit there smoking pipes, chewing pompee and drinking coffee while they talked. I, being the oldest child, was made to stay close by and serve them coffee or water or whatever else they needed. In winter they moved off the porch and sat beside the fireplace and drank coffee—and sometimes a little homemade brew—while they talked. But regardless of what time of year it was, under whatever conditions, they would find something to talk about. I did not know then that twenty or twenty-five years later I would try to put some of this talk in a book which I would title *The Autobiography of Miss Jane Pittman.*

Too, there was much talk on the river bank, especially during cane season, and around the fireplace at night. The flood of 1927 and Huey Long's assassination in 1935 were popular topics, both indoors and out.

Gaines denies that he is a storyteller, as such, despite his backlog of tales. When asked if he considered himself a humorist he replied:

> I don't tell jokes. Whenever I do tell a joke no one laughs . . . . I think I am more of a listener, really. I listen. I like to listen to the way that people talk, and I like to listen to their stories. Then when I get into a little room some place . . . I go to my little desk, and try to write something down. But I'm no story-teller. I'm only a listener.[4]

He said more on the subject in his address to the Modern Language Association meeting in 1981 in Los Angeles.

[4]Fitzgerald, "An Interview," 333.

There are several good story tellers in my family. My brother Lionel is very good, one of the best story tellers I know, and my brother Charles is good, and my mother is good, too. And she can also sing. I've heard that my grandfather could tell good stories, and one of my great-grandfathers was a big rascal, so it was necessary at times to tell big lies to get out of bigger trouble. Story telling and music (but no professionals) it seems have been in the family for as long back as anyone can remember, according to Pete [Walter Zeno.]

Pete was this old man who lived on the plantation for ninety years. He knew my people, five generations of them, and he told me they were great liars—he didn't use story telling—as I'm doing now—he said great liars. And he also knew the ones in the family who liked music. He could name them, and he could name who could beat who singing.

Well, we buried Pete in May [1981]. Two days before he died I was talking to him. . . . He had over twenty-five children . . . and over 84 grandchildren that we could count. . . . He was a great story teller, because he knew so much about the old people, and how it had been long, long ago. I used him as a helper-outer for *Miss Jane*. He used to tell me how the people used to sing. Because on this plantation was a church, and no matter where you were you could hear the people at the church singing. And of course the people sang in the field while they worked, and he used to tell me about that, too.

I wrote letters for the old people and I read the letters they received, and I read the Bible and the comic strips, and I ordered from Sears Roebuck and Montgomery Ward catalogues for them. But I remember most writing their letters for them. They could never get it down right. Letter-right, I mean. They would talk and talk but it would not be the way you put it down on a letter. That's another thing about the writer—he must be a form-a-lizer. He must be able to put it down right, readable. He must be able to sift through, catch the

> essence. It would've been better, I'm sure, if the old people could just talk to one another and not have to worry about letter writing, depending on somebody like me. But that was impossible. . . . Someone had to write for them. I was paid nickels and dimes and tea cakes.

By the third grade Gaines was more educated than the older folks would ever be. Often in his own words as he wrote and re-wrote, he helped them phrase the letters to say exactly what was intended and to make it literate enough to suit himself. He would write on a narrow tablet with a pencil and then read it back to them. They would ask him to "Tell Viney" or "Tell Aunt Clara I'm all right," and similar messages. His imagination and learning skills were put to good use by Miss Augusteen and others who called on him not only to write and read letters for them, but to read the newspaper to them as well. They depended on him in many ways, and looked up to "E. J." or "Jay," as they called him. Young Gaines felt that he was expected to make something of himself, that he had been singled out by his people as somebody that would do something special.

Miss Augusteen spoke some Creole, thereby communicating with the older Creole men and women who came to visit. Young Gaines absorbed the sounds of this patois, as well as that of the Negroes and the Cajuns. Another aunt who sold cosmetics often took Gaines with her to parts of Pointe Coupée and West Baton Rouge parishes. He recalls,

> I met all these people who put these things on their faces and made themselves smell sweet, and they spoke French because my aunt spoke Creole. . . . A writer from North Louisiana would not have had the same experiences I had in South Louisiana. I never think of myself as number one a black writer, quote black, or Louisiana black, but as a writer who happens to draw from his environment what his life is, what his heritage is.[5]

[5]Carl Wooton and Marcia Gaudet, "Talking with Ernest Gaines," *Callaloo,* XI (1988), 234-235.

* * *

One summer afternoon when he was twelve, Gaines was baptized in False River by the Baptist preacher, and though he began attending a Catholic school for blacks at about this time, he was not particularly attracted to nor swayed by either religion. The same year of the baptism his budding creativity blossomed in the form of some short plays, which were presented at the church. Like Jimmy's play in *Miss Jane Pittman*, Gaines' presentation was humorous. His favorite subject was mock weddings with himself as the minister and hissing prompter for forgotten or flubbed script. Most of the roles were played by his siblings, who were made up with black and white shoe polish and given funny lines.

Gaines later described these early efforts at writing to an interviewer for the *New Orleans Review* in 1973:

> I can go back to when I was 13 or 14, and remember that I put on little plays and all. I put them on in this church, and I had to rewrite everything. Not only did I have to rewrite, but I had to be the director. I had something like a little mock-wedding going on. My back was toward the audience and the people who were getting married—and the best men and all—faced the audience, I had my script over the Bible, and I would read my part, because I never learned the damned part. So that's the way I started trying to write from the time I was about 13 years old.[6]

By the time Gaines was a teenager and had begun to write, he was convinced that religion neither prevented problems nor solved them, though he always felt it important to believe in something higher than oneself.

[6]Forrest Ingram and Barbara Steinberg, "On the Verge: An Interview with Ernest J. Gaines," *The New Orleans Review*, III (1973), 344; © 1970 by Loyola University, New Orleans. Reprinted by permission of the *New Orleans Review*.

For three years before leaving River Lake Plantation Gaines attended St. Augustine, the middle school originally opened for Catholic Negro children in New Roads in 1932. Preceding the school's founding had been the establishment of the St. Augustine Mission, due to the efforts of Father E. P. Hartnett some ten years earlier. When Father Hartnett first arrived in New Roads he found no house, no school, no church and no money. For the following two years he conducted his church duties in St. Mary's Church, a kindness allowed him by its pastor, Father John Hoes, who also housed him in the rectory. Until St. Augustine was established classes for the children in religion, writing, reading, and arithmetic were held in the rectory. As the enrollment grew, the need for a larger plant was apparent. Plans were soon begun to build a school to which many northern benefactors contributed.

Initially there were three classrooms, three lay teachers, and 120 Catholic children. Teachers' salaries were paid with tuition and generous donations from benefactors. By the time Gaines entered St. Augustine in 1945, however, the enrollment was obviously no longer limited to Catholic children. Though he conformed to the school's discipline by going to Mass, he was not required to take the Holy Sacrament nor go to confession.

Gaines recalls that the school bus would not go the extra distance to pick up students who lived as far away as River Lake. Many a time, in order to attend school, he stood on the riverbank hitchhiking or caught a ride on the little country bus that passed. Sometimes the sheriff of Pointe Coupée Parish, whom Gaines remembers fondly, would give him a lift to school. Once he offered to give the sheriff a shoe shine to pay for the rides, but the sheriff appreciatively declined.

By 1951 the Sisters of the Holy Ghost had taken over the teaching at St. Augustine. The school grew and prospered until 1969 when the parochial schools were integrated and it became a part of Catholic Elementary and High School of Pointe Coupée. But when Gaines left the plantation in 1948 there was no high school for blacks in New Roads, nor admittance to its public library, which establishment now has an autographed copy of one of Gaines' books. It appeared as if the blacks, who knew nothing except working in the fields, would have no use for a full education, either in Pointe Coupée Parish or elsewhere. Finally, in 1951, three years after Gaines had left River Lake, the first parish high school for blacks, four-room Rosenwald, opened in New Roads. It was built almost entirely with funds from black organizational groups and tax monies raised by both blacks and whites.

Recreational activities for blacks on the plantation were limited and restricted. But Gaines found his own escape in the natural beauty of the plantation, where he ran, played, fished, and blew off steam. Too, he made occasional trips with friends to New Roads, "the big city," to see cowboy movies on Friday nights.

HEADING FOR A NEW LIFE

It was now time for young Gaines to go, time to begin a new experience. In 1948, when he was fifteen, having finished the eighth grade at St. Augustine, he left River Lake. As the oldest, he would be the first of the children to join his mother and stepfather in Vallejo. He said:

> Not all kids had the chances I had. It was luck. Those who stayed here [on the plantation], most ended up with very little education, not going to high school at all. Some were luckier. Some could go to high school and some went on to Southern University or to a university in New Orleans.

Gaines values education highly, disputing the idea that a hard life is a good one, though admitting that it gave him thought and material for writing.

He continues, regarding the school situation in Pointe Coupée Parish:

> I'm pretty sure the talent I had was average. I knew kids there who were athletic, who would have been great baseball players or fighters or actors or maybe writers or stand-up comedians, or singers. They never got a

> chance living in a place like that. . . . I hope it [the hard life] never happens again to anyone. Even when I was growing up there I never thought it was the worst sort of life because everybody else around me was the same way. Everybody was poor, wore the same clothes, ate the same food, went to school five months, did the same work. That was life. But the older people always thought it was something else and wanted me to do other things.[7]

Actually, at that time, gifted young blacks were either ignored or considered dangerous; if they spoke up or deviated in any way from their racial plantation stereotype, they could easily be killed. Though some of Gaines' younger brothers and sisters did not finish an education, his half-siblings born in California did, and have seen that their own children attended school.

Years later Gaines vividly described the poignant occasion of his departure from River Lake to journalist Ruth Laney. It could easily be a scene in one of his works. Well supplied with Miss Augusteen's good food, layered in bags between his scanty wardrobe in a battered suitcase, he was overcome with mixed feelings.

> I remember the day I left. It was Sunday. It took me all day to pack, unpack, and repack the old brown leather suitcase. I didn't have many clothes . . . but for some reason I could not get it done. Maybe it was the bag of oranges, or the shoebox of fried chicken and bread, or the tea cakes and pralines wrapped in brown paper, or the bag of unshelled pecans—maybe it was one of these or all of these that kept me opening and shutting the suitcase. But, finally, I got it done and came out onto the porch. Everybody was there: the old people on the porch talking to my aunt and the children in the yard waiting for me to come down the steps so they could follow me to the road. I went to each one of the old people, shook their hands, and

[7]Steve Culpepper and Mary Broussard, "Writer Draws on Pointe Coupée Childhood," *Sunday Advocate,* December 4, 1988.

> listened to their advice on how to live 'up North.'
>
> Then I went to my aunt [Augusteen]. She sat on the floor—just inside the door. 'I'm going, Aunty,' I said. I did not lean over to kiss her—though I loved her more than I have loved anyone else in my life. I did not take her hand, as I had taken the other people's hands, because that would have been the most inappropriate thing in the world to do. I simply said, 'I'm going, Aunty.' She looked up at me from the floor. I saw the tears in her eyes. She nodded her head, and looked down again. When I came out into the road, I looked back at her. I waved and smiled; she waved back. The old people were silent all this time—but I'm sure that before I reached the highway to catch the bus they were talking again.[8]

He flagged down a Trailways bus headed for New Orleans, where he would use the train ticket sent by his mother and stepfather to get to Crockett, California, across the bay from Vallejo. Gaines' stepfather, Ralph Norbert Colar, Sr., had once worked on Parlange Plantation, not far from River Lake. He later became a merchant seaman and contributed to the support of Gaines and his younger siblings. In 1947 Gaines' mother moved with him to Vallejo, California, near San Francisco, where she worked in a military plant. (The majority of Adrian Gaines Colar's twelve children, five of whom were by Mr. Colar, still live in the Bay Area.)

* * *

Gaines' first California home was in government project housing where he readily found friends of all ethnic groups—white, black, Mexican, Filipino, Japanese, and Chinese, who had moved into the area after WW II. He heard a variety of languages, and was exposed to different conversations,

[8]Ruth Laney, "The Last One Left," Baton Rouge *Sunday Advocate Sunday Magazine*, October 30, 1983, p. 7.

concerning everything from food to school and family problems. He realized now that people could not be categorized as simply black or white, but that a combination of people made the world go around. He considered himself lucky not to have moved to a place like southside Chicago, Harlem, or even Watts, California, where he might have been swallowed in a large black ghetto.

Gaines recalls his feelings at the time:

> I made friends quite easily, and most of the time, especially during the day, I was very happy. But at night when the new friends had gone, I sat alone in a room and thought about home. Many times I wished that my aunt would write my mother and tell her to send me back. Or that some wise man would come up and tell me how futile an education was when I had to sacrifice so much for it.[9]

Seldom at home because of his profession, Gaines' strong, handsome stepfather, Mr. Colar, was also a wise and strict parent who commanded the utmost respect. The family soon moved to Vallejo, first to old Carquinez Heights and later to the 200 block of Florida Street. Though at the time Vallejo was integrated, it was a typical rowdy navy town. Gaines' friends here were not as plentiful, nor as wholesome. He ran for a short time with some rough, trouble bound boys. Mr. Colar soon advised him to abandon the gang, get off the streets, and spend his time exploring the library. Since Gaines had worked out at the YMCA long enough to get "punched around a bit" in a "dismal session with boxing gloves," he was willing to see if librarians were a gentler breed.

This was an important beginning for young Gaines who had previously read no more than two novels. The Vallejo library proffered a whole new world in which to broaden himself. He recalls having checked out two to three dozen books during the first month after receiving his library card. At first he chose books indiscriminately, maybe just because he liked their dust jackets. But when schoolwork got heavier, as well as the

[9]Gaines' 1971 speech at Southern University.

carrying of the books, he selected only those he knew he would read.

Reading became his passion, just as writing fiction was to be his passion later. He resented the stereotyped "bad nigger" character drawn by witless writers, preferring instead their descriptions of a barking dog, a distant train whistle, the red dust in Georgia, the black mud of Mississippi, and the smells of rain, a wet dog, or sweaty clothing on a field worker. With those he could well identify. He knew that this was the sort of thing that would appeal to him if he were a writer, the sort of thing that he would choose to express.

"I didn't know what books to read. I read anything at first," Gaines has frequently said to interviewers. Within a few months he realized that he preferred reading about rural life in the South, but literature was limited. Moreover, there were no books available by or about blacks. In his loneliness to identify with the blacks he had known, he continued to read all authors who had written about rural life. Gradually a thread emerged. He read, studied, wrote, and began to understand, to clarify questions about himself in relation to his ethnic past.

After reading all the Southern writers whose works were in the Vallejo library, Gaines selected those who wrote about nature or people who worked the land. This is when he discovered John Steinbeck and the Salinas Valley, Willa Cather and her Nebraska, and others who would say something about the dirt of the earth, trees, clear streams and the infiniteness of the sky.

Soon Gaines found Hemingway, Faulkner, Twain, and then Turgenev, Tolstoy, Chekov, Joyce and De Maupassant, all of whom were to influence his own writing style strongly in various ways. Reading was a definite improvement over hanging out with the gang, or getting punched around at the gym.

By the time Gaines was sixteen, lonely for his people in Louisiana, he was certain that he wanted to be a writer, to write about them as he knew them. He later expressed these feelings to Gregory Fitzgerald:

> When I went to California . . . I was terribly lonely for my friends and relatives. . . . I read and read, but I did

> not see myself and my friends and family and relatives in the stuff that I did read. I didn't see us in the Southern writers. I didn't even see myself in the Russian writers, although the Russians came close. So I began to try to do it myself and of course, I went back to my childhood to write about. I suppose that most writers, when they first start out try to write about their childhood, and this is what I did.[10]

Suspecting that his step-father lovingly thought he was a little crazy, he nevertheless began his first novel, one long aborning, which would eventually become *Catherine Carmier*. He worked at it twelve, sometimes fifteen hours a day, writing by hand on yellow typing paper. Then on a rented typewriter, using two fingers, sometimes one when exhaustion overtook him, he completed the novel to his satisfaction. He does not recall whether it was single or double spaced. He cut the pages down to book size, wrapped the sheets, tied the parcel with string, and mailed it to a New York publishing house. He has told interviewers:

> I thought you just sent it [a manuscript] to them and they put it between covers and it was a book. It came back in that same old string, too. I figure they must have shaken and smelled it and been afraid to try. When they found that it was not food, they probably played football with it a couple of weeks, then decided to send it back to me.

A rejection slip was enclosed with the manuscript. (He does not recall whether it was pink, blue or yellow.) Gaines' disappointment was inconsolable. In an undated draft of a speech, ca. early 1970s, Gaines said of the experience: "I had visioned thousands of dollars, a nice place to live, a car, clothes, money to send back home to my younger brothers and sisters. I was let down, but I was determined to go on. I had only lost the first battle, not the war—at least not yet." Page by page he

[10]Fitzgerald, "An Interview: Ernest J. Gaines," 333.

burned the manuscript in the incinerator. Shortly after this first failure, he persuaded his mother to buy him a used typewriter, which he proceeded to work away on, continuing to use the two-finger system. (In 1964, some sixteen years later, a much reworked version of his first manuscript emerged as *Catherine Carmier*, Gaines' first published novel).

THE MATURING GAINES

After graduation from high school in 1951 Gaines enrolled at Vallejo Junior College, the first male in his family to enter college. While there he received numerous track letters and awards, having set a record for the 220-yard dash which stood twenty years. But during his athletic activities he injured a knee badly, a situation which still prevents any involvement in strenuous sports. In 1953 he received an Associate of Arts in Journalism from Vallejo Junior College (now Solano College).

That same year he was drafted into the army, and served a two-year stint in Guam. He wrote of his experiences with the military but was not pleased with the results. In an interview in Lafayette in 1983 Gaines says of Guam, "I was there physically, but I wasn't there spiritually. Spiritually, I'm still in Louisiana. Early life is the most important part."

In an undated speech among Gaines' papers he comments further on his writing efforts while in the military, admitting that he preferred softball, pool, and pinochle to the tedious and confining process of writing a novel. However, while he was on Guam, one of his short stories was selected for a second prize ($15), one which later got honorable mention ($10) in a GI competition by the US Far East Command in Japan. He said,

> I cashed the ten dollar check but the fifteen dollar check is at the house in a little glass bank that belonged to my aunt [Augusteen] who died on that Louisiana plantation in 1952. After her death, the little glass bank with a few coins were given me to remember her by. I put the check in the bank when I was discharged from the Army in 1955, and it's been there ever since, because in

> order to get it out I would have to break the bank open, and that I'll never do.

Neither has Gaines been pleased with what he has written about California. The *San Francisco Examiner*, June 20, 1978, quoted him as saying, chuckling: "Everything I have written with a California subject has not been published. Maybe after I am dead they [the writings] can be put in a collection so students can look at them." For subject matter Gaines has always preferred to draw from his early years on the plantation, where he has returned periodically since the early 1960s, still considering Louisiana the most romantic and interesting of all the states.

* * *

Immediately after military discharge Gaines enrolled at San Francisco State College, taking advantage of the $110 per month offered on the GI Bill. Gaines recalls his first days there in an undated speech:

> When I entered San Francisco State College in the fall of '55 and told my advisor I wanted to be a writer, he asked me what else I wanted to do. I told him nothing else. He broke down the percentage of those people who made a living writing—and it was frightening. My being black, he said, the chances of making a living writing would be much harder. I told him I didn't care how hard it would be, I couldn't think of anything else I wanted to do. He saw that I was not going to change my mind and he said, 'You can't study writing here because you cannot get a degree in writing. And in order to stay in college on the GI Bill you must work toward a degree. Well?'
>
> I must have rubbed my chin, then. People usually do when they're making such decisions. 'What's the closest thing to writing? ' I said, after I had rubbed by chin two or three times. 'I would say English,' he said.

> 'When you fail at writing you can always teach English.' 'Give me that,' I said. 'You'll need a minor,' he said. 'What goes good with English? ' I asked. 'For a writer I would suggest History or Social Studies,' he said. 'Well, sign me up for one of them,' I said, without rubbing my chin. 'Listen,' he said, seeing that I was being sarcastic. 'Don't let me force anything on you.' 'I'll take Social Studies,' I said.

Gaines majored in English and minored in Social Studies and remembers suffering most of his first year. But compensation came from his introduction to good writing and other students who were likewise hoping to be writers. At the time, 1955, San Francisco State had classes in creative writing, poetry, drama, the novel, and the short story, but no Bachelor of Arts in creative writing was offered. Gaines and his fellow students were taught to read such exemplary authors as Hemingway, Faulkner, O'Conner and Joyce, while writing their own pieces which were read in class and then criticized constructively.

Off campus Gaines, the only black in the writing class of twenty-five, did not run with the fellow students, most of whom were at that time into the hippie movement. This less serious group sat on the beach or on the floor of someone's pad, drinking wine and talking endlessly about writing. Gaines preferred to be by himself, thinking, writing, and thriving on any encouragement given by his professors, most of whom obviously felt him superior, took an interest in him, and gave him extra help.

He hoped to show his younger siblings that he could be successful, an incentive to them to work hard. If he should not make it as a writer, teaching would be a paying and respectable alternative. But he was not doing well in Expository Writing class, taught by Mr. Stanley Anderson, until he submitted a short story, "The Turtles," as a fiction assignment. It concerned a growing young man's first sexual encounter. The story caught the attention of Anderson, who suggested it be named "The Voice of the Turtles." But Gaines stuck to his original title, and "The Turtles" was published in 1956 in the first issue of *Transfer*, San Francisco State's first literary magazine. The following year, 1957, another of Gaines' stories, "Boy in the Double-Breasted Suit," was published in *Transfer*. In this comical piece a widowed father is about to take a new wife, who has taken a shine to his boy.

During his college years Gaines took odd jobs, such as shining shoes, dish washing, and cab driving. Sometimes he thought of himself as a "bum," due to his disinterest in earning money and because he spent every spare moment writing on whatever paper was handy. In an interview with Paul Desruisseaux, Gaines said he really did not want to be a bum, and certainly not a lousy writer, but as he continued to write the more he realized how little he knew about writing. For some months he worked as a night mail clerk, and as mail clerk for an insurance company, during which time he wrote a first draft of "A Long Day in November" on paper towels from the insurance company's men's room. Until interrupted by his supervisor he had written 250 pages of paper towels in two to three weeks.

Besides Anderson, other professors at San Francisco State were impressed enough with "The Turtles" to suggest a New York-based literary agent. Professor Mark Harris contacted Dorothea Oppenheimer, who agreed to help Gaines. "Dee" Oppenheimer, for whom Gaines has maintained the utmost respect, has been his sole agent and has offered editorial help for most of his six books. Gaines knew that this lady knew her business. Though in some of their correspondence she fondly calls him "Old Eee," her detailed letters of recommended revisions indicate that she gently insisted that he meet her professional criteria at all times. Gaines dedicated *Bloodline* in 1968: "For Dee with my deepest love."

Gaines told Desruisseaux,

> She [Oppenheimer] had some long, lean years, I'll tell you that, because there was really nothing much until 1967, so for about eleven years she helped me out a lot, reading my stories, criticizing them, sending them out, getting all the rejection slips and not letting me see

> half of them.[11]

(Oppenheimer has come to Lafayette on occasion, and Gaines' colleagues are cordially received by her when they are in New York, according to USL professor James Wilson.)

AT STANFORD

Shortly before he graduated from San Francisco State in 1957 with a Bachelor of Arts in Language Arts, Gaines was encouraged to submit three stories for the Wallace Stegner Creative Writing Fellowship at Stanford University. Doing so, he received one of the fellowships. Gaines has said that Stegner, one of America's great discoverers of literary talent and later (1972) Pulitzer Prize winner for *Angle of Repose*, could "really smell out promising writers. He found so many of us," for example, Ken Kesey, Wendell Berry and Luis Harss, also on fellowship that year. Tillie Olsen had studied under Stegner two years earlier.

Gaines had barely enough money to support his modest life style without working full time, but these were wonderfully exciting semesters for him. His professors there, including Richard Scowcroft, were genuinely interested in his efforts, and took time to make constructive suggestions. Gaines continued to read, read, and read more—not the latest best-seller trash, but more of his Russian, French, and American favorites.

The Beat Era was imminent. Gaines said:

> All the races . . . shared all kinds of ideas. You'd go into these nightclubs and hear all these different readings of poetry and prose with jazz in the background. . . . Not that I was influenced by the Beat stuff, the Kerouacs and all these kinds of guys. I thought they were all crazy in the first place. But I didn't mind being there to see what they were doing. I sat back and

[11]Paul Desruisseaux, "The Making of Ernest Gaines," *Black Times,* IV (September, 1974), 10.

> watched it. . . . Many of the young black writers, even my age and younger ones, were influenced by the most successful of black novels and that was Richard Wright's *Native Son*. They all tried to imitate this kind of urban thing. I was not urban. . . . Finally I realized, hey man, you gotta be what you are. . . . I think if I'd gone to the eastern part of the country, I probably would have gone into playwriting. My earlier teachers said I had that sense of place, using small areas and then a lot of dialogue and that my whole scenes were place and then dialogue, place and dialogue.[12]

Of his aspirations at the time Gaines said in a speech in November of 1969 at Chapel Hill, North Carolina:

> I wanted to say something that no one else had said, something that no one else talked about. It was inside me. . . . When I wrote stories at San Francisco State and at Stanford I was always told that I had potentialities. Yes, I would do it, but, no, I had not really clicked yet. It would take time. . . . My inside boiling, boiling with impatience to put it down—how much time would it take?

Though he was most appreciative of the direction in good writing which he received at Stanford, he remembers sitting in class "drawing stars." In an undated news item he was quoted:

> They didn't teach me how to write. No one does that. It just helps to have people who are in the same thing to talk to occasionally. It seems to me there is only one thing to do about writing: dig into it. You've got to get in a little room with a desk by yourself and do it. You know? Do it.

But in a later interview with University of Southwestern Louisiana professors Marcia Gaudet and Carl Wooton (cited above), Gaines attributed a good part of his technical writing

[12]Wooton and Gaudet, "Talking with Ernest J. Gaines," 231.

skills to his professors in California. They did not tell him what to write, rather *how* to write it *better*. "I was not pushed with a lot of political ideas [nor] . . . with demands to write about race or anything else. They said write what you want to write about, bring it in and we'll discuss it. And they discussed it more from a technical point of view," Gaines said. This is pretty much the method that Gaines now uses in his own teaching.

In 1973 he said during an interview for the *New Orleans Review*:

> A prof would come by and tell you, hey, that was a good story! Now, that's the greatest thing in the world that can happen. Of course, nobody generally does that until you begin to publish and get some recognition. After I'd gotten some recognition, I got several monetary awards: Guggenheim, Rockefeller, and others. But the teacher, if he's sensitive, if he cares, can be extremely valuable to the student. . . . I would agree that there's no way to teach a writing class to someone who's not interested in writing. To help him at all, I think it would be necessary that he's been writing.[13]

Continuing the subject, Gaines wrote in an undated, untitled page found in his papers:

> What the writer needs most is freedom to do the work that he feels he was put here to do. The fellowship to Stanford gave me that freedom for a year. It also gave me the opportunity to meet other young writers who were having the same problems with their work as I was having with mine. A few of us had published a story or two, but most of us were still waiting for that first one to be accepted. We had begun to feel that there was a conspiracy by magazines against our stories. If there were no such conspiracy, then what were the necessary ingredients to make a story acceptable. Both Wallace Stegner and Richard Scowcroft told us 'Work.' So we

[13]Ingram and Steinberg, "On the Verge," 344.

> went home to our desks and worked, then came back to the lecture room to talk some more. We tore into one another's stories like madmen, but we got no enjoyment from it; because the flaws we found in the other person's story, we saw in ours also. So we went back to our desks to work, to work, and to work some more.

Certainly Gaines' fellow students Ken Kesey, Wendell Berry, Luis Harss, John Christopher Brookhouse, and Tillie Olsen, have made names for themselves as writers. In a speech which Gaines gave in late 1969 in Chapel Hill, North Carolina, at the request of Joe Ritok, Gaines had more to say about these student friends at Stanford:

> It was at Stanford that I met Chris Brookhouse. Many days we had breakfast, lunch and dinner together at Encina Hall. Chris, myself—there must have been a half dozen of us who used to meet and eat at the same table for every meal. I remember one morning while we were eating breakfast—we were having dry cereals. Chris asked me who was my favorite writer. I told him Schultz.

Chris said:

> 'Schultz?' I nodded, 'Schultz.' Chris, I'm sure wanted to know me better, that's why he had asked me the question in the first place. He could see that I was a loner, he could see that even though I was eating with them all the time, being around them all the time, I was not part of the Stanford crowd. But now he looked at me curiously. Here was a guy who had just lucked in at Stanford on a writing fellowship, not academic—and he thinks he's a wiseguy. 'What Schultz?' he said. But before I could answer he had either looked down at his cereal box or he had looked at one of the others sitting at the table. I'm pretty sure Carrie Walls was there. Grove Powell, Ross Brackney—and others. Ross Brackney is the only guy I've ever met who could tell jokes that early

in the morning. I did not answer Chris till he looked at me again. 'Charles Schultz,' I said. 'Peanuts. The best thing in fiction today.' Chris smiled and went on to eat his cereals.

Ken Kesey was at Stanford then. Wendell Berry, a writer from Kentucky was there also. I remember one day Wendell asked me if I hated Whites. I told him no. He did not believe me. He could not understand why I did not. I suppose he had been taught directly or indirectly to hate Blacks and Yankees. Wendell at that time was far from being 'liberal' but he was trying to see things for himself. Still he could not see why I did not hate a Southern White boy sitting in the class with me while in the South the problem to integrate schools made headlines every day. I told him I did not hate him, as a matter of fact he and I had something in common that no Northern White and I could have: and that was the south which was in both our bloods.

I met Wendell only recently at Richard Scowcroft's home at Stanford—Scowcroft is now head of the writing program there—and I found that Wendell had become very liberal, maybe even radical, by Southern standards. I'm leary [*sic*] of liberal Whites, or radical Whites—I've met so many phonies—but I do feel that he had become as liberal in his thinking as he appeared to me that night. He told me that night things that he was trying to do for both races that he could not have imagined ten years ago. I'm sure even if someone had told him this ten years ago he would have denied it possible.

Besides myself, Wendell Berry, and Ken Kesey, another fellow, an Argentinian, by the name of Luis Harss was also there. Of course there were others in the class, but the ones mentioned have gotten some bit of fame or notoriety—especially Ken Kesey.

Now, I mentioned these three other guys and myself because at that time I feel that we were all trying to do the same thing—trying to find something of value in the old people, the old customs, the old ways—the homes we had left. I suppose all except Kesey. At the time he was interested in writing about Bohemia. This was the time of the Beats around San Francisco, or just after the Beats, and Kesey who had come from far away, and not to HIP Oregon, was very much interested in the Beats. His hero at that time was Jack Kerouac, and of course, we know, according to the people who write about Kerouac that he fathered the word 'Beat', or if not the father, the main exponent of it, and that the subject of his works, especially the novel *On the Road* was rediscovering America. The Walt Whitman of his time. When you look at Kesey's *Cuckoo's Nest* and realize that the story is told by a very slick Indian, you can see that Kesey went back even farther than Kerouac in his bid to rediscover America. Wendell Berry was writing about the people of Kentucky, Louis Harss was writing about Argentina, and I, of course, was trying to write about my native Louisiana." [See Appendix 2 for additional material on these writers.]

AFTER STANFORD

In 1959 Dorothea Oppenheimer sent Gaines' stories "Boy in the Double-Breasted Suit" and "The Fight" to *Texas Quarterly*. They were rejected. But that same year Gaines received the Joseph Henry Jackson Award for the "Best Novel in Progress," *Catherine Carmier*. Actually it was an arduous reconstruction of the draft which he burned when he was sixteen. The novel was not published until 1964, for Gaines works methodically without hurrying. Among his papers there are at least ten drafts, or fragments of drafts, of this first novel, which underwent several title changes.

Of the Jackson Award boost, Gaines wrote in an undated speech (c. 1969-70) found in his papers:

> In January of '59 I started writing on 'The Little Stream' book again. Later in the spring I won the Joseph Henry Jackson award for a section of the book [published as *Catherine Carmier*]. After winning this award I felt that the rest of the book should be easy and that I should finish it later that same year. How wrong I was. It turned out that only the first quarter of the book was easy; everything else that followed was but one obstacle after another. My plot was unreal, the dialogue was untrue, and action that I was imposing on my characters was forced. The people and the place were cardboard figures. So everything I wrote one day, I destroyed the next day. Wrote and destroyed, wrote and destroyed.

Gaines was still reading other writers to discover their secrets—Turgenev's *Fathers and Sons* for style; Faulkner for dialogue; Joyce for rhythm and stream of consciousness; Hemingway for clarity and paragraph development, as well as the Bible and Shakespeare. "All of them helped in some way, I suppose, but still I was having the same old problems with my book," he said. "My Southern character and place just did not ring true."

While a college student, realizing that writing was to remain his first priority, even above good health, Gaines decided against marriage for himself. He has said that he felt unprepared mentally to support a family, and refused to be supported by a wife. He has, however, missed not having children of his own, especially when he visits his family at Christmas and other times of reunion. Since the early 70s he has spoken of "my lady Linda," a San Francisco woman, and her daughter, Rozzi. Speaking of her in an interview with Ed Levitt of the Oakland *Tribune* in 1977 he said:

> I have my place and she has her place. But we're together most of the time. I'm very old fashioned about marriage. . . . When you're married somebody has to be in the home to keep things going. And I'm not going to be the guy who is Ms. so-and-so's husband. My house is going to be mine. I'm going to run it my way.
>
> Oh, I've had romances. I've been very popular with the opposite sex. I think the laws concerning marriage are antiquated. Times have changed the attitudes of people. Now a woman will say, 'I have the right to do anything I want to do.' Well, writers, artists, painters, actors, musicians—we all get quite selfish. We're not ourselves until we're doing our own work. We think that's the most important thing in the whole world. Now who's going to put up with that kind of crap?[14]

GAINES THE WRITER

By the early 1960s Gaines had settled into a $175 per month three-room, no frills apartment in San Francisco's Fillmore district. He could not afford a phone. Supporting himself with odd jobs, he remained determined to be a writer, often jotting notes on paper scraps and toilet paper at the workplace. His self-imposed regime of a five to six hour work day was relieved by long daily walks, usually in San Francisco's Golden Gate Park, which he has termed the "most beautiful urban park in the world." Speaking of his hand to mouth existence, he admitted

[14]The date of the Levitt interview, found in Gaines' papers, is incomplete.

that no one twisted his arm to be a writer. He chose the profession for himself.

Having decided that he wanted money only from writing, Gaines saw some lean times in the mid-60s, as he was beginning *Of Love and Dust*. One Christmas he could not even buy a gift for his mother. Later, recalling his pathetic situation, he told one interviewer in 1969 that his girl dropped him, but he did not blame her, since he was too broke to buy her a hamburger at MacDonald's. *Of Love and Dust* came slowly at first; he could not decide where to go with it. Unlike his usual method of beginning with a certain character, he sketched out a whole plot and then filled in with extra people and situations. He admits that his imagination really starts moving when he begins writing.

He had already completed the extended short story "A Long Day in November" in 1958, though it was not published until 1964 by *Texas Quarterly*. In 1962 he wrote "Just Like a Tree," followed by "The Sky is Gray" in 1963. The latter was published that year by *Negro Digest*. Gaines had hoped to publish these three stories as a book, but Professor Malcolm Cowley, whom he knew at Stanford, advised publishing "A Long Day in November" separately. It was subsequently published by Dial Press in 1971 as a children's book.

Gaines wrote in an undated speech (ca. 1969) found in his papers that during the late 50s and early 60s many of his young writer friends were leaving America for Europe, Africa, and South America—and especially Mexico—to "discover" themselves away from America, now "so insanely involved with materialism." One friend left San Francisco for Mexico with his wife the summer of 1962, became a successful writer, and was able to live the good life in Spain. Gaines was invited to join them at the end of the year to write his "big novel" about Louisiana, but meanwhile needed to keep his job in the post office. He said:

> All summer long I thought I would go to Mexico. But something happened at the University of Mississippi in September of '62 that changed my mind. I kept thinking and thinking about this brave, very brave man [James

> Meredith]. And I told myself then that in order for me to ever write that book I would have to take the same chances in Louisiana that Jim Meredith was taking in going to Mississippi.

On January 3, 1963, he packed clothes, books and records and went to Baton Rouge, Louisiana. This would be his third visit to the area since leaving in 1948, but this time he would try to stay there a few months. "A week or so after I had been there I was stopped and questioned by the police. Who was I, what was I doing? I explained that I was visiting relatives. They accepted that answer."

Among other indignities he suffered were segregated bus stations; colored eating sections, which were sometimes in the basement; stores that prohibited trying on clothes before paying for them; and refusal by white cab drivers to carry him. Despite this situation, Gaines continued,

> I do feel deep down in me that the six months I spent in Louisiana definitely saved my writing and quite possibly my life . . . in that I could never have written *Catherine Carmier* if I had not gone South, and maybe I would never have written any other book . . . because my writing is my life. For me not to write is for me not to live. So I went there, put up with many things I hated, but I learned much, much about the people and the place that I wanted to write about. . . . Six months after I left Louisiana the book [*Catherine Carmier*] was finished and it was published about eight months after that.

Gaines soon realized that the Mexico stay would only have afforded an escape from America's problems, some of which were his own as well. His six months in Louisiana proved invaluable.

Gaines may not have particularly enjoyed the next two years, as he continued to drive himself at his writing, which was not in any way lucrative at that time. *Catherine Carmier* by his own admission did not make money. He said in a speech at Southern University in Baton Rouge in 1971 that though he tried hard to think of another novel about Louisiana, he could not. He began one dealing with bohemian life in San Francisco, a scene he confessed to knowing little about. "Within a year and a half or two years, I had written three novels about San Francisco—which were probably three of the worst novels that have ever been written by a published writer," he said in the speech. They were "pretty bad," "unpublishable," because they "don't ring true." The cause might be that, though he said "physically" he is a Westerner, he is still "soulfully" a Southerner.

> I realized from those three efforts that I was not a San Francisco writer—or at least not yet. And if I were not, then what—what then? Since I could not think of another Louisiana novel, what could I do? So I got a job working with a printer [early 1965]. And when anyone asked me what I was doing I told them I was learning the printing business. . . . But even when I was saying this, my mind was only on writing something else about Louisiana. I knew that I had more to say—and eventually it would come—but when and how—I didn't know.

He only knew more strongly than before that he must write about his own black people because that is what he knew about. Too, there had been a scarcity of literature about blacks. He has had more success with writing about the familiar—for him, scenes from his earlier life. He continues to draw on Louisiana, a place rich in tradition, stories, myths, and superstitions, and on his own experiences and the tales that his people told.

Though Gaines felt that the professors at San Francisco State thought he was wrong to write about proud blacks who lived on a Louisiana plantation, he was determined to write about them in order to *see* stories about blacks in print. Besides the fact that he *knew* about them, he also *cared* about them. He saw himself as a writer who was black, rather than as a black writer. Since he was still a sports fan, he wanted to be as good a writer as Willie Mays, Bill Russell, and Wilt Chamberlain were athletes.

This was a time when other black writers were voicing their militancy and selling it with such books as *The Autobiography of Malcolm X* and *Native Son*. Gaines' occasional lectures and readings were sparsely attended, especially by blacks. He feared they might have thought him an Uncle Tom type, or in any case, slightly out of touch. He had as much anger as any other black, but his approach to it was different.

By his own admission his

> first ten years of writing were hell. Growing up in the South, I know the last thing in the world that whites wanted to see was humanity in blacks. . . . I knew the way to show that humanity was to do something positive. Some guys get angry and go to a punching bag. . . . I try to use the anger in a positive way, to create a lasting punch, one that will have a longer effect than just screaming or calling somebody . . . [a] son of a bitch.[15]

In August of 1964 Gaines registered for a five-day class on "The Negro Writer in the United States" at the University of California in Berkeley. In a letter, dated January 20, 1965, from Hoyt W. Fuller, managing editor of *Negro Digest*, he was asked to write a paragraph on "What is the task of the Negro writer concerned with creating a work of art in a segregated society and how does this task differ from that of the white writer—if it differs at all?"

Gaines' response, along with that of a dozen other black writers, appeared in *Negro Digest* for January, 1968. Fuller's introduction said: "Relatively unknown on the writers conference circuit, he [Gaines] nevertheless is highly regarded by his fellow writers. . . . Mr. Gaines agrees with those who feel that Richard Wright lost touch with the 'living American exile' by remaining so long abroad." Gaines said: "Wright was a man of strong passion—not an intellectual. He had to get his material out of the American soil, not out of a European library." Fuller asked whether there is a future in the "black aesthetic" concept, and Gaines replied: "As long as they [black writers] write about *people*. *People*. *People*. *People*. And not just about problems."

[15]Carter, "Ernest Gaines," 72.

Fuller's next question was: "Should the journey toward Art lead consciously and deliberately through exploitation of the black experience?" Gaines replied: "I've always said that a man, black writer or not, should do what he can do best." Fuller asked: "Should black writers direct their work toward black audiences?" and Gaines concluded:

> No more than French writers should. The artist is the only free man left. He owes nobody nothing—not even himself. He should write what he wants, when he wants, and to whomever he wants. If he is true, he will use that material which is closest to him. Those people who have experienced much of what he (the artist) has will see themselves in his work. If they don't then no amount of preaching by the artist will do any good.[16]

In the mid-60s Gaines received a two-book contract from Dial Press who wanted to publish *Bloodline*, a collection of five stories, but insisted on the completion of a novel first. The novel, *Of Love and Dust*, was the swiftest written of all Gaines' books, requiring slightly over a year, but it was nevertheless a time of pressure for him. He knew that Dial meant business and he needed the money. It was published in 1967, and though the royalties were modest, Gaines was brought to the reading public's attention for the first time since *Catherine Carmier* was issued in 1964.

Of Love and Dust concerns a black prisoner, Marcus, who is taken to a plantation to work out his time under a merciless white overseer, Sidney Bonbon. Marcus is restless, rebellious, resentful, and after failing to seduce Bonbon's black mistress, goes after his white wife. A hot affair ensues, ending in Marcus' death as the lovers plan to escape. It is a beautifully written novel, powerful and suspenseful. To Gaines dust symbolizes the absence of love.

In 1967 Gaines received a National Endowment for the Arts Study Award. A letter from Carolyn Kiser, director of literary

[16]Hoyt W. Fuller, "Black Writers' Views on Literary Lions and Values," *Negro Digest*, XVII (1968), 27.

programs of the National Foundation on the Arts and Humanities, to former fellow student Tillie Olsen indicated that Olsen had recommended Gaines for this award, one which she received herself the following year. Kiser's letter, dated February 9, 1968, reads in part: "Somewhat belatedly this will inform you that Ernest Gaines received one of our study awards. . . . Thanks for telling us about him."

In Gaines' papers is a congratulatory letter from Stephen L. Schlesinger, assistant secretary of the Guggenheim Foundation, saying that his receipt of this NEA Study Award would not affect his application for a Guggenheim, which he was not awarded until 1972. Supportive letters for the Guggenheim include one from Hoyt W. Fuller, an obvious admirer of Gaines. (For his glowing and eloquent letter, dated November 8, 1967, see Appendix 3.)

Dorothea Oppenheimer sent one of Gaines' stories to *Freedomways* in 1967. Though its title was not specified in the correspondence between her and Gaines, it could have been one later published in the *Bloodline* collection. A letter of rejection from *Freedomways*' editor, dated June 22, 1967, objected to the length of the story, but said it was good, "though not the best story by Ernest Gaines that I have read. The four-letter words and the situation that the story revolves around did not bother us. We would like to publish a piece by Ernest Gaines. When you have a shorter piece, please let us see it." Concerning four-letter words, Gaines uses them sparingly and never to clarify a situation.

Though *Bloodline* was under contract with Dial for the following year, its completion was less frantic, because three of the stories it would contain had already been published: "The Sky is Gray" (*Negro Digest*, August, 1963); "Just Like a Tree" (*Sewanee Review*, Autumn, 1963); and "A Long Day in November" (*Texas Quarterly*, Summer, 1964). The other two, "Three Men" and "Bloodline", were probably in Gaines' head by this time, waiting to materialize on paper. The arrangement of the stories could be viewed as a man's life cycle from childhood to adulthood, and *Bloodline* has been described as an "episodic novel." It was published in 1968 and brought Gaines wide acclaim.

Shortly after the publication of *Bloodline* in 1968 Gaines' sister, Lois Dixon, hosted an autograph party for Gaines at her home in Campbell, California, near San Jose. Some sixty guests attended. A reporter was invited to write up the event for the *San Jose Mercury,* September 1, 1968. His account read in part:

> Mama, [Gaines' mother, Mrs. Colar] dressed for a party, was hiding out in the kitchen. An ethereal blonde flitted from room to room in the unusual household. Mr. Lee Dixon [sister Lois' husband] was being assigned various tasks by women. That is what happens to hosts and husbands before parties.

* * *

The 60s had brought a cadre of writers like Jack Kerouac, as well as militant black groups and anti-war protesters into Berkeley and the San Francisco Bay area. Though well aware of such turbulent scenario, Gaines stayed apart from it, wanting only to write his book about Louisiana. In 1968 he was urged to carry a placard, to get into civil rights activities, to write something for the press, the magazines. He told the agitators he was working on *Miss Jane Pittman*, but they had no patience for such "junk." They wanted him to pick up a gun. He was not angered by this urgency, but rather chose to keep on with his work rather than to simply turn out a sociological piece of equipment, as many contemporary writers were doing. Writing on subjects important to him was his personal form of protest.

One positive influence on Gaines' attitudes at this time, mentioned earlier, was James Meredith's courageous integrating of the University of Mississippi. It clued him to return to his native land for research, to give way to the subconscious tug that had not fully surfaced. He was indeed interested in black rights, but not in a militant way, evidenced by the fact that he thoroughly researched the subject for *Miss Jane Pittman*, gathering data on Louisiana history, legalities imposed on blacks, reconstruction, and the like. Since his return to River Lake in 1963 he has made the trip a yearly pilgrimage.

The late 1960s mark the beginning of Gaines' travels as a public speaker and reader. Recognition was on the way, especially after the publication of the *Bloodline* collection in 1968. He has remained in demand with audiences of all backgrounds, all ages. Though outwardly composed, he has admitted to nervousness when speaking.

On one such trip, in March of 1968, Gaines read at McKinley Elementary School in Baton Rouge. Several fan letters from the students are among his papers. One to "Dear Mr. Gaines" from "Yours truly, Mary Lee" said:

> I am writing to let you know that I enjoyed your reading to us and I want to thank you for your time at McKinley Elementary library, Tuesday afternoon. It was very interesting. I would like to read that book you read to us before. I am in the 5th grade. My teacher's name is Miss S. L. White. I hope you'll come again. When you are back in Baton Rouge stop at McKinley Elementary School, even if I still don't go here any more.

Gaines was chosen in 1968 as one of the guest lecture series speakers for the Black Writers' Workshop, established that year under the auspices of the San Francisco Arts Commission. Besides the lecture series the organization afforded a facility for authors and playwrights to read and present their dramas. On November 2, 1968, he spoke at the Western Addition Branch Library in San Francisco. Flyers announcing the event had been distributed.

In February of 1969 Gaines gave a lecture/reading from *Of Love and Dust* at State University College in Brockport, New York, under English Department auspices. Later that year, when asked if he preferred writing about his homeland from such a distance, Gaines told an interviewer:

> Well, in San Francisco if someone's against you, they know how to vote you out of an area. If someone's against you in Louisiana, or if I wrote a book and they

> did not like it or me in Louisiana, they might shoot me anytime. So it's much safer to live in San Francisco than it is in Louisiana. . . . If I were to live in Louisiana and write about an inter-racial love affair, I should be brave enough, myself, to love; and brave enough to stand beside anyone else who tried. In San Francisco, I could do these things. In Louisiana it might be a little problem to do the same things. So, as you know, I live in San Francisco.

In the same interview, when asked if Louisiana's old social patterns were breaking up or changing, Gaines said:

> Yes, in some cases. . . . The physical makeup of the country is changing. People are chopping down more trees and plowing up more land, but the people themselves are pretty much the same. In the cities . . . more people are eating at the same counters, blacks and whites together. There are more black people working as clerks. . . . This was unheard of two years ago.[17]

Referring to an eatery, he commented that now a black boy could not only clean off tables, but be a cashier as well. "But just across the street—well that's another story."

LIFE AFTER MISS JANE PITTMAN

Obviously Gaines had given much thought to Miss Jane Pittman's story during his yearly visits back to Louisiana. Ever since the early 60s, when he compiled a list of the most significant happenings in the state since 1900 (see Preface), the wheels were turning, even if subconsciously at times, for *The Autobiography of Miss Jane Pittman*, the story of a 110-year old ex-slave, her joys, sorrows, loves, her independence and survival. Copious research by Gaines in both Louisiana and California libraries had continued over the years in preparation

[17]Fitzgerald, "An Interview: Ernest J. Gaines," 335.

for this book. Its actual writing took approximately two and a half years. *Miss Jane*, published first by Dial Press in 1971, carefully incorporates history accurately, but history interpreted by an uneducated, natively intelligent black woman. Complex and panoramic in its time span and cast of characters, it is unlike Gaines' previous books. His labors resulted in a much accepted, humanly appealing novel, which confirmed even more solidly his reputation established by *Bloodline*.

Gaines received some financial help for *Miss Jane Pittman* from a Rockefeller Grant-in-Aid in 1970. In a letter dated June 24, 1969, Gaines had written to Gerald Freund of the Rockefeller Foundation about his proposed use of such monies: "The money will not write the book—that I must do on my own—but it will surely solve many problems . . . pay food, pay rent, clean clothes, pay insurance and doctor bills, and move me around in Louisiana so that I can talk and listen."

With the success of *Miss Jane Pittman* in 1971, Gaines was financially able to move to a second floor, unpretentious eight-room flat in the same section of San Francisco on Divisadero Street, a section where average hard-working people lived. Not minding that the flat was plain-looking, nor in a particularly swank part of the city, Gaines has since kept it as his spring and summer residence. His living room overlooks Divisadero Street. His office is in the back, revealing a more scenic view of San Francisco and the Bay. To insure privacy while writing he hangs a sign on the door saying, "Don't bother me."

At first he had few belongings except books and records. There was plenty of space and freedom to work. At one time his walls were papered with maps of California, Louisiana, Africa and the United States. Later, besides photos of his family and River Lake Plantation, he hung those of his favorite authors and one of Martin Luther King.

Early on Gaines accumulated books for his continually increasing library, now totalling thousands of volumes. By 1974 he had accumulated about 7,000 books. His kitchen table was used as a desk. To one interviewer he mused about having a "real lot" of money—enough to move to the Pacific Heights section. His life style had not changed noticeably, though he gradually indulged in some niceties, such as new pieces of furniture and on occasion in a better brand of liquor. Speaking about monies from *Miss Jane Pittman* to journalist Ed Levitt, who interviewed him at his larger apartment in 1977, he said, "It made me comfortable. It bought that leather chair you're sitting in." Gaines received $50,000 for the TV rights to *Miss Jane*. "My agent grabbed his share," Gaines continued. "Uncle Sam dug in. If I got $35,000 I'm very lucky."

Levitt wrote that Gaines "had a well-fed look," and that he used frequent hand gestures when talking, "like an artist painting a picture." To Levitt Gaines confided the hope that his and Alex Haley's books might change the course of black writers. Black writers, according to Gaines, should study history, go to archives, travel. Then they would have something else to write about besides "prostitutes, drug addicts or whatever else in the big city ghettos."[18]

* * *

Believing that a strong body helps the mind to work, Gaines walks about three miles each morning before he starts writing. First he writes in long hand, quickly, and then again slowly. Then he revises on the typewriter. Anything that his agent, Dorothea Oppenheimer, sees is actually a fourth writing, but one which he himself considers a first draft.

Gaines has often said that the different styles of music have influenced him as much as have styles of literature. While writing *Miss Jane Pittman* he played Modest Moussorgsky's "Pictures at an Exhibition" daily. His San Francisco flat is usually filled with musical sound from his enormous collection of records and tapes. His tastes encompass everything from the classics of Beethoven to the blues of B. B. King and contemporary jazzists.

It is not surprising that blues guitarist/singer B. B. King (born Riley B. King) is a favorite of Gaines. They have much in common. King was born in 1925 on a plantation in the

[18]Copy of a newspaper item found in Gaines' papers with incomplete date and title of paper.

Mississippi Delta, worked in the fields, and later became a sharecropper. He played guitar on the streets to supplement his meager income. In his early twenties King left home for Memphis to sell his blues style to recording studios, working hard at the thing he loved most. He *had* to make music, just as Gaines *had* to write. King is not a screamer. He moans, he cries, he wails for the whole black race, just as Gaines does when he writes.

Also high on Gaines' performer list is saxophonist Lester Young, "Prez" or "Pres" to those who knew him best. "Prez," for President, was the name given Young by singer Billie Holiday, to whom he gave the name "Lady Day." Gaines has said that Holiday is his favorite female singer. (For more information on King, Young and Holiday, see Appendix 4.)

* * *

Though admitting to newspaper interviewer Paul Desruisseaux that Louisiana still exerted an attraction, Gaines had not thought seriously of ever going back there to live, certainly not in the plantation area.

> If I could have the things I *want*, maybe I could live in Louisiana or the South. I don't know exactly what those things are, but I want to be someplace where I can do *whatever* I want. I mean if I want to do it, damn it I want to do it! And I don't want anything preventing me from doing it.

Gaines considered San Francisco that kind of place, saying, "Some people put it down, but San Francisco is probably the greatest goddamned city in this country. I love San Francisco. I live here and I work here. *This* is my home."[19]

A piece titled "Chapter One of *The House and the Field*, a novel" was published in the 1972 winter issue of the *Iowa*

[19]Paul Desruisseaux, "Interview with Ernest Gaines, Mill Valley (Calif.), *Pacific Sun,* November 7-13, 1974.

Review. It concerns a black servant left alone in the big plantation house for a few hours, during which time he fancies himself as The Master, drinking the master's choice whiskey, trying on his expensive clothes, and pompously giving orders to the older black woman servant. Then he takes the woman's pass and goes out into the field to think about how he can escape. The novel apparently did not materialize.

This was the year (1972) that Gaines received a Guggenheim Fellowship. The honors had begun to pour in. He was given the Louisiana Library Association Award on March 25, 1972, for *Miss Jane Pittman*. Mrs. Juanita Bridewell presented the award at the association's Book Dinner, a highlight of the Baton Rouge convention, held at the Capitol House Motor Hotel. Gaines was the first writer of fiction to receive this award in twenty-two years. At that time *Miss Jane Pittman* was on the American Library Association's Notable Book List and was being considered for several other awards.

This same year, on June 16, 1972, Gaines received the California Gold Medal for the best book by a Californian, his *Miss Jane Pittman*. The Commonwealth Club of California, which presented the award, was established in 1931. Any Gold Medal winner must have been a California resident at the time his book was delivered to the press. A telegram to Gaines, dated May 25, 1972, from Durward S. Riggs, the Commonwealth Club executive secretary, follows:

> I have pleasant honor to advise you your book *The Autobiography of Miss Jane Pittman* has been awarded the Gold Fiction Medal of Commonwealth Club of California as one of seven best books by California authors in 1971. Please hold this confidence until we notify you of public release date. Award will be made by club president Justice Murray Draper at luncheon at which you and your wife will be seated at head table in Gold Ballroom, Sheraton-Palace Hotel, San Francisco at noon, Friday sixteenth (Business dress). Please send biography including education, previous writing, etc. Would appreciate receiving glossy photograph for publicity purposes. Please advise by collect wire whether

you can be present.

At the Third Annual Awards Banquet of the Black Academy of Arts and Letters at the Hilton Hotel in New York on October 7, 1972, Gaines received the Letter Award for *Miss Jane Pittman.* The evening was quite a to-do. The guest speakers were Alex Haley, Loretta Pauker, and Dr. Herman O'Daniel. Harlem Philharmonic artists and the Daphne Weeks Orchestra provided music, and an elegant, multi-course dinner was served. Gaines' award was presented by Dr. Wilfred George Onslow Cartey, making him one of the group's sixty-eight Fellows in the fields of music, painting, sculpture, literature, dance, and scholarship. Others receiving the Letter Award were Samuel Yette, Michael Harper, and Dr. Chancellor Williams. Each recipient was given a $100 honorarium.

* * *

By now Gaines was more than ever in demand as a speaker for universities, clubs, and writers' groups. In March of 1973 he spoke at Southern University in Baton Rouge, Louisiana, and the following September he was one of five guests at a YWCA sponsored "Authors Read Their Works" series at the University Methodist Church in that city. A reporter for the Baton Rouge *Sunday Advocate* called him the "possessor of a low key delivery."

In early November of 1973 Gaines read from and discussed his works at a mini-series, "The Written Word," at Fresno City College. In announcing the event, *Rampage*, the college newspaper, quoted the famous comment by Melvin Maddocks of *Time* magazine: "Ernest Gaines may just be the best black writer in America. He is so good, in fact, that he makes the category seem meaningless." A reporter for the *Fresno Bee* (undated) described Gaines as "a soft-spoken man, a powerfully built man with soft, sensitive eyes," and quoted him at the lecture as saying: "I had to work and work and work. But I finally reached a point where people began to notice me. It's hard work and it's lonely. But if it is what you really want to do you'll do it. [A writer must] learn to write honestly about familiar topics." This was the goal Gaines had set for himself, to write truthfully about the black experience in America, and to recognize black characters as human beings.

In May of this same year, 1973, as a "celebrated alumnus" he read from "Just Like a Tree" at the Solano College Hour in Vallejo. A flyer for the occasion read in part:

> Following Mr. Gaines' reading there will be videotape excerpts from *The Autobiography of Miss Jane Pittman*, a resume of his Vallejo school experiences by Mr. William Wilson, and an award in recognition of his achievements given by the Board of Commissioners of the Associated Students of Solano College. All persons present are then invited . . . for a reception at which they may meet Mr. Gaines and at which there will be refreshments served.

* * *

From 1974-78 Gaines was a member of the literary panel for the National Endowment for the Arts. Also, in 1974 he was appointed library commissioner for the city and county of San Francisco, a position he chose to leave before his term ended, due to differences with San Francisco's Mayor Joseph Alioto in 1975.

On August 19, ninety percent of the San Francisco police force went on strike, demanding a thirteen percent salary increase. An offer of 6.5 percent had been rejected. Many of the city's fire department employees joined the strike. (Though city transportation employees threatened to strike two days later, their plan was averted by a 6.9 percent raise.) Rather than call in state troopers, the National Guard, or other police personnel to quell the strikers, Alioto, a friend of the local unions who had supported his mayoral race, persuaded the San Francisco Board of Commissioners to meet the strikers' demands for the full thirteen percent, effective as of October 15.

Evidently Gaines disagreed with Alioto's handling of the matter. A part of his letter of resignation as library commissioner reads: "I cannot serve under a man for whom I have no respect," a quote from the *San Francisco Chronicle,* August 29, 1975. In the same issue librarian Kevin Starr's reaction stated: "We are just heartsick at the loss of this major American writer who was also, incidentally, one helluva Commissioner." An undated item in the *San Francisco Examiner* reported: "Mayor Alioto yesterday accepted the tart resignation of author Ernest J. Gaines from the Library Commission." His letter to Gaines said:

> I accept your resignation with regret. Someday your experience or your study will convince you that the use of state police against local strikes is as offensive as is the use of state police against civil rights workers. In any event, I thank you for the good service you have rendered to the people of San Francisco.

In 1974, at the request of New Orleans journalist Jason Berry, Gaines joined the editorial advisory board for a book review supplement to the New Orleans *Vieux Carré Courier*, a New Orleans paper no longer viable. Berry thought such a board "would elevate its [the supplement's] credibility." He asked Gaines, Alice Walker, Jim Whitehead, George Garrett, Walker Percy, among a few others,

> though I wasn't on close terms with any of them, having but one book of my own out at the time. They agreed, since it basically didn't require much beyond lending one's name. Ernie [Gaines] replied with a long, handwritten letter explaining that he didn't have enough time for his own writing and didn't see how he could do this; so I wrote back explaining that he didn't have to do any real work, etc, and he said yes.

The book review supplement lasted only two or three issues. Berry and Gaines did not actually meet until 1978.[20]

In 1974, the year *Miss Jane Pittman* was filmed, Gaines was

[20]Letter from Berry to Anne Simpson, November 24, 1989.

given a tribute by the Southern California Motion Picture Council. For the occasion he spoke on the writing of *Miss Jane*. Despite repeated inquiries to libraries, newspapers, and various organizations in California the exact date and the nature of Gaines' tribute have not been ascertained.

* * *

In February of 1974 Gaines was invited back to Baton Rouge under the same YWCA auspices as the preceding year. At this time Gaines said he had no further interest in future filming of his works, that he wanted to keep away from it. (However, a few years later his short story, "A Long Day in November, " and his novel, *A Gathering of Old Men,* were filmed.) At this same session he said that he was not influenced by the Harlem Renaissance writers because he had already set his style before he read them. Asked if black literature should be a separate discipline he said, "I believe everybody should be able to read everybody's work, if it is good work. I hope everyone can read mine for what it's worth. I try to mold my work to give readers a feeling of human experiences."[21] Later that month Gaines spoke at the Western Addition Branch Library in San Francisco, where he had done so in 1968, during Black History Week.

Gaines spoke in Atlanta at a session titled "The South—Life and Letters," April 17-19, 1974, arranged by the American Society of Newspaper Editors. On the panel with him were novelist Doris Betts (*Beasts of the Southern Wild and Other Stories*, 1973) and writer/editor Willie Morris. Gaines was commencement speaker for San Francisco State's June, 1974, graduation ceremony, and was also named "Alumnus of the Year." San Francisco State honored him with a cocktail buffet in the Alumni Association's Offices on the Embarcadero, and during the event he was asked to draw the winning raffle tickets for the Alumni Association Raffle.

Signs of nostalgia were evidenced in Gaines' comments in

[21]Baton Rouge *Morning Advocate,* February 22, 1974.

an August, 1974, issue of *Southern Living*. He needed to come back to southern Louisiana, to "the land," as he called it. "I have to touch, I have to be. You melt into things and you let them melt into you—the trees, the rivers, the bayous, the language, the sounds." His coming from the south made him feel "closer to nature, to the earth, and to both good and bad attitudes." At this time he was still writing drafts in longhand, better able to "think and strike out" faster in pencil.

In October of 1974, Gaines, along with poets Michael Harper, currently at Brown University, and Sterling Brown (d. 1988), spoke in Portland at Lewis and Clark College for that school's Awards Ceremony. Not only was Brown an outstanding literary scholar but an historian as well. Though Gaines and Harper knew each other from previous award ceremonies, this was the first time Gaines had met Brown, then fifty-two and teaching American Civilization at Howard University. *The Pioneer Log*, Lewis and Clark's bulletin, reported that on first observation Gaines thought Brown was white. Some repartee overheard at a party preceding the ceremonies follows:

> Brown: You're not wearing a tuxedo.
> Gaines: No, I don't believe in stuff like that.
> Brown: That nigger over there don't have a tuxedo on either. What the hell am I wearing this thing for?
> Gaines: The only excuse I can give for my ignorance is the education system of this country as well as the government who has not in the past, and to this day, recognized the black intellectual.

Gaines was totally impressed with Brown, sensing that his knowledge of the common man enabled him to write as he did. Brown preferred Gaines' *Miss Jane Pittman* to the movie version, remarking that in this novel Gaines pulled the past up "from the deep well of his consciousness." The *Log* reporter described Gaines' voice as "very soft. He seems shy, and does not use a great amount of inflection when reading."

On November 11, 1974 Gaines was guest of honor at the California Librarians Black Caucus held in San Diego's Town and Country Hotel. The invitation to this affair by Robert

Chrisman, editor of *The Black Scholar,* stated that he would not need to make a speech, but as guest of honor would be presented with an award for *Miss Jane Pittman*, in conjunction with a viewing of the film. His expenses were paid and he was given a small honorarium, plus a plaque.[22] Though he undoubtedly appreciated this token, Gaines remarked sometime later about having his name on similar plaques: "Hell, I don't care one way or the other. I want the flowers while I'm living. It'd be nice to have a path or walk, 'This is where Ernest Gaines Walked,' or something like that. But I don't know that I really care."[23]

Just three days later Gaines was back at San Francisco State College to read "The Turtles," his first publication, for George Price's "Writers on Writing" course. A few weeks afterward an interview with Gaines in the *San Francisco Bay Guardian* provided some insight on the author's lifestyle. Gaines did not have much to do with other Bay area writers. Many of them were his friends, however, though he had no weekly routine about bar-hopping with them. He reiterated,

> Writing is done in a little room all by yourself. If I'm not writing, I'm wanting to get to the desk. I'll walk by, sit down and look at something, maybe strike out a word. Instead of that 10 minutes, I'd like to spend four hours there. I've never felt, never, never, that I didn't want to spend an hour at my desk. Never. I've never felt so depressed—or so happy—that I didn't want to go to it.

* * *

Though the 1971 publication of *Miss Jane Pittman* and the subsequent filming of it in 1973-74 made more money for Gaines than all of his previous books combined, he evaded questions about its success with a *Guardian* interviewer in 1975.

[22]Letter from Robert Chrisman to Gaines, October 3, 1974, in Gaines' papers.

[23]Undated, unidentified news item in Gaines' papers.

> I finished 'Miss Jane' four years ago and I'm trying to write another book [*In My Father's House*] that is taking all my time and energy. A book is finished when I'm finished with it. If I'm alive ten years from today, and someone should ask me about Miss Jane Pittman, I'll say I don't know about Miss Jane Pittman. I hope that by then I will have written some other books so I won't be remembered as the person who wrote 'Miss Jane Pittman.' As long as they don't put that on my gravestone—'Here's the guy who wrote Miss Jane Pittman.'

Gaines went on:

> People ask me what do I really want? I think I'd like to be able, if I had the money, I'd like to have a home with a half acre, an acre of ground, and I could just get out there and dig, plant a row of flowers, beans. Many of your Southern writers, they always say they're gentleman farmers and all that kind of bull. I'd like to have a little piece of ground where I could just plant something sometime.[24]

The *Los Angeles Times*, February 9, 1975, carried a long item by Gaines concerning the black writer's task. It is important for its thoroughness and reflection of the literary scene since the unrestful 1960s. Gaines prefaced the piece, titled "Black Writers Should Get Off the Soapbox," with his discovery as a teenager of the library. He continued:

> Good fiction about blacks was almost impossible to find in 1948, even in the libraries of a great urban center like San Francisco. There were two reasons for this. One was that white fiction writers either were hostile or condescending or did not thoroughly understand the subtle nuances of rural black life. The other reason was

[24]Item from Gaines' papers, date incomplete.

that black writers themselves had not been able to strike a proper balance between their legitimate social and political obligations and the need to create good art.

However, things are different today from what they were when I first went into the libraries in search of fiction about blacks. There is an abundance of good books available, and the black writer is himself emerging as a new social, cultural and intellectual force in American society. Thanks to television, and Broadway, the movies and black studies, Afro-American writers are rapidly approaching the day when they can take their places alongside ministers, athletes and entertainers as shapers of images and opinion. Neither is the influence of the black writer confined to the black community. Such successful television presentations as CBS's "The Autobiography of Miss Jane Pittman" have also made the white community conscious of the artistic talents and intellectual power of the black writer.

This makes the black writer a spokesman of sorts, whether he chooses to be or not. The dramatic emergence of Afro-American novelists and playwrights from decades of isolation, neglect and even ridicule may have brought long overdue recognition, but it also has imposed new social responsibilities. They will—and should—be judged by stricter artistic standards while, at the same time, their role as political spokesmen for their people is more complex than in the days of cultural exile.

One by-product of Afro-American writers having been isolated and ignored for so long is that they have had things pretty much their own way with regard to artistic standards. Few critics complained about the quality of their work, because few of the critics cared. As for their readers' attitudes, blacks demanded protest novels and whites simply would not read anything else by a black writer. The end result was that black writers paid more attention to political matters than to developing the technical and creative aspects of their writing.

There is nothing wrong with political ideas in literature. I hate to even think of where fiction would be without politics—without Charles Dickens, Leo Tolstoy, Ralph Ellison, Upton Sinclair, James Allen McPherson and John Steinbeck. The trouble with many young black writers, though, is that they are still trying to dabble in politics and social criticism without having actually learned and developed the basic technique of fiction writing. This is evident in the massive numbers of 'Superblack' but shamefully written works that can be found in almost any bookstore.

For the black writer, bad literature—no matter how socially inspired it may be—is bad politics. And this is not just literary shop talk. For the fact is that we have a number of whites traveling the country trying to convince the American people that blacks are genetically inferior, and this makes everything we do a political and social issue. This is especially true when it comes to fiction, poetry, theater and other intellectual enterprises. There are ways of speaking out against racism without preaching, lecturing or otherwise sacrificing one's artistic integrity; one way is through the quality of one's work.

We do not necessarily have to exaggerate the value of the black experience in our writing, not if we just write well about any subject we choose. . . . The lesson we should learn from this is that good art does not have to be 'angry' or 'militant' to be good politics—just creative, accurate and precise. This, then, is the social and political responsibility of the black writer. He must create books and plays that will withstand the biased scrutiny of his oppressors. He also must produce work that can be handed down through the ages and serve as inspiration to the thousands of black and white youth, who, like myself in the 1940s, are turning to the libraries, bookstores and the media, not only for leadership and direction, but also for intellectual stimulation.

* * *

On March 1, 1975, Gaines was the keynote speaker at the annual installation of officers dinner for the Justice Police Association in San Francisco. He spoke about the poor, black, and minority folk in America, the criminal justice system, and the need for such groups as the Justice Police Association. He told of his childhood experiences and answered questions about the movie of *Miss Jane Pittman.*

Gaines spoke at the Black Student Union at the University of Delaware April 21, 1975. The campus publication, *Pamoja,* reported that "those not in attendance missed an extremely gratifying experience." Later that year *Outcry*, organ of the Bay Area Council on Soviet Jewry, reported that Gaines marched in a demonstration with the International Council on Soviet Jewry in support of Andrei Sakharov, 1975 Nobel Peace Prize winner.

A letter dated June 13, 1975, from Barbara Wright of the Poetry Center at San Francisco State asked Gaines for purchasing rights to the videotaping of his reading from *Miss Jane Pittman* for $200. If he agreed, which he most likely did as an alumnus of that school, he was to be included in the Poetry Center's Video Tape Library of living authors.

* * *

By 1976 Gaines' nostalgia for Louisiana had surfaced again, though he was not quite ready to move back there permanently. After all, he had made strong ties in San Francisco as well. His personal belongings were all there. A Baton Rouge *State-Times* interviewer visiting San Francisco in February of 1976 described Gaines' apartment as "choked" with blues records. Friends periodically suggested that he move to a nicer apartment. His success with *Miss Jane Pittman* had obviously impressed the neighbors, but they were still shy in approaching him. He admitted to two favorite neighborhood bars, identifying his drinking buddies as an Irish police patrolman, a Spanish high school teacher, fellow black writers Ishmael Reed and Al Young, and an Irish bookie. Still preferring to write about Louisiana, he pointed out that no one else was doing it.

Gaines said to Blake Green of the *San Francisco Chronicle,* about San Francisco: "I'm used to it here, I like the neighborhood." Everytime he has returned to Louisiana he has been asked why he doesn't live there. "There are things I could not tolerate if I lived in Louisiana," he said, admitting that now he would be welcome at the big plantation house where his grandmother was the cook—a house he was not allowed to enter as a young black boy living on the plantation.

During the interview he referred to "my lady Linda," very proud to point out the carved ebony walking stick which she had given him. Green said: "When he writes of the problems of inter-racial relationships, he has his own with Linda to draw upon." Gaines went on, "I'm a lonist—so caught up in my work that I could not be at all times what I should be. If I'm a celebrity nobody ever tells me. I can afford to drink Tanqueray gin and Jack Daniels now and I have a car."[25]

Again, in mid-February of 1976, Gaines returned to Baton Rouge as the first speaker for a new YWCA series, "Authors Read Their Works." (He would be followed on the series the next month by his friend, the respected author Alice Walker.) At this meeting he said, in disagreement with author Thomas Wolfe, that a writer "must" go home again. He described his writing regime:

> I fall out of bed, throw some water on my face, drink two or three cups of black coffee, go to my little table in the hall and start writing. I don't sit there waiting for trumpets to sound and rockets to blast. I get up to write. If you want to do something you have to sacrifice other things.

Later that month Gaines spoke at Indian Valley College in Novato, California, reading from *In My Father's House*, then in progress. He had already worked on it five years and rewritten it six or seven times, a fact confirmed by Dorothea

[25]*San Francisco Chronicle,* April 29, 1976.

Oppenheimer's letters of suggested revisions. An account in the *Indian Valley Echo* for February 24, 1976, quoted Gaines: "I work on one thing at a time. I beat it or it beats me. It's not all the time you can see your errors. Publishers are in control like a coach." He told the audience that he nearly always begins with a character and the story comes later. *Of Love and Dust* took about a year from start to finish, and the *Bloodline* collection was a six or seven year process, with the story titled "Bloodline" being the most difficult, he said.

Jesting about inspiration, he said: "I'm most inspired when the landlord knocks on the door and wants the rent." Then seriously he said that inspiration came simply by wanting to write and doing it well, by being creative in one's own special way. Rejection slips of all colors have been a part of his life. When he reads his own works, he has seemed pleased when the language flows the way people actually talk. The *Echo* reporter commented that his audience rapport was due to a "warm sense of humor and honesty. It seemed that the subdued browns and blacks of his clothing were selected so as not to outshine his story telling. And what a story teller he is!"

On February 26, 1976, Gaines read from *In My Father's House* at the Library of Congress, an event sponsored by the Gertrude Clarke Whittall Poetry and Literature Fund.

The following April he spoke on "Miss Jane Pittman: Messages through Fiction," to a symposium, "Discourse and Discovery in Freshman English," in Lubbock, Texas, at Lubbock Christian College. In the program brochure Gaines was called a "struggling novelist," his own term. A few weeks before he was scheduled in Lubbock the *University Daily* quoted him in a humorous mood. Hoping to tell the class something of the plot of *In My Father's House*, his novel in progress, he planned to finish with "and the rest of the story will cost you $8.95." That same month Gaines spoke for a Writers Conference Workshop at Clark College in Atlanta.

In May, 1976, he read from *In My Father's House* at the Ortega Branch Library in San Francisco. The next month he presented the awards for the University of Texas at El Paso's Literary Awards Competition. While on campus, he held a discussion on contemporary writing in America, and read something from his own works. On June 20 he was in San Luis Obispo, reading from his works and discussing writing at that city's second annual poetry and jazz festival.

On November 1, 1976, Gaines read from *Miss Jane Pittman* at "A Salute to Zimbabwe," a cocktail benefit, held in the home of Mr. and Mrs. William Moore in San Francisco. Guest speaker was Congressman Ronald V. Dellums.

* * *

A letter from Michael Harper to Gaines, dated February 5, 1977, indicates that Harper's exam papers for the previous semester were essays on *Miss Jane Pittman*. The letter said in part:

> I think you're already being read where it counts, in the best programs of literature in the country, and this will result in the readership that changes attitudes, deepens perception. Have you been watching 'Roots'? I expect you won't get the audience Haley's gotten, but perhaps the one you've already gotten is more lasting; you're certainly a better writer, a better story-telling stylist, and soul-articulator that's a fact.

Gaines continued to supplement income from his writings by filling speaking engagements. In March of 1977 he addressed students at Northwestern State University of Louisiana in Natchitoches, reading from the opening chapters of *Miss Jane Pittman*. During the address he answered questions from the audience concerning the book's section on the assassination.

> I think the period in our country's history from 1958 to 1968 is so rich that any writer, white or black, could spend the rest of his life writing about it. I've intentionally bypassed the period in my own work. If I were younger and more courageous, maybe I'd tackle

it.[26]

A special tribute was given Gaines in June of 1977, when he was inducted into the Blacks in the West Hall of Fame, under the auspices of the African American Historical and Cultural Society. He was one of seven to be so honored for giving "unselfish public service toward their community." At the occasion Alex Haley was presented a key to the city of San Francisco. The *Sun Reporter* called the meeting a "plush event." Though Gaines may not have been in attendance, on July 21 of that year a program presented by middle schoolers and their teachers at St. Paul's Center in Baton Rouge was dedicated to Gaines, Alex Haley, Dr. Martin Luther King, Jr., Dr. Mary McLeod Bethune, and Dr. George Washington Carver.

On August 3, 1977, the *San Francisco Chronicle* mentioned as "one of the year's unique and interesting events" a program in the Little Theater of the California Palace of the Legion of Honor. Participating were Gaines, reading one of his early short stories, "My Grandpa and the Haint," and Ghanian drummer Kwaku Daddy with his group in a segment of rhythm, melody, and voices. As an experimental venture being considered for college campus presentation, it was comparable to the jazz/poetry days on Upper Grant Avenue in North Beach.

The following September Gaines was a panelist for the session titled "The Teaching of Fiction Writing" in a four-day Conference on the Teaching of Creative Writing, auspiced by the Institute for Study of History, Life, and Culture of Black People in Jackson, Mississippi.

For a few months (unspecified) in 1977 Gaines evaluated the tutoring for various ethnic groups at St. John's Episcopal Church between Mission and Valencia streets in San Francisco. The program, funded by a grant from the federal government, promoted multi-ethnic cooperation and communication and multicultural education, and stressed English and mathematics. Tutor and student, of dissimilar languages, worked on a one-to-one basis. Ethnic backgrounds included were Negro, Latino,

[26]Ruth Laney, "A New Approach to Black Writers," Baton Rouge *Sunday Advocate,* April 17, 1977.

Chinese, Hindu and Filipino. The children shared their writings and stories which ultimately went into a collection.

* * *

Gradually Gaines had begun to relax his work schedule, if only slightly. Though he remained a stickler to his work day and his walking habits, he still found time to sail, talk with friends at his favorite bar, read, listen to music, and spend time with his "lady," breaking the loneliness of the writer's life which he had chosen for himself.

In My Father's House was completed in 1977, to be published the following year. This dramatic book was six years aborning—it had not come easily. Set in south Louisiana its painful subject is that of an immature father who unfeelingly abandoned his first family, and later made a new life for himself as a respected minister, family man, and black community leader. After several years his oldest, estranged son, bent on revenge, mysteriously appears. Once the father recognizes him they still are unable to communicate fully. During several tense pages the father's sanity is in jeopardy. His agony is almost unbearable as the truth about his first family unfolds. Ultimately the son, jailed for a time, eludes him again and is found dead in a nearby swamp.

A humorous business letter to "Dear Old Ee" from Oppenheimer dated December 15, 1977, concerning the book and some photos reads in part:

> Here are your contact sheets back with my 'first' and 'second' choice. In my second choice you look a bit like a Jew which is probably why I like that one. Anyway, I think the first choice is ok. I'm sending your dedication over to Knopf exactly as you wrote it. Except that I've retyped it. I can't send it without also sending them your letter which starts: 'Stinker." I don't think that would be quite right. I'm glad you're going to get skinnier again. Big loving hug, [signed] Dee O.

Another letter from Oppenheimer, dated January 25, 1978, reported on some of Gaines' earnings from translations, reading tours, and royalties, as well as her percentage as agent. "Hope you get some money back from old Uncle Sam," the letter said. "It sure was nice getting that $75.00 [commission], as this has been the roughest year that I've ever had, and every little bit helped. Let me know if there's anything you don't understand. Take care old Skinny-o. A hug, Dee O."

Though the exact date and nature of the honor are not known, at sometime in 1978 Gaines was honored in San Francisco by the California Press Women. Repeated inquiries to California libraries, newspapers, and the California Press Women by this author have failed to get these details. The Newspaper Department of the San Francisco Public Library wrote: "We can find no articles about Mr. Gaines and the California Press Women in any available indexing for the San Francisco papers."[27] However, Gaines' speech for the occasion, found in his papers, concerned the writing and televising of *Miss Jane Pittman*, and read in part:

> I wish to thank the California Press Women for inviting me here tonight to say a few words about another lady. Though she is fictitious, not fact, not based on any one person, nor a composite of several, I would not have been able to write about her had not someone, many black women, shared this experience.
>
> I have been accused of writing a hundred years of black history in *The Autobiography of Miss Jane Pittman*. I disagree entirely. I'm not so egotistical, arrogant, to believe for a second that I could write the history of blacks in America through the eyes of one illiterate black woman. *The Autobiography of Miss Jane Pittman* is a novel. The character is a creation of my limited imagination. Not only was I not trying to write the history of Black America, I was not even trying to write the history of one person. No one person, not even the black woman herself can write that story in its entirety. No one person can write all the pain, anguish, suffering, sorrow of that hundred year old black woman.

[27]Letter to Anne Simpson, dated January 26, 1990.

> Not even she herself.
>
> So I wrote just a little bit of it. Because of my limited imagination, and because of the necessity of form. Form must play as important a part in the novel as should content. So much of what could have gone into the book had to be left out, omitted, because of the necessity of form. Therefore, it is not history, but a novel. Let us just say that the novel is about a lady who had been left out of history by historians who did not think she was important enough to be included.

Gaines then spoke of his early life in Louisiana, and of his brave, energetic Aunt Augusteen and her physical condition, continuing,

> I should point out now, and definitely so, that Miss Jane is not my aunt. My aunt was crippled, and could not even go out of the yard. Miss Jane travelled all over the State of Louisiana—walking, running, even horseback riding. What I did with Miss Jane was give her my aunt's courage, her moral strength. To me, my aunt was the bravest person who ever lived. I tried to make Miss Jane brave, moral, tough, durable, resilient and above all funny. I cannot recall that my aunt had too much of a sense of humor. But to live to be a hundred and ten, as Miss Jane had to be, a sense of humor was definitely needed. You can't make it without humor.
>
> It took me two and a half years to write *Miss Jane Pittman*. I started the spring of '68 and finished the fall of '70. I can't recall how many books I read, probably a couple of hundred, or part of, let's say. I made use of the archives at LSU, the library at Southern University, as well as the state library in Baton Rouge. After returning to San Francisco, I could always write back to these different institutions for additional information when needed. While in the South, I also went out into the field. There were then, and still are, a few people on that Plantation where I grew up. There's a man there, Mr. Walter Zeno, who has known five generations of my

people. I go back to Louisiana at least twice a year, I visit him each time, and we sit, have a drink, and talk. Wine is his favorite, but he'll drink vodka, too, and I'll take either.[28]

Miss Jane caused a row from the beginning. My agent submitted the galleys to a very popular magazine known to publish writings about women [*Cosmopolitan*]. The editors were interested in serializing the novel, or at least publishing parts of it in two consecutive issues. However, there was some concern as to whether the book was fact or fiction. When the editors found out that it was fiction, that a hundred-and-ten-year-old woman had not actually talked into a tape recorder, that a man made up the whole thing, it was immediately, regrettably unpublishable by the magazine.

The book as it is now was published in '71, and a year later we were contacted by Hollywood. At first, very little money was offered for the right to film the book. It took two or three months of bickering between my agent in New York and the people in Hollywood before they could reach a reasonable agreement. Later, after the contract was drawn, I met with the screen writer and producers in a restaurant here in San Francisco. We talked about what would go into the film, and later we met again in Louisiana to scout for possible locale where the film could be shot.

Tracy Keenan Wynn [script writer] was quite possibly seeïng the South for the first time. He had been to Florida, but never to my part of Louisiana. So it was a revelation for him—cultural shock, I think they call it. And later when the film was made, you saw, I saw, that Miss Jane was revealing her story to a white newspaper man, blond, blue eyes, instead of that black schoolteacher as I had earlier written it. (I've been told, not by Tracy, by others, that America was not ready yet, for a total black show, without one sympathetic white character from beginning to end. Remember, this was

[28]Walter Zeno died a few months after Gaines gave this speech.

just a little over four years ago.)

Anyway, I've been criticized and criticized for the white character in that particular role. As if I had anything to do with it at all. I was not officially involved with the script, and did not see it as a whole until they had started shooting it in the South. And even if I had seen the script, and objected to the character—because we had no clause in the contract about character interpretations—any opposition of mine would have meant nothing.

Originally, the producers had wanted to make the film for the theaters. But no major movie company was interested in a story about an old black woman talking into a tape recorder, no matter what she was talking about. The producers then turned to television. The first network, ABC, turned the script down even though they had paid for first option. (Later whoever the person was in charge of special programs would admit in TV Guide that he had made a big mistake.) The script was then taken to CBS. A young man there in charge of special programs liked the script very much and convinced his bosses that they ought to try it. They felt they were taking a big chance, but they decided to give Miss Jane two hours of prime time.

Tracy Kennan Wynn had wanted in the beginning to write a story that would cover a period of two nights. Because he felt, and rightly so, that it would need that much time to tell the story in its entirety. But the producers knew that they could not get that kind of time, nor that kind of money. They knew they were setting a precedent, and they had to take whatever they could get. But after the popularity of Miss Jane, other shows, of course, did better. Not only did they get more money, they got twice, four times, six times as much time. And ABC, the very network who would not take the chance at first, seems to be the leader in producing the novel on television today.

The film is very good, no doubt about it. Some critics have said, including Pauline Kael, that it quite possibly might be the best film made especially for television. But there are drawbacks. Many. And I think the main drawback is because of money and time. The book covers a hundred years in time—on television—we had a hundred and ten minutes—just over a minute to a year. Tracy had written a script for at least three or four hours. To edit the script down to two hours was to eliminate many good parts, and much good acting. As the film is now, we find that we have many peaks, but few valleys. No gentle slopes leading up to the dramatic points, no gentle slopes leading from the dramatic points.

Couple of examples, then I'll sit down. In the book the Cajun assassin, Albert Cluveau, is a very good friend of Miss Jane. As a matter of fact, the only friend in the world he has is Miss Jane. No one else would tolerate him. After he has killed the schoolteacher, Miss Jane's adopted son, Albert Cluveau gradually loses his mind. This is the way it is in my book, the way it was in the script, and the way it was filmed. But when the film was taken back to Hollywood and edited, the mad scenes, the actor's best scenes, were left out. In the film we never ever see him again after he killed the teacher, which was a crime to this man's acting.

There were other cases like that. There's a tender love scene between Joe Pittman and Jane Pittman just before he leaves to recapture the horse that would eventually kill him. That particular scene explains where he would die—but you never get to see it. You witness the death—and that's all. There's another tender and tragic love story between a white boy and an octoroon school teacher. This is in the book, it was actually filmed, but later edited. Because there was not enough money to pay for time.

Yesterday, I was reading the newspapers about the fifty most popular shows that have been on television. Football games, baseball games, the film Roots and many other shows. Miss Jane was not one of them. But we don't mind—she and I. She knows what she's done—

and I'm very proud of that.

And I wish to thank you again for being proud enough of her to ask me in her stead to be here tonight. Thank you.

* * *

Recommended by Senator John F. Dunlap, Gaines became a member of the California Library Services Board for 1978-80. His letter of intent concerning the position read:

> Until I was sixteen years old I had never walked inside a library, public or private. Where I come from in Louisiana there were no libraries for blacks, and I could not go into the ones for whites. It was in Vallejo, California, that I went into my first library. That was in 1949. Since then I have spent as much time in libraries as I have in any other place except my own house. It was there that I discovered the writings of Hemingway, Faulkner, Twain, Joyce, Shakespeare, Tolstoy, Flaubert, Chekov, de Maupassant, and so on and so on. It was there that I tried to imitate them, and later my own books would be shelved somewhere between those of Faulkner's and Hemingway's. I supposed the main reason I would like to serve on the California Library Board is that I love books, and would like to have something to say about keeping them around.
>
> The second question, What do I hope to accomplish? falls under the answer above. I would like to have a voice in keeping libraries open and available to everyone. I would like to find a way to make more people come into libraries. Most people are afraid of libraries, because they are afraid of books. Since I do a lot of reading in public libraries, colleges and universities, I think I am in a good position to speak of its benefits. I have done so in the past, and I have used my own experience in the library as an example of what one can accomplish there. As for my qualifications for serving, I can only say that I've been involved with books daily

> the past twenty years. I have a library of my own now, so I am forever reading. I am also the author of six books. I have served as a library commissioner for the city and county of San Francisco. And I have been recognized by libraries both in my native state, Louisiana, and my adopted state, California, as a worthy contributor to our national literature. [Signed, Ernest J. Gaines]

The society column of the *San Jose Mercury News* gave an account of a party honoring Gaines in mid-July, 1978, at the home of the Russ Hofvendahls in Los Gatos Hills, celebrating the publication of *In My Father's House*. Three of Gaines' sisters, five brothers, and his mother, Mrs. Colar, were among the 120 guests on the "covered deck that looks across the swimming pool on a lower level and wooded hillsides to the valley below." In attendance were Gaines' literary friends Jeannie and Jim Houston (author of *Return to Manzinar*); Paul Desruisseaux, editor of the *Daily Californian*; and his wife, Pam Coakley, West Coast representative of Knopf publishers. Cicely Tyson was invited but was in Taiwan making a film. The party's highlight came when Gaines read the first chapter of *In My Father's House*.

September of 1978 marked Gaines' first speaking engagement, one of many to follow, on the University of Southwestern Louisiana campus at the Deep South Writers Conference. On this occasion he met Jason Berry for the first time.

On November 5 Gaines read from *Miss Jane Pittman* at the John F. Kennedy Library in Vallejo. He was one of the honorees at the Oakland Library's open House celebration of its hundredth anniversary on November 15, 1978. His photo and biographical data appeared on the back of the January, 1979 Oakland Library Newsletter. The Oakland *Montclarion* commented on Gaines' fans who wanted autographs on copies of *Miss Jane Pittman*: "Literary star Ernest J. Gaines comes in with such a crowd it is impossible to talk to him."

Apparently his opinion of televising another of his works had altered, since the first bittersweet reactions to the filming of *Miss Jane*, for just a few days earlier he had spoken with a

Vallejo Times-Herald interviewer on the subject of how to choose his favorite one: "That's like asking a parent who is his favorite child. Each book has its own merits—each has something to give."

A letter from Oppenheimer, dated November 20, 1978, and Gaines' own remarks found in his papers, indicate that he was asked to speak at the Modern Language Association Convention in 1978, but declined. Oppenheimer's letter read in part:

> Dear E, You shouldn't have hung up on me. I've been trying to call you back to tell you I talked to Stepto [Howard University professor] and he's going to try and straighten it all out. E, what's the matter? I have something terribly wrong with my tooth—the one that supports a bridge and this has not been one of my happiest days. . . . My jaw hurts and also my head, and, E, I really want to quit being an agent. I only have a very few good years left. So I'll hang on one more year, ok? Please call me about the MLA thing. . . . Take care, DO.

(Gaines did not speak at the MLA until 1981, though he was asked a second time before then, according to statements in his papers, saying that he had turned down two previous invitations, because he did not know what was expected of him. The reference to Stepto is not clarified).

Gaines served on the Board of Education for the Oakland Unified School District in 1979. The draft of an undated letter in Gaines' papers, probably written in 1979, indicates that he might have applied for a teaching position in some California school at this time. It was typed on yellow paper and read in part:

> I have been writer in residence at several universities, including Denison University for three weeks, the University of Arkansas for one week,—as well as Ohio State, Yale, Lewis and Clark, the University of Texas, Brown and others. . . . I should prefer working in the evening if possible. If not, then

> anytime that there might be vacancy.[29]

In April, 1979, Gaines presented readings from his works at the University of Texas in the Academic Center Auditorium, an event sponsored by the university and the Texas Union Afro-American Culture and Ideas/Issues Committee.

* * *

Gaines read and lectured at the Library of Congress on February 26, 1980, on a series entitled "Poetry Readings, Lectures, and Dramatic Readings," sponsored by Gertrude Clarke Whittall. A brochure for this particular series of lectures said of Gaines:

> Gaines, who thinks that the artist is the only free man left in the world, has so far been concerned in his fiction (usually about rural Louisiana) with individuals determined, often heroically . . . to maintain their codes of conduct among debasing or confusing forces or to face the consequences of changing with the times.

In early March of 1980 Gaines volunteered and was accepted as a speaker for the Honors English class in San Francisco's School Volunteers Community Resource Service, a federally funded project for Career Education which provided extra speakers, lecturers and performers for public schools. Apparently he had already done community service previously by speaking in the schools, for in November of 1979 the Oakland Unified School District, as the result of Gaines' visit to one of their schools, presented him with a compilation of ten essays and poems based on *Miss Jane Pittman*. The foreword of this tribute stated:

> Ernest J. Gaines, author of *Miss Jane Pittman* and

[29] Gaines did teach creative writing at Stanford in 1981, possibly as the result of this application.

> other works, is the first visitor for the 1979-80 school year. Since writing is a vital part of our language arts thrust, Mr. Gaines' visit will assist in motivating students to participate in creative writing and improve skills in this area. Former speakers, such as Maya Angelou, James Baldwin, and Alex Haley, have also been an inspiration to students in creative writing.

On April 9, 1980, Gaines received the first of his five honorary degrees, a Doctorate of Letters, from Denison University in Granville, Ohio, where he had been writer in residence for three weeks in the winter of 1971. Denison, founded in 1831, is a private, coed university of medium size. The following kudo appeared on the Honors Convocation program for the occasion: "Ernest J. Gaines, able student of literature and writing, artful recorder of our history and our aspirations, gifted creator of fictions that speak the truth."

On April 21, 1980, Gaines read at the College of Alameda in that California city, as part of Black History Week. A report in the *Alameda Times Star* stated: "Gaines laughed. It was the laugh of a man who is proud of what he has done, who knows he has captured his early youth in memory and print." He read from his story "Grandpa and the Haint," which is about a young boy and his parents who "encounter a stiff dose of Louisiana Voodoo."

That same month Gaines read from *A Gathering of Old Men*, then in progress, at Unity of Connecticut College and Genesis of the U. S. Coast Guard Academy in New London. Jointly presented by the Department of Humanities and ECLIPSE, the annual cultural program of Genesis and Unity, the event was titled "An Evening with Ernest Gaines." After reading Gaines answered questions about "The Sky is Gray". A report in the *Eagle's Nest* for May, 1980, quoted a cadet as saying:

> I was grateful for the opportunity to listen and talk to Mr. Gaines—he made my goals for achievement seem attainable, seem real. [Mr. Gaines is] a rare person who enjoys great success without losing humility. Anyone

> who had listened to this gentleman was touched by his sincerity, spirit, and especially his class.

It was obvious from his speech that he loved people, "had a contagious spark, a simple background and approach to life."

A letter from Oppenheimer, dated December 22, 1980, to New York attorney Frank R. Curtis, stated that Gaines would receive $5,000 from *Reader's Digest* for permission to print a condensation of *Miss Jane Pittman.* Curtis was to receive a $500 fee. The condensation has not been published, however, according to a telephone spokesperson in the Indexing Department of *Reader's Digest*, November, 1989.

* * *

Evidence of Gaines' collaborative effort on a musical in 1980-81 is found in a letter to the National Endowment for the Arts, dated January 13, 1981.

> This letter is in reference to Dr. Valerian Smith's request for aid from the National Endowment for the Arts. Dr. Smith, Ms. Lynn Smith Whitfield, Ms. Hedi Wilmore, and I have been working on a musical for the past several months. We had been promised enough aid from other sources, but this did not materialize. Therefore we are turning to you for help.
>
> The project is a musical titled *Supper*. The plot concerns the effort by church members to raise enough money to pay off a church's debt, and the action takes place in present day Louisiana. Any black person who has grown up in the South has gone to a Supper. On any given Saturday night somebody nearby is giving a Supper. There is much 'Soul' food—fried chicken, fried fish, gumbo, chittlin, pralines, pies and cakes—available for little money. There is also soft drinks for children, and hard drinks for the old. There might be some gambling, craps or poker, in another room of the house. The Lord does not frown upon this, because all of

> the money, or most of it, will go to help the church. All kinds of characters from all social backgrounds are present. A doctor of medicine, a professor at the local college or university, a lady of the street, her pimp, the man who picks up garbage, and the maid who makes beds in motel rooms are all there. It is probably the only time when people from the various backgrounds will all meet under the same roof.
>
> In *Supper* there are several subplots, comic and tragic. There is much singing and dancing. *Supper* is original in both idea and locale. Nothing like a Louisiana Supper has been put on stage before, because there is no place like Southern Louisiana for its food, its people, and its various dialects. We are hoping that the Endowment may aid us in presenting this project soon. [Ernest Gaines, author.]

There is no evidence that "Supper" ever materialized, if the above letter, in fact, was actually sent to the NEA. A letter to Anne Simpson from Jillian Miller of the NEA Opera-Musical Theater Program, dated December 6, 1989, stated:

> I have looked through the Endowment's Annual Reports in an effort to locate information on Ernest J. Gaines and/or 'Supper.' There are no records of his receiving funding from the Opera-Musical Theater Program. Unfortunately, we do not keep records past five fiscal years in the office and since he did not receive funding, it is impossible for us to tell if his application was rejected or if he simply did not apply.

In 1981 Gaines served as a member of the editorial board for the California Bar Association's magazine, *The California Lawyer*. He taught a graduate course in creative writing at Stanford University in the spring of 1981, "the same one that he had taken as a student some twenty-two years earlier, when he was a Stegner Fellow at Stanford," according to Director of

Creative Writing Nancy H. Packer.[30]

The following fall Gaines spoke again at the Deep South Writers' Conference at the University of Southwestern Louisiana in Lafayette, where he would remain as visiting professor creative writing for the fall semester. At the same writers' conference Gaines' poet friend Wendell Berry spoke on the intricacies of poetry, a form he would like to see extended. Gaines' talk mainly concerned the writing of *Miss Jane Pittman*. He recalled that one strong influence in preparing it was *Lay My Burden Down*, a collection of interviews with slaves, published in 1945. Some of these short pieces are quite humorous, while others depict the slaves' oppression and fear.

He told the audience that *Miss Jane Pittman* was at first to be titled "A Short Biography of Miss Jane Pittman," but it grew as he began to fall in love with Miss Jane's character. Gaines pointed out that few black writers follow through with their Southern traditions. "Writers must care for people in their stories . . . and write dialogue using normal conversation. Fiction can be true without being entirely factual."[31]

* * *

Before the fall of 1981, Gaines' exposure as a lecturer on the college/university level had been expanded to Yale, Brown, Stanford, Lewis and Clark, San Francisco State, and to the Universities of California, Arkansas, Texas, Louisiana, Southwestern Louisiana, Southern, Virginia, Kentucky, and North Carolina at Chapel Hill, to mention only a few of his engagements. He had also read for a second time at the Library of Congress.

Written from San Francisco his acceptance letter for the position at USL to English Department chairman Dr. Albert Fields, dated May 4, 1981, read:

[30]Letter from Nancy Packer to Anne Simpson, January 21, 1990.

[31]*Morning Advocate*, September 22, 1981.

> I am very happy and deeply honored to be offered the position of Visiting Professor of English to the University of Southwestern Louisiana for the academic year, 1981-1982. And I hereby accept the offer under the agreements stipulated in your letter of 24 April 1981. Attached was the customary vita.

In December of 1981, Gaines spoke at the West Coast Modern Language Association meeting, held in Los Angeles at the Westin Hotel. Excerpts follow from the somewhat low-key speech, which in essence was a series of stories.

> Recently I read an interview with Theodore White—a man who has made a lot of money writing about other men—and in the interview he said there's nothing more demeaning than promoting a book about one's self. I agree with Mr. White wholeheartedly. The next most demeaning thing I can think of is trying to explain one's own art—be he writer, musician, painter—athlete—whatever.
>
> Neither Joe Louis nor Willie Mays could explain his art. And Muhammed Ali, in an interview, will talk about everything else but fighting. And that's the way it should be. The artist should do his work as well as he can, and let it be at that. Nothing else is necessary. Willie Mays occasionally dropped a fly ball, but he hit home runs more often. So why should we ask him why he committed the error, or how he could possibly hit a ball coming at him at 97.5 miles an hour. Let other men explain that. Those who sit in press boxes with little speed timers, let them explain it. That's what they get paid for. Mays was paid to swing, to connect, and that's what he did, and he did well. Joe Louis said enough for all athletes, all artists, when he explained to a reporter just how he would whip the fleet footed Billy Conn. Quoted Mr. Louis: 'He can run, run, run, but he can't, can't hide.'
>
> The artist is too busy creating to explain it. Once he starts explaining it, he no longer creates, he becomes the

> critic. The greatest creator of all, the one we all try imitating, created the world in six days, and on the seventh day he did not meet critics, he rested. Now I think most of us feel that he did a pretty good job. Of course we do wonder why He created some of the things that He did. I for one have often asked myself why in all his wonders he created mosquitoes and Mississippi. And still I don't think it's necessary for him to have to explain it to me.
>
> I ignored the first and second invitations to come to the MLA convention, because I had no idea what was wanted of me. I called this friend [Michael Harper] who knows more about these things than I do, and I asked him: 'What the hell is this oral to writing stuff, anyway?' He said, 'It's what we talk about when we get together.' I said 'But we're doing nothing but bs-ing most of the time. We're drinking, listening to jazz, blues—bs-ing like dogs.' 'Well, talk about that,' my friend said. 'Just be natural.'

Gaines, as aforesaid, considers himself a poor story teller. He continued the speech by saying that when he tries

> people will go to bathrooms, order drinks, or start talking to someone else. Some would come out directly and tell me, 'Oh, cut it out, Gaines. Go home and write a book.' But there are a few who would stand around and listen to me—not that they were interested, but they felt they should show some courtesy to the author of *Miss Jane Pittman*. I've had about five hundred offers to write biographies since that book came out."

Everywhere he went he met

> at least one person who had a story to tell so fantastic that it would put Miss Jane's puny little story to shame. Several ladies of the street have offered me a 50-50 deal [to write theirs], and besides there would be fringe benefits. . . . I listen to all of them. One day, maybe

> twenty years from now I'll be able to sift through it all and do something with it. You catch a little here and a little there, and you let it sink in, and try to do something with it later. At least that's how its worked for me.

In closing Gaines said,

> I would bore myself to death trying to write the way I speak. I prefer trying to imitate others. I told my buddy Mike Harper that I'd talk about the things he and I talk about when we're together. That I've tried to do. I hope I didn't bore you to death. Thank you, thank you very much.

* * *

On January 14, 1982, Gaines read on two programs in Modesto, California, highlighting that city's observance of Martin Luther King's birthday. The *Modesto Bee* reported that of his own works Gaines said,

> Perhaps militant writing has made white people more aware of blacks. I think a scream can reach ten times as many people in a hurry as a book can. But I hope my books will be around awhile. When I'm angry I sit down and try to write the perfect paragraph, the perfect sentence. That's how I strike back. I hope that in my works I do write about the things King [Martin Luther, Jr.] stood for.

After the event Gaines said, "It is more important for a man to be a man for a moment than to be a non-man for the rest of his life. A woman should be feminine rather than a feminist; a mother and a wife."

In late February of 1982 Gaines spoke in Indianapolis on "The Art of Writing" as part of Black History Month. The Indianapolis-Marion Company sponsored the event, in connection with the Public Library Foundation. About his pace of writing Gaines said, "I cannot hurry the process. Every word, every line of dialogue must be the best I can do. I write to be read aloud." The film of "The Sky is Gray" was shown at this meeting.[32]

Gaines, in his mellifluous voice, made a perfect narrator for "A Lincoln Portrait" by American composer Aaron Copland when the work was presented on May 2, 1982, by the University of Southwestern Louisiana's symphony, "L'Orchestre," in Angelle Theater on the campus. As stated in the program notes, the narration included direct quotes from Lincoln with directions to the speaker, who is

> cautioned against undue emphasis on the delivery of Lincoln's words. The words are sufficiently dramatic in themselves; they need no added emotion in order to put them across to the audience. They are meant to be read simply and directly, without a trace of exaggerated sentiment. It is the composer's wish that the Speaker depend for his effect, not on his acting ability, but on his complete sincerity of manner.

Gaines' participation in this campus activity was well received. A reception followed the concert, honoring Gaines and benefactor Andrew Jumonville.

Stipulations in Gaines' contract with USL, which was renewed for the fall of 1982 term, required that he speak at USL's annual fall Deep South Writers Conference, as part of the university's Black Visiting Professor program. The USL administrators had no intention of curtailing, locally or elsewhere, his speaking engagements, which continued apace. On October 1, 1982, Gaines spoke at LeMoyne-Owen College, a private, church affiliated school in Memphis. Program notes for the occasion said of Gaines: "In his home state, he developed 'his perfect pitch for the sound and sense of people's speech.' "

That same fall the public schools of Pointe Coupée Parish, Gaines' native area, sponsored an "Ernest J. Gaines Literary Contest" for grades 9-12. The guidelines stipulated:

> Write an essay not more than 500 words long on some

[32]*Indianapolis News,* February 27,1982.

> aspect of your own personal experiences and observations of Pointe Coupée Parish, such as work, school, recreation, religion, changes you notice, what you like or dislike, etc. Originality is important. Provide your own title.

Judges for the contest, which drew forty papers, were ten of Gaines' colleagues of the USL English faculty. Prizes to the winners were presented at the Parish Fair on October 23, 1982.

* * *

Teaching responsibilities at USL have allowed Gaines the spring semesters and summers off, at which time he returns to San Francisco to pursue his writing and fulfill more speaking engagements. Gaines was visiting professor at Whittier College in California for the spring semester of 1983, where he held the Richard M. Nixon chair. At the time he told a *Los Angeles Times* journalist that he had no trouble with that politically: "I'm here to teach creative writing."

On March 10, 1983, Gaines spoke at the University of Houston with co-guest writer Evangelina Vigil, professor of literature at that institution. (Vigil's *Thirty an' Seen a Lot* won the 1982 American Book Award.)

The following May, having returned to California for the summer, Gaines was speaker at the Eleventh Annual Festival of Children's Books in Fresno. The *Fresno Bee* well covered the event in its May 13, 1983, issue. Gaines admitted the need for more black children's books, but said that though he had often been associated with children's literature, frequently writing from a child's point of view, he did not really know how to write children's literature. "I can go back and get a child's voice when I want to," he said.

He told the audience that *In My Father's House* was received "coolly." James Baldwin had written him from Paris concerning the book, saying "Mon cher, mon cher, it seems like you're selling out." Gaines, however, did not feel that he had sold out nor slumped on it, saying that if someone else did not like it, it was that person's problem, not his. He had never intending writing a sequel to any of his books, because after giving each one his best, he moves on, even though the new project may not at first seem as good as the previous one.

While speaking he used the word "sweat," applying it to his craft as a wordsmith. Gaines said:

> I'm not one of those cerebral writers . . . who can sit in a classroom and talk and talk about all the psychological and philosophical things that go into my writing. I create characters, then make those characters do whatever my philosophy happens to be through character action.

He cited as an example Miss Jane Pittman: what she said and did carried the action. When someone in the audience pointed out to Gaines that his characters all were either going somewhere or returning from somewhere, he said, "You're damned right they do!" His role models are based on rural people and their philosophies, people who stuck to what they believed in. He has wanted, above all else, to please his Aunt Augusteen.

* * *

Gaines continually renews his stylistic thoughts by re-reading his favorite Russian writers, the Bible, Shakespeare, and poetry. Periodically he has met for rap sessions with contemporary writers Gwendolyn Brooks, James A. McPherson, Alice Walker, Toni Morrison, Al Young (*Sitting Pretty*), and Ishmael Reed. Some of these gifted writers, along with Larry McMurty (*The Last Picture Show, Terms of Endearment, Some Can Whistle*), Gaines says are among his extremely talented collection of "drinking buddies" from Stanford days.

Walker's friendship with Gaines dates back to the 1960s, when she lived only a few blocks from him in San Francisco. Author of the novels *The Color Purple*, *Meridian*, and most recently *The Temple of My Familiar*, to Walker's credit also are volumes of poetry, *Revolutionary Petunias* and *Once*. Some of the poems from *Once*, in typescript, are in Gaines' papers. (See Appendix 5 for additional information on Walker.)

In San Francisco on June 24, 1983, Gaines was one of eleven artists honored at that city's Arts Festival for his/her exceptional contribution to the cultural achievements in the Bay Area. Works of each of the eleven honorees were displayed from June 24 through July 3 in the SFMO Gallery at the Bank of America World Headquarters on California Street in San Francisco. The awards were presented by Mayor Dianne Feinstein and Arts Commission President Roselyne C. Swig. Established in 1971, the Commission originally honored only one person.

This same year, at the first Bay Area Writers' Conference held in San Rafael, Gaines read from *A Gathering of Old Men*, his latest novel. Parts of a glowing letter of thanks, undated, from conference coordinator Judith Greber follows:

> On behalf of everyone who had the opportunity to hear you read from *A Gathering of Old Men* and answer questions, I thank you. You were the highlight of the first Bay Area Writers' Conference, and your presence helped make the conference the success it was.
>
> It was a thrill hearing you and meeting you and the only sad part of the evening was learning that you will be leaving San Francisco soon. If you are ever back in the area, I would hope that we could again lure you into the conference.
>
> You were a memorable and inspirational speaker to every writer in that room, and all of us thank you and wish you great happiness in Louisiana—and we all look forward to the work that will come out of your new locale. Thank you.

A Gathering of Old Men resembles a skillfully drawn murder mystery. There is plenty of suspense as it unravels. Set on a plantation, each of Gaines' many characters, from a small boy to the very old men, tells a story, providing clues to a killing, but in doing so, some of them feel protective enough of the real killer to assume the blame themselves. By taking a stand against the "system" for the first time, the old men have gained self-respect by speaking out, thereby asserting themselves as "men."

Shortly after the publication of *A Gathering of Old Men* in the summer of 1983, Gaines' sister Lois Young, gave a party for him in her home in Mount Hamilton, overlooking San Jose. Gaines, dressed in a white suit, read to about fifty friends and family members gathered in Mrs. Young's front yard. In an undated, unnamed news item book editor Constance Casey wrote of the occasion:

> He [Gaines] read quickly but distinctly, in the language of an 8-year-old boy in this section, then of a middle-aged black woman and a young white man in others. The effect was like listening to a piece of music in which three different instruments—a flute, a trumpet, and then a trombone, perhaps—which advance the same theme. . . . Here in San Jose Gaines' voice was drowned out for a few minutes by the quintessential suburban sound, a neighbor's power lawn mower. 'Don't hit him,' Gaines called after his young brother-in-law, Jesse Coval, running down the hill to get the neighbor to stop. 'Invite him up. Tell him we've got some drinks up here.'

Casey mentioned one of the guests, novelist Bill Broder, a fellow student with Gaines at Stanford, as saying: "Of all the writers I knew then, Ernie was the most unwilling to compromise, not for fashion or for politics. In the 60s, black radicals gave him grief for not being sufficiently political. But he wrote about what he felt he was meant to write about." Another guest, author Joe Gores, said of his longtime friendship with Gaines, "As a writer you really don't meet that many people who are real writers."

Don Thackeray, celebrated author of *Masada* and *Fate is the Hunter*, was also at the party. He recalled first meeting Gaines on an interview in 1967: "You want Ernest K. Gann," Gaines said to him, as he answered the door. "Don't tell me who I want to interview," Thackeray stormed back at him. After going up the block for a drink, they became friends, and since have co-owned a twenty-eight-foot sloop. Another acquaintance, San Francisco upholsterer Ricky Weathersby, who did some work for Gaines, was at the party. Curiously, Weathersby was born about 100 miles from Oscar, Louisiana.

It was undoubtedly a rewarding day for Gaines in many ways. He autographed forty books. Journalist Casey was amused at a conversation related to her by Gaines' brother, Mac.

> Mac: "Will you be selling books at the party tomorrow, E. G.?"
>
> Gaines: "Yes."
>
> Mac: "Save me four or five. How much are they going for?"
>
> Gaines: "$14."
>
> Mac: "I'll take one."

The day after Mrs. Young's party Gaines talked about *A Gathering of Old Men* on a TV show in Los Angeles. Also on this same circuit he spoke to a group in Oakland, encouraging young people to do more reading. Now it was time to assume his new teaching duties in Lafayette, Louisiana.

GAINES AS PROFESSOR

Having been a guest writer at the University of Southwestern Louisiana between 1981-83, Gaines joined the English faculty in the fall of 1983. With an eye to the future and financial security, he decided to stay at USL for at least a few years.

In 1982 when Gaines was asked to donate his papers to the archives of Dupré Library, he agreed. He brought two heavily insured trunks of them when he came for the Deep South Writers Conference in September of that year. Another four to six foot-lockers were left in San Francisco awaiting shipment. USL English professor Joseph Riehl designated that the papers be used by scholars at Dupré, honoring Gaines' restrictions on reading some of the sections containing unpublished manuscripts. Painstaking and meticulous cataloging has been done by Dr. Bruce Turner, Dupré archivist, with the assistance of Riehl, Dupré director Donald Saporito, and English professor Dr. Albert Fields.

There is still a large amount of papers which will not be available to the public until after Gaines' death. According to the present agreement with Dupré Library, Gaines still owns the papers, though ultimately Dupré hopes to secure permanent ownership. A contract states that USL has the first right of refusal in case some other library or individual wants to buy them, depending on the amount of the monetary offer.

* * *

USL was the first state university in Louisiana to desegregate (1954), a move which may have had some influence on Gaines' coming there. In 1983, out of the 16,000 enrollment, 16.3 percent were black students. The December 3, 1983, *Los Angeles Times* carried some of Gaines' comments on the matter: "Not only am I here [at USL], have a good teaching job here, but I am teaching a lot of kids whose parents probably fought against my being in any school at all. There's so much the students can learn from each other that can break down stereotypes." Gaines was "not bitter at having grown up without the opportunities that were available to whites, but is relieved that the change is occurring." Gaines had begun to see and applaud the changes brought about by the civil rights activists in the last twenty-five years, remembering how formerly the blacks had no courage to back their feelings for fear of being bombed. Periodically he is encouraged by desegregation efforts in Southern schools, but only if they result in integration.

Dr. Carl Wooton, USL English professor, was quite instrumental in persuading Gaines to come to USL. Wooton continues to introduce Gaines each year when he speaks at the Deep South Writers Conference. Gaines still confesses to being slightly nervous each time he speaks in public. A reporter for The *Times of Acadiana*, March 23, 1982, said, "It's as if he's afraid his listeners may boo loudly if they don't like the story.

Or maybe he fears they simply will fall asleep in their seats." Anyone who has ever heard Gaines would consider either of these actions unlikely.

By 1983 Lafayette's university and business communities were well aware of the author's talents, and rightly so. *A Gathering of Old Men* had just been published and had received favorable reviews. *Miss Jane Pittman* had sold a million copies and had been translated into several languages. Both *Catherine Carmier* and *In My Father's House* had been reissued in paperback. *Of Love and Dust* and *Bloodline* were still in print and selling. Attention was turned toward living accommodations befitting the author, who for the past two years had lived on campus in Cajun Village, a housing area for married students.

Gaines returned to the USL campus in August of 1983, unaware that a surprise awaited him. He was met at the airport by some English Department colleagues, brought to Arbolada, one of Lafayette's older residential areas adjacent to the campus, and presented with the keys to a lovely brick home. Lafayette attorney F. Ray Mouton, Jr. (descendant of a Confederate general, Alfred Mouton, and Jean Mouton, the founder of Lafayette) and his wife Janice, both USL graduates, had given the home to USL. It is to be Gaines' permanent home as long as he stays on the USL faculty, with the stipulation that only a family member may live there with him. The Moutons' generosity may have been influenced by their young son, who talked about the movie of *Miss Jane Pittman* for five days after he had watched it some ten years earlier. Mouton said, "For the story to have that type of impact on a young white boy in the South, it had to be exceptional."

Tasteful furnishings for this gracious house were donated by local merchants, a project chaired and implemented by Dr. Joseph Riehl. Money for yard upkeep has been provided by USL. Adding to the home's decor is a portrait of Gaines in his beret by area artist Larry Wilson, done from a photo taken by Philip Gould. The garage was remodeled as a repository for Gaines' manuscripts and other papers as they were shipped from San Francisco. Gaines gradually moved these to Dupré Library, footlocker by footlocker.

A letter presented to Gaines from the Moutons read: "Please

accept the gift of this home in honor of Miss Jane, Catherine, and the Old Men." Gaines accepted the home "in honor of all the Jane Pittmans . . . and Old Men of the world who have worked hard and suffered." Gaines now admits that some of his best friends are Cajuns, the group whom he had formerly made villains in his books. His appreciation runs deep.

* * *

GAINES AS PUBLIC SPEAKER

Shortly after his installment in the new home, Gaines was again featured at the Deep South Writers Conference, at which time he read from *A Gathering of Old Men*. In the following weeks he spoke twice in New Iberia, Louisiana. Once he read from *Old Men* at the Iberia Parish Library. Then at a less formal presentation, in reminiscing about his lack of boxing prowess, he told the audience, "I undid the laces of the gloves with my teeth, took them off, and went to the library." A letter to Gaines, dated November 22, 1983, from the Iberia Parish Library director, Carla Klapper, was quite complimentary. In part it said:

> I believe that your discussion with the RATs group opened a new view of life to that mostly white group. As for your second appearance, that is the best representation that we have ever had from the black community for any library program since I arrived here last year. I know that we gained a few Friends that evening, and I found you as one of them.[33]

The Bayouland Library System held its regional meeting in December of 1983 at the Lafayette Hilton Hotel. As guest speaker Gaines' topic was "Libraries—A Writer's Perspective." More in demand than ever as a speaker, Gaines scheduled in the

[33]Ms. Klapper clarified RATS, "Readings in American Themes," as a Louisiana Endowment for the Humanities funded literature program. At the time the story under study was Gaines' "The Sky is Gray."

Lafayette area alone two to five speaking engagements, autograph sessions, or other professional commitments per week from October, 1983 through May of 1984, confirmed by his itinerary handwritten on a calendar found in his papers. At one of these engagements when St. Anthony's Church in Lafayette celebrated Black History Month, in February of 1984, Gaines read at a brunch from *Miss Jane Pittman*.

On April 6, 1984, he was the keynote speaker for a Festival of the Arts, held on the Shreveport-Bossier City Southern University campus. Afterwards an autographing reception was held in Gaines' honor at the Barnwell Art and Garden Center in Shreveport. On display were copies of *Miss Jane Pittman* and *In My Father's House*. Later in April, when Texas Women's University in Denton held its forty-sixth annual Writers Conference, Gaines was the featured speaker. After his comments a video of *Miss Jane Pittman* was shown. In May of 1984 Gaines was made an honorary life member of USL's chapter of Phi Kappa Phi Honor Society.

Two quite significant and prestigious honors came to Gaines in 1984. In March of that year he received a letter from Dr. Howard R. Swearer of Brown University, notifying him that Brown would confer upon him an honorary Doctor of Letters in May. Swearer's letter read: "The Fellows desire to recognize in this manner your outstanding career as a writer who has spoken eloquently for the voiceless in our society." Formal invitations were to be sent to any of Gaines' family whom he wished to invite to the ceremony.

Also of national note, for the second time Gaines was the recipient of the Commonwealth Club of California Award. The event, held in the Gold Ballroom of the Sheraton Palace Hotel in San Francisco on June 8, 1984, was broadcast over National Public Radio. This time the award went to Gaines for *A Gathering of Old Men*, chosen during 1983 as the best work of fiction by a California writer. At the time Shirley Temple Black, who presented the award, was president of the Commonwealth Club. Her letter informing Gaines of this honor read in part: "I am looking forward to meeting and hosting you and your guests. Congratulations on your outstanding work. We are particularly pleased to present this award to you for a second time." (Before receipt of Black's letter, Gaines had received a mailgram in March from Director Michael Brassington, asking him to be the featured speaker at this fifty-third annual program for California writers.)

A draft of Gaines' acceptance speech for receiving the honor was found in his papers. (Evidently he later deleted all except the first paragraph, according to the Commonwealth's bulletin published subsequently.)

> Madame President, Mr. Director, Members of the Dais, Ladies and Gentlemen: I wish to thank the Commonwealth Club of California for this award. It is an honor indeed to receive this award a second time, to stand where such writers as John Steinbeck, William Saroyan, Wallace Stegner, C. S. Forester, others whose name are as familiar, stood before, writers whose works I had to study in college and the university, and one in particular, Wallace Stegner, who helped develop my craft as a writer while I was a student of his at Stanford. Again, Madame President, Mr. Director, I thank you.
>
> At the same time, this is a sad moment for me, because I have to say goodbye to my apartment on Divisadero Street where all the seven books were written. I have been offered the position of writer-in-residence at the University of Southwestern Louisiana—and which I have accepted. Come January 1985 my permanent address will no longer be on Divisadero Street, but Buena Vista, in Lafayette, Louisiana. It is ironic, but this same institution which now offers me that position would not have allowed me entrance through its front door when I left the South in 1948, but only through its side door or back door, and only then had I entered with a mop and a bucket.
>
> But I will go back, to continue my writing, as well as teach, and I only hope that I can give to a student, white, black, male or female, the kind of help, encouragement in his or her writing as I received from my instructors at San Francisco State and Stanford.
>
> This is not to say that I'm saying goodbye to San

> Francisco. Don't close your Golden Gate to me. It gets awful hot in Louisiana in summer months, and I will be happy to return to San Francisco for its cool weather, to walk through the park, and to go with my buddies out on the bay, to sail around Alcatraz and Angel Islands. I will always come back to San Francisco.

Gaines then read from *A Gathering of Old Men*, which excerpts were also printed in the Commonwealth's bulletin.

Gaines received another honorary doctorate in the spring of 1985 from Bard College in Annandale-on-Hudson, New York. Bard, established in 1860, has hosted such writers-in-residence as Ralph Ellison, Mary McCarty, and Saul Bellow. In a letter from Bard's president, Leon Botstein, Gaines was given the honorary Doctorate of Letters "in recognition of your outstanding and distinguished contributions in the field of literature and to the literary heritage of this country." Gaines was the unanimous choice for speaker at this event, held on June 1, 1985. Author Philip Roth also received an honorary doctorate at this time.

In July of 1985 Gaines spoke at the Barnwell Garden and Arts Center in Shreveport, Louisiana, giving his much quoted advice to aspiring writers: "Read, read, read, and write, write, write." He emphasized the importance of continuing to write, despite rejections; re-writing then becomes real writing. He said that one must allow, as he himself did, the influence not only of other writers, but of athletes, musicians, and teachers, who all practiced discipline in their own ways to achieve individual goals.

Gaines shared some of his reflections, his enjoyment of the students, and mixed feelings about the amount of time teaching takes from his writing, with journalist Ruth Laney. As he teaches, he frequently reminds his black students that as a black, at their age, he would not have been admitted to the University of Southwestern Louisiana. Though the revolutionary fervor of the 1950s and '60s no longer exists, it did change things. The black-white situation has now become a matter of self, one not to do with color.

Continuing with Laney, he confided one of his visions for a

large scale novel which he felt strongly should be written. It would cover the period between 1958 and 1968, to include the deaths of Martin Luther King and the Kennedys. This novel could either be a series of vignettes with short chapters, or follow the more massive structure of *War and Peace*. As a representative American novel, it would include all basic elements: lynching, murder, assassination, and destruction of homes, property, and churches. Gaines has not wanted to spend time in research for such a book himself, but would willingly help a worthy student undertake the project. Gaines is not very sympathetic with a student writer who discredits his own experiences as a subject for writing.

Reflecting on changes within himself Gaines told Laney he felt he had begun to accomplish something, to contribute something to the world. Rather than compulsively jump into writing a novel with no overall plan, he prefers *thinking* through it carefully, then writing.

HONORS AND MORE HONORS

Whittier College, where Gaines had been visiting writer in 1983, honored him with its highest degree, Doctor of Humane Letters, at commencement exercises on May 25, 1986. A letter from Eugene S. Mills of Whittier requested that Gaines also be the commencement speaker for a $500 honorarium. Mills' letter assured Gaines that most anything he wanted to say would be acceptable:

> I think there would be a very great interest in remarks about your own life and distinguished career as a writer; or about the work of the writer as artist; or about the conversion of writing into film; or about the South and your background as a basis for literature. . . . You should feel free to speak personally and to say whatever you think might be especially informative to the graduates.

Another significant event, perhaps a more personal one,

occurred the following fall. On October 11, 1986, Gaines presented the Fourth Annual Literary Awards for Pointe Coupée Parish, the place of his birth.

* * *

In early April of 1987 Gaines participated in a panel discussion, "Tell About the South," in Chattanooga, under auspices of the Arts and Education Council's Conference on Southern Literature. On April 8 he was in New York City, having been chosen by the American Academy and Institute of Arts and Letters to receive a $5,000 award at this group's annual dinner. He was one of eight persons to receive a monetary award, to "honor and encourage writers in their creative work."

May of 1987 was another month of honors for Gaines. On May 10 an elaborate reception was held for him in Lafayette's Cajundome for the screening of *A Gathering of Old Men*. The list of 300 to 400 invited guests from the city and state also included Gaines' family. This same evening the film was shown on CBS. The local and area media coverage was generous.

It is not surprising that Gaines' salary at USL for the coming year increased considerably. On May 20, 1987, Louisiana State University in Baton Rouge conferred upon Gaines an honorary Doctorate of Humane Letters. A page in the commencement program devoted to Gaines gave some insight into his nature:

> It's not often that a Louisianian of fame remains in his home state. It's not often that he can bring positive recognition to his home and people. But Ernest J. Gaines has done just that. . . . He had a wish, and he made it come true. 'I want to smell that Louisiana earth, feel that Louisiana sun, sit under the shade of one of those Louisiana oaks, search for pecans in that Louisiana grass in one of those Louisiana yards next to one of those Louisiana bayous, not far from a Louisiana river. And I wanted to hear that Louisiana dialect—that combination of English, Creole, Cajun and black. For me there's no

> more beautiful sound anywhere. I wanted to read about the true relationship between whites and blacks—about the people I had known.'
>
> Gaines hasn't just heard about Louisiana. He's written about it. . . . In recognition of his national and international reputation as a writer who was born in Louisiana, who lives in Louisiana, whose short stories and novels are mostly set in Louisiana, who gives unceasingly of his time in reading and talking to children and citizens in Louisiana—and for the truth about our lives that he helped us see through his fiction, Louisiana State University considers it a privilege to confer upon Ernest J. Gaines the honorary degree, Doctor of Humane Letters, *honoris causa*.

There has rarely been a lull in Gaines' activities. In October of 1988 he received the Southeastern Library Association Award for *A Gathering of Old Men*, for his "significant contributions . . . not only to the culture and literature of the South and of America, but also to the body of international literature." SELA is an eleven-state membership association which strives to promote library and information services in the southeastern region of the United States. The Outstanding Southeastern Author Award was presented to Gaines at the opening session of the joint conference of the Virginia Library Association and SELA in Norfolk, October 26, 1988. Chairperson was Charles Beard, and the award presenter was Diane Guilford, chairperson of the selection committee.

As explained by Claudia Medori, SELA executive secretary for 1989, the award is presented every two years, unless the committee decides that none of the authors nominated is of a high enough caliber. The recipient is awarded an engraved plaque, a $500 honorarium, and his/her expenses are paid to the biennial conference to accept the award. Criteria for the recipient states that 1) authors considered must be native to or bona fide residents of a SELA state at the time the work was written or published; 2) caliber of author should be considered and if no deserving person is nominated the award may be omitted for the biennium; 3) author's works should be considered on the basis of their significance and important to the general public as well as on their literary excellence; and 4) two awards may be given during each biennium—one in fiction and one in non-fiction. In each category works must have been published within five years prior to December 31 of the year preceding the biennial conference.

First given in 1978, the Outstanding Author Award had previously been received by Eudora Welty that year; Richard Beale Davis, 1980; Dumas Malone, 1982; and Gail Godwin, 1984. There was no recipient in 1986.

In early November of 1988 Gaines accepted an invitation to speak at the Louisiana School for Math, Science and the Arts in Natchitoches. Outstanding students in their junior and senior high school years attend LSMSA through selective screening. Gaines read from his then unpublished short story, "Christ Walked Down Market Street," its first public reading, and received a roomful of 'thumbs-up' in response. He discussed specific points of his most famous works, and answered questions from the audience. After the event Chris Lyons, journalist for *Renaissance*, the school paper, wrote: "We were very fortunate to have this opportunity to speak with such a noted author."

GAINES HONORED WITH PUBLIC DRINKING FOUNTAIN

In May, 1989, plans were laid by the Freddie Thomas Foundation of Rochester, New York, for the erection of a drinking fountain named after Miss Jane Pittman and honoring Gaines. The Lafayette *Daily Advertiser*, August 28, 1989, gave an account of the project:

> The symbolism in the works of Ernest J. Gaines will always make an impression on the people there now that the city has named a new public water fountain after one of Gaines' characters, Miss Jane Pittman. . . . The idea for a public fountain came after a community leader could not find a water fountain to drink from while in the downtown area. The Freddie Thomas Foundation

> donated the structure, which has three fountains connected to one base. The foundation's board of directors felt the fountain symbolized the community's and Pittman's ideal of humanity, liberty, and equality. Earlier this summer [May 18] Gaines was guest of honor for a fund-raiser for the construction of the fountain. Before the benefit Gaines read some of his works to members and guests of [Writers and Books] a Rochester writers' club.

Writers and Books has endeavored to promote among the general public a better understanding and appreciation of contemporary writing. A source of encouragement to creative writers of all ages, Writers and Books provides a setting in which established writers can come together with aspiring writers and interested readers for both instruction and creative interchange of ideas. In 1974 Writers and Books literally began as a bus, travelling throughout the northeast United States, bringing contemporary writing and book arts to new audiences. Now it has its own center at 740 University Avenue in Rochester.

The Freddie Thomas Foundation is a non-profit charitable organization founded in 1974, in honor of Dr. Freddie Thomas of Rochester. Dr. Thomas was an educator, a scientist, a biologist, and a humanitarian. The Foundation's 1989 President was Margaret Thomas, widow of Dr. Thomas. Managed and operated by professional and non-professional volunteers, it supports and subsidizes approximately 200 needy groups.

The Miss Jane Pittman fountain, a three-spigot bronze monument, designed and sculpted by Calvin Hubbard, stands in Liberty Pole Plaza in downtown Rochester. It is the city's only downtown public drinking fountain. The elaborate benefit for its construction, at which Gaines was guest of honor on May 18, was titled "The Lilac Gala." Held at the Top of the Plaza Restaurant it featured dinner, dancing, and musical entertainment.

Gaines' appearance in Rochester for these events got excellent news coverage. Mrs. Thomas was quoted in the June 1, 1989, *Brighton-Pittsford Post*: "Gaines was very impressed with the event, especially the community participation. He has even volunteered to return for the dedication in July." There was a concurrence of opinion among those involved in the fountain project that Miss Jane and the fountain stand as strong symbols of courage and freedom. One woman remarked: "She [Miss Jane] could have easily been my great-grandmother, and she stands as a model for us all."

* * *

Gaines has been a featured speaker at nearly every Deep South Writers Conference since 1978. On September 24, 1989, shortly after the fall semester began, Gaines once again honored the Conference by reading, this time from his coming novel, *A Lesson Before Dying*, to an attentive and appreciative audience. The book, set in 1948, concerns a black teacher who is asked to visit an illiterate younger black man in jail, where he is about to be electrocuted for a crime which he did not commit. Gaines' delivery was both dramatic and amusing, as he read in first person as the teacher, who recalled his own days in a small black school.

Another of Gaines' many speaking engagements for the fall of 1989 included one at Lafayette's St. Thomas More High School. For the session the students, who were prepared to discuss Gaines' *A Gathering of Old Men*, saw a film of "The Sky is Gray." A question-and-answer period followed, during which Gaines was asked about his boyhood in Louisiana, his reasons for becoming a writer, and the themes and ideas of his works. Again, he gave his six words of wisdom: "Read, read, read, write, write, write."

GAINES RECEIVES HUMANIST OF THE YEAR AWARD

On December 7, 1989, Gaines received the Humanist of the Year Award from the Louisiana Endowment for the Humanities. As early as the previous May two glowing letters in Gaines' behalf were issued from the USL administration, recommending him for the prestigious award. One dated May 25, 1989, was written from the dean of Arts and Humanities,

Richard Cusimano, to Dr. Michael Sartisky, director of the Louisiana Endowment for the Humanities. In part it read:

> Gaines is a humorist to the core, and the pages of his books reflect his deep commitment to the high moral values taught in the disciplines of the humanities. His students are privileged to learn their craft from an individual of deep understanding into the nature of writing and creativity. They learn that good writing results from long hours of rewriting and hard work. He is not merely a writer, but a doer and a helper.

Cusimano further pointed out that Gaines gives freely of his time in lectures to the students on all educational levels, and that he has formed a group of fellow black faculty members who meet in his home periodically to discuss social problems of blacks.

The other letter, dated May 30, 1989, from USL president Ray Authement to the chairman of the Humanities Scholars Subcommittee bears quoting in toto:

> I wholeheartedly endorse the nomination of Ernest J. Gaines for the LEH Humanist of the Year Award for 1989. As a Louisiana author of pre-eminent stature whose works are translated into a great number of languages, he has brought to the attention of the world those issues important to the humanities. In his classes here at the University, in his speaking engagements across the state and the nation, and in his participation in activities in our community, Gaines has also shared his vision of a world where individuals act according to right principles and achieve dignity by those actions.
>
> By the conduct of his life and through his fiction, Gaines embodies the essential concepts of humanism. Motivated himself by a deep concern for the well-being of his fellow man, he inspires in others compassion for human suffering and respect for human integrity. He has proved to be a worthy role model for minority and non-minority students alike on campus and in his

> public readings in area schools. Both Louisiana and Acadiana are indeed richer for his presence.
>
> For all his contributions to the spreading of humanistic ideals, I recommend that you give serious consideration to the candidacy of Ernest J. Gaines for the 1989 Humanist of the Year Award. He well deserves such an honor in recognition of his unstinting service to the humanities.

Gaines did indeed receive the award as its fifth recipient, on December 7, 1989, at the Bellemont Hotel in Baton Rouge. Preceding the event press releases from the LEH director of communications were laudatory. The following material, gathered for them, is "Used with the Permission of the Louisiana Endowment for the Humanities," with this writer's special appreciation to Dr. Michael Sartisky, executive director of the LEH.

"Gaines is at once an historian, psychologist, and sociologist of the Louisiana he loves so much," says Dr. James Olney, LEH board chairperson. "He [Gaines] epitomizes the model of the teacher-scholar: easily approachable, encouraging, honestly critical, and open to discussion in the highest Socratic spirit," concurs A. David Barry, head of the USL Foreign Languages Department and LEH board member.

Barry was also quoted in the *LEH Chronicle* for September, 1989: "Ernest Gaines, the internationally recognized writer, is also Ernie Gaines, the caring, sensitive individual. What better blend of greatness for the Humanist of the Year in Louisiana?" The writer of the *Chronicle* article said that Gaines "has not only held his ground in Louisiana, but has helped the humanities in this state to gain ground. We honor him for his past contributions, as we look forward to his future ones." Gaines' contributions were well summed up by LEH's 1988 Humanist of the Year, Dr. Huel D. Perkins, who said, "We know through all of this he [Gaines] has helped to foster an understanding of the humanities which has made us better persons, better citizens, and better Louisianians."

Other recipients of this award have been historian Stephen Ambrose, 1985; the late historian Joe Gray Taylor, 1986; and literary critic Lewis Simpson, 1987. Simpson recalled for the *Chronicle* Gaines' "humanizing influence" when he heard him read at a local church:

> I don't remember so much what was said as I do the way in which, with no pretension whatsoever, Ernest, establishing himself in the eyes of his youthful audience as an image of the literate, perceptive mind at work, awakened these young people to the possibilities of written expression in relation to their own lives. Multiplied many times over, such occasions as the one I recall have had an influence that is difficult to calculate, even in general terms, but must be reckoned as vital, an influence that may well be tangibly embodied as time goes on in any number of lives, perhaps indeed already is so embodied.

The Louisiana Endowment for the Humanities is the state affiliate of the National Endowment for the Humanities. It is a non-profit agency, which awards grants throughout the state for humanities programs. Keynote speaker for the award presentation was Nancy Stevenson, chairperson of the Federation of State Humanities Councils Board of Directors and wife of former Illinois U. S. senator Adlai E. Stevenson III. The Humanist of the Year Award carried a $1,000 honorarium for Gaines.

Lafayette's *Times of Acadiana*, December 13, 1989, spoke of the event as

> the latest in a series [of awards] given to the novelist, but it serves to remind us of the top rank which Gaines holds among current American writers. Gaines is one of the truly authentic voices in contemporary fiction. His presence at USL is a boon to students of literature, as well as a great enhancement to the university's reputation nationwide.

Gaines' award banquet speech, printed in *Cultural Visions*, Spring, 1990, was titled "The Autobiography of Mister Ernest

Gaines," and relates the first fifteen years of his life. Unlike most of Gaines' works it contains very little conversation and is written in third person.

* * *

Early in 1990 Gaines was selected by the Miller Brewing Company to be one of twelve African-American authors featured in the Gallery of Greats portrait collection and calendar. Other authors honored by Miller were Maya Angelou, Amiri Baraka, David Bradley, Rita Dove, Charles H. Fuller, Jr., Toni Morrison, John A. Williams, August Wilson, James Baldwin, Langston Hughes, and Richard Wright. Titled "Black Authors: A Voice for the People," the collection was unveiled in Washington, D. C., on February 7 at the Duke Ellington School of Arts. The Negro Ensemble Company of New York City presented a ninety-minute performance highlighting selected works by the authors featured in the calendar collection.

In a USL news release preceding the occasion, Noel Hankin, Miller Brewing Company's director of marketing relations, said:

> We salute these 20th century storytellers both for their contributions to our nation's literary wealth and our understanding of African-American culture. We know they have struggled. And we know they have opened doors for those who will follow. They truly are a voice for the people.

Spencer Lawrence, portrait creator for the calendar, has produced several portrait series, including one of forty jazz greats and another on the Civil Rights Movement.

Gaines was given much attention during Black History Month, February, 1990, especially by the colleges and universities in Acadiana. On Lake Charles' TV Channel 7 he was given special tribute by a black spokeswoman. And Gaines himself, who was back in Louisiana for a few days in February, made a beautiful cameo for TV Channel 9 in Baton Rouge. In the scene he is walking over beautiful old plantation grounds, wearing his beret, and speaking of his heritage.

On February 23, 1990, Gaines was among thirty black political, social, and cultural leaders selected for induction into the newly formed Louisiana Black History Hall of Fame. Ceremonies honoring the inductees, including civil rights activists, educators, politicians, athletes, musicians, and other writers, took place in June, 1990, on the campus of Southern University in Baton Rouge. Some of the honorees, such as Louis Armstrong, Clementine Hunter, and Louisiana's only black governor, P. B. S. Pinchback, were honored posthumously.

An explanatory item in the Lafayette *Daily Advertiser*, February 25, 1990, read:

> The thirty initial inductees span a wide range of time and represent a variety of endeavors and diverse geographic areas of our state. Their similarities, however, are more important. Each has enjoyed great personal success, and more importantly, each has positively and significantly impacted the broad fabric of our state and /or nation.
>
> The Hall of Fame is intended to bring an awareness of the contributions blacks have made to the state. Until a permanent site . . . is secured, it will be housed at Southern University's John B. Cade Library.
>
> The organization plans to take an active role in the initiation, support and promotion of programs to reduce illiteracy and high school dropout rates. It also will seek corporate sponsorships to pay tuition, books and supplies for college students and set up a clearing house for information on financial aid for attending college.

Gaines filled two engagements in Louisiana in March of 1990, one at Northside High School in Lafayette, during its observance of Black History Month, and the other as speaker on *Miss Jane Pittman* for the Tennessee Williams/New Orleans Literary Festival in that city at Le Petit Théâtre du Vieux Carré.

GAINES IN THE CLASSROOM AND OUT

Gaines' strict writing regime was unavoidably relaxed slightly when he began teaching creative writing at USL in the early 1980s. Instead of writing five or six hours a day, he has been hard pressed to get in two or three. He continued to hold office hours, and to give freely of his time at speaking engagements and to interviewers. Coming to USL has solved his financial worries. In 1982, *A Gathering of Old Men* was far enough along that the physical move from San Francisco to Lafayette was not detrimental to its progress. He said: "It was a time when I knew where the novel [*A Gathering of Old Men*] was going. If I were at the beginning of a novel, not knowing anything about the novel, it would have been a very bad time."

Gaines has said that he continually learns from his students, "things about background, accents." Above all he stresses two things in his teaching: to write well and to respect each other in class. His six basic words of advice to young writers, "read, read, read," and "write, write, write," have often been quoted. Gaines says that in reading one discovers how sentences, paragraphs, and descriptions are formed, such as the sky at different times of the day. Then the writer should apply these techniques to subjects that he wants most to write about.

In Gaines' creative writing course a student reads aloud to the class, either a short story or a chapter from a book that he is writing. Comments from the class are then called for before Gaines gives his own. If he sees that the student is getting defensive with the constructive criticism, he urges him to "take what I say with a grain of salt, because I disagreed with my teachers, too."

In a taped interview in Baton Rouge in March, 1978, later edited by Charles H. Rowell and titled "This Louisiana Thing That Drives Me," Gaines was asked what advice he would give contemporary black writers. Gaines' answer, not confined to just black writers, incorporated much of the classroom philosophy that he continues to use. "I don't know what to tell a writer to do," he said to Rowell.

> One of the things I believe in is that the writer should

> be free to do whatever the hell he wishes to do. I only hope that he writes about the human condition. If he is black, he should write about the black condition. I don't know how in the hell he can avoid writing about white conditions if he is an American. If he is a black Southern writer, how can he avoid writing about the Southern condition? If he is a Northerner, how can he avoid writing about Northern conditions? As long as he writes truthfully about the human condition, his experiences, whether these experiences are direct or vicarious, I'm pleased. . . . Play the game as well as you can possibly play it. . . . In order to do it well you are going to have to sacrifice . . . to put a lot of time in. . . . Read good writers, whether they are white or black, Chinese or Japanese, or Russian, or writers from Mars or wherever. Read the best to see how they do things, because any good writer can help you. . . . Study hard and spend a lot of time at the desk. . . . You must read, and you must write.[34]

To an interviewer for the *Daily Advertiser*, September 25, 1983, Gaines confided: "I like teaching when people are interested in what I'm doing. It's fun to exchange information with people who really want to write. I encourage students to write about what they know and feel. Nothing bothers me more than a kid who doesn't think his experiences are worth writing about."

* * *

Student praise for Gaines has been high. Richard Bier, who, "by an extraordinary piece of good fortune," took Gaines' creative writing course in the fall of 1981 said in an undated news item found in Gaines' papers:

> During this time I learned more than a little about

[34]Charles H. Rowell, "This Louisiana Thing That Drives Me," *Callaloo #3,* I (May 1978), 50-51.

> writing and about Gaines himself. Both in the classroom and at the rap session which we held afterwards (the location of the latter ranging everywhere from dark corner bars to fellow students' pads and punctuated with cigarettes—no, no pot: Gaines isn't into that kind of drug scene) the writer patiently listened to our efforts, and we eagerly listened to suggestions about them. Not the least advantage was that while it is questionable to this very day how he found talent in us, we at least had the advantage of learning something of value about writing and about him. . . . He also has a superb sense of humor, but is a bit reticent about exhibiting it unless he knows one rather well. He is also so kind and hates to say 'no' so much, that he was eternally being asked to come here, to speak there, to do this, to help out with that. Through it all, though, I never once heard him complain, even as he went about complying with as many demands on his time as he possibly could. . . . He is fond of wearing a Hemingwayesque beret outside the classroom.

In a lengthy feature article in the *Times of Acadiana*, March 25, 1982, other students were quoted. Miles Hawthorne, a former *Daily Advertiser* editor who was in Gaines' class, said of him:

> As a teacher, he's better than most I've run into. Of course, he's not a professor, he's a writer. He has a very serious and professional interest in what he's doing—he's not a stick in the mud about it. He's got a sense of humor and he's willing to listen to what other people have to say. He's careful to say that we're free to argue with him or ignore him, because he used to argue with his teachers.

Ruth Foote, an undergraduate, said that she had learned much from Gaines' teaching, mostly that she was not working to her full ability, that she must work harder.

* * *

Ernest Gaines does not lack for respectful colleagues. Longtime friend, author/professor Michael Harper required term papers on *Miss Jane Pittman* in 1977 for one of his classes at Brown University, as did editor/professor William Decker when he taught at New York University in 1980. USL professor James Wilson who taught English in Beijing, China, in 1988-89 under Fulbright auspices, included Gaines' *A Gathering of Old Men* as required reading for his course.

Colleagues at USL have marvelled at Gaines' literary strengths, evidenced in the previously quoted feature article from *The Times of Acadiana*, March 25, 1982. Most impressive to Carl Wooton, another creative writing professor at USL, is Gaines' honesty, and "his ability to capture another voice, a very separate kind of voice that tells the story. . . . His control of the language, the style itself prevents [his writing] from being angry. It's not screaming or shouting; it's just very true."

Patricia Rickels, professor of black literature at USL, likes best

> the way he captures people's language, . . . the sounds of Louisiana people really talking, black people, white people, Cajuns, Anglos. . . . He's got the rhythms . . . the vocabulary . . . the cadences and the nuances of Louisiana talk down so well. And it sounds so natural. . . . It's the art that conceals art. It not easy to write in a way that sounds natural. It's the sort of thing that Mark Twain did so well.

Rickels, however, very gently pointed out that Gaines "had a problem with *In My Father's House*. . . . He somehow lost hold of his touch that he has with the ordinary people's sense of the comic." His best work, she feels, is serious writing laced with tragic elements and comedy. "He's very good at his comic touches . . . it's very much in *Miss Jane Pittman* . . . [and] in the better stories . . . the stories in *Bloodline* that have humor are better than the ones that are more solemn. . . . It gives that blues tone, that half-comic, half-tragic thing."

During Black History Week in Lafayette in February of 1990, Rickels spoke about Gaines' imagery in "Just Like a Tree" (one always returns to one's roots), and of the relationship between the oral black folk tradition and the literary tradition.

Professor Jane Bonin, who began a critical biography of Gaines, commented:

> I think his strength is his ability to create characters and situations that are universal . . . experiences that many of us have never had or even thought about, but that when you read them, you know that they're true and that they are what it is to be human. You may have never stood out in the cold and waited for a bus to take you into town to get your tooth pulled [as in "The Sky is Gray"], but you know the truth of that experience when you read it.[35]

* * *

Gaines is well liked, both on and off campus. Some say he is more shy and modest than anyone would believe, considering his fame and experience. He has been described as "gracious, generous," and even "courtly." He is upbeat, cheerful, and manages to find some good in most everything. He enjoys watching and talking about football, baseball, and other sports, and playing card and dice games, especially "Liar's Dice" a popular game in San Francisco bars. It is played with a cup and five dice, similar to a poker hand, except that the players lie about it. One of his favorite sipping drinks is cognac.

When he was first introduced to Aggie jokes, Gaines was quite amused. According to some of his Lafayette friends, he most enjoys talking about anything and everything with a small, comfortable group, though is sometimes reticent to talk about his work in progress. When he is in San Francisco he enjoys sailing on the bay in his co-owned boat.

Once Gaines came back to Louisiana in the late 1960s to do

[35]Lafayette, La., *Times of Acadiana,* March 25, 1982.

research for *Miss Jane Pittman* he returned annually to visit his kin and friends, and to enjoy Mardi Gras festivities. As a small boy he was not allowed inside the River Lake plantation house, but in recent years he has been a welcome guest there.

In the previously cited interview with Charles H. Rowell in March, 1978,[36] Gaines spoke of his visits to Louisiana.

> I come back not as an objective observer, but as someone who must come back in order to write about Louisiana. I must come back to be with the land in different seasons, to travel the land, to go into the fields, to go into the small towns, to go into the bars, to eat the food, to listen to the language. As I said, I don't come back as a scientist, strictly as an observer; I come back to absorb things.

Rowell asked, "Does that mean you have not absorbed California, or does it merely mean that Louisiana interests you as a place to write about?"

Gaines said,

> I'm not one of those intellectuals who can explain the creative mind, but I do feel that the early impressions on the artist are the most lasting. I'm thinking of such writers as James Joyce . . . [and] the Russians. . . . About California—I . . . . suppose I have written four or five novels about California, but they are not very good books. They will not be published during my lifetime, if I have anything to do with it. . . . I doubt that I will be able to write a good book about California . . . . until I have gotten rid of this Louisiana thing that drives me, yet I hope I never will get rid of that Louisiana thing. I hope I'm able to write about Louisiana for the rest of my life.

Gaines is rarely angered, but gets a little miffed when he fills an engagement, expecting feedback, and the audience has not done its homework. He does not wish to be put on display as a

[36]Rowell, "This Louisiana Thing," 39-40.

star. He simply wants to be known as a writer, and he wants to be read, particularly by the people for whom he is going to speak.

He cares about caring people. Human injustice can provoke Gaines' anger. He reacted strongly to former president Reagan's budget cuts, and looked upon the Jonestown mass suicide in Guyana, about which he feels everyone should be angry, as a great tragedy. In the profile of Gaines in The *Times of Acadiana* his feelings on the matter were explained:

> Gaines has a personal reason for deep feelings about the Guyana tragedy. Several of Jones' older followers lived in Gaines' apartment building before they moved to Guyana. In fact, Gaines often spoke with a woman who later was put in charge of Jones's elderly followers in Guyana. The old people's barracks in Jonestown was named 'Miss Jane Pittman Garden.' Gaines still believes he might have been able to do something that would have saved those people from their untimely deaths. 'I thought I should be howling, screaming, so that this could happen never again. And yet it will happen again . . . . because we're not angry enough.'

To the same interviewer he confided his views on marriage. Since he had decided early to devote all his time to writing, he would not let anything take away from that, not politics, religion, or another person. He has not lacked for sincere and lasting relationships, however, and said, "I think if the right person came along today, that could be something different. But I suppose my demands are so high now, and I'm not very easy to get along with. But it may happen."[37] These statements were made in 1982. Gaines is still single.

New Orleans journalist Jason Berry, mentioned earlier, heard Gaines speak at Loyola in October of 1989, and wrote:

> I am very fond of Ernie. . . . There is a kindness and sensitivity about him that is rare among human beings, much less novelists. . . . I've visited him a few

[37]*Times of Acadiana*, March 25, 1982.

times in Lafayette, and remember the party he gave in 1985 for the Deep South Writers Conference at his house in Arbolada. . . . Ernie was playing jazz tapes.

It may have been that conference, in 1985, when he spoke to one of the conference sessions about his childhood, the poverty on the plantation where he grew up, and his aunt, who couldn't walk. I was deeply moved by his reflections before he read that time. For by any objective measurement, Ernie's route to literary stature beat the toughest of odds. That may explain his extreme courtesy as a listener, especially to blacks. When he signed books at Loyola the other day I realized how serious his expression was; he asked several people if they wanted his San Francisco address, and wrote it down in the books as part of the autograph signing. I wasn't sure about the meaning of that, or whether he'd done it a long time (I suspect he has), but it struck me as a way of conveying a certain intimacy between writer and reader. Here was one of America's leading novelists giving out his address to people, and short of adding one's phone number, you can't get more open-minded. Most writers as they achieve fame search for serenity, privacy, and calm spaces away from interruptions.[38]

* * *

Gaines' novel in progress is titled *A Lesson Before Dying*, a chapter of which will be included in *Something in Common*, a forthcoming anthology of Louisiana writers. During his life Gaines expects to come full circle, to be buried back on "that little patch of Louisiana land" on River Lake Plantation. But he has much to do, much to write, much to give before that time. He continues to write, to speak, to share his wisdom and insights.

[38]Letter from Berry to Anne Simpson, November 24, 1989.

PART II

WRITING STYLE: INFLUENCES AND CHARACTERISTICS

INTRODUCTION

Ernest J. Gaines could be called a philosopher as well as a novelist, though in his works he does not preach, nor judge, nor does he try to inflict his personal views on the reader. He does not need to. The reader immediately senses the feelings of the author's finely drawn characters, convinced from the first sentence that Gaines' inner man is present.

The several quoted passages included in this section have been selected for their pertinency to Gaines' stylistic approach.

LITERARY INFLUENCES

Since Gaines had read almost no black writers at the time he began writing, he does not consider that any particular one has consciously influenced him. Though he admires many of them, he deplores the fact that some of them deny having learned anything from preceding writers. Gaines has been especially impressed by Jean Toomer (1894-1967), and he has mentioned the works of writer/ethnomusicologist Zora Neale Hurston (1891-1960) as peripheral influences. Of Toomer's poetic novel *Cane*, published in 1923 and reissued in 1975, Gaines says, "To *me* that's the Black American novel. That *is* my novel." He was particularly taken with Toomer's structuring of *Cane*, in which he combined short chapters of poems and short sketches, mostly about women.

Initially, 500 copies of *Cane* were printed. As an Afro-American writer Toomer caught the attention of editors and critics with *Cane*, but his later books were not popular. The introspective Toomer, brilliant, eccentric, and tortured, is a fascinating writer, particularly in descriptive passages from *Cane*: "Karintha is a woman. She who carries beauty, perfect as dusk when the sun goes down." Of another woman, Esther, whose lover has left, Toomer writes: "Her hair thins. It looks like the dull silk on puny corn ears. Her face pales until it is the color of the gray dust that dances with dead cotton leaves. . . . Her mind is a pink meshbag filled with baby toes."[1]

In retrospect Gaines realized that Toomer had been an innovator, and ventured that Ernest Hemingway and Gertrude Stein strove to do what Toomer had begun only a few years earlier. Gaines says of Toomer,

> This man has a combination of prose and poetry that we *ought* to have, Black writers ought to have. We're full of music, natural rhythm, you know, music, music, music. And he has more music in his prose than any of us. Unfortunately for me, I discovered him after I had already sort of established a style of my own. But if I had not, I know without a doubt that he would have had the greatest influence on me.[2]

De Maupassant was one of the first writers who interested the young Gaines, "because," Gaines has said, "he wrote so beautifully about the young, and told good stories, used the simplest language, and most times made the stories quite short."

Gaines has repeatedly admitted the profound influence of Tolstoy, Dostoevsky, Turgenev, Chekhov, Faulkner, Hemingway, Joyce, Shakespeare, Twain, and the dramatists of ancient Greece upon his own writing style, a fact almost belabored by analysts of Gaines. Though of different locale, generation, and race, the Russian writers, in particular, addressed themselves to the peasantry and its struggle for dignity, a theme also pervading most of Gaines' works, for Gaines knows that the black man *is* America's peasantry.

[1]Jean Toomer, *Cane* (1923; reprint ed., New York, 1975), pp. 2, 23, 24.

[2]"An Interview with Ernest J. Gaines," 49.

In a speech in 1969 in Chapel Hill, North Carolina, where he was invited by Professor Joe Ritok, Gaines defined the American peasant, asking

> But why this fear [of other writers] to write truly about the American peasant? Is there no such thing as a peasant in America? Then what do we call the man who works the land and does not own it? The man who lives in a one room shack and works and works and barely makes enough to eat? If you don't want to call him a peasant, call him something else—the name does not matter—that he exists does, and that he has not been properly described is true. In Hollywood, as in our novels, he is either ignored or romanticized. Today if Hollywood wants to make a movie about peasants, they must go to Mexico or to some oriental or European country. Never Mississippi, Alabama, or Louisiana. They can find the most peasant of peasants a hundred miles out of Hollywood, but they prefer moving their millions of dollars of equipment to film peasants in Mexico, Europe, or the orient.

He considered *The Grapes of Wrath* the only good movie that Hollywood made about American peasants,

> and the only time you can see that is on the late, late show—as if they were afraid that it might shock the more sensitive. I doubt that it would, but I do think it would make them think and ask questions. . . . Once you start asking questions about the Joads, you might ask questions about the conditions of the blacks.

In Baton Rouge at Southern University in 1971 Gaines expanded on the Russians' expertise in writing about the peasantry.

> Their peasants were not caricatures or clowns. They did not make fun of them. They were people—they were good, they were bad. They could be as brutal as any man,

> they could be as kind. The American writers in general, the Southern writer in particular, never saw peasantry, especially black peasantry, in this way; blacks were either caricatures of human beings or they were problems. They needed to be saved, or they were saviors. They were either children, or they were seers. But they were very seldom what the average human being was. There were exceptions, of course, but I'm talking about a total body of writers, the conscience of a people.[3]

Gaines continued by pointing out some of the Russian contrasts to his own culture which were fascinating but confusing to him, such as their icons and religious worship, their four and five syllable names, their greetings, their food and customs.

> I had eaten steamed cabbage, boiled cabbage, but not cabbage soup. I had drunk clabber, but never kvass. I had never slept on a stove, and I still don't know how anyone can. I knew the distance of a mile—never have I learned the distance of a verst. The Russian steppes sounded interesting, but they were not the swamps of Louisiana. Siberia could be just as cruel, but still it was not Angola State Prison. So even here, those whom I thought were nearest to the way I felt still were not close enough.[4]

* * *

Of the American writers Gaines especially champions Hemingway's understatement of things, which he considers as profound as Count Basie's musical understatements. Hemingway's style, which is relatively free of adjectives and

[3]This speech, later titled "Miss Jane and I," *Callaloo #3,* I (May 1978), 27.

[4]Speech given at Southern University, Baton Rouge, 1971, found in Gaines' papers.

adverbs, and the stoicism of many of his characters who always "came through gracefully under pressure" have provided a bible for Gaines. For who knows better than Gaines that *no* one has experienced as much pressure as the black in America, and managed to come through more gracefully? In each of Gaines' works, a black person is given a heavy burden and is expected to "come through." He always shows the strength and pride of his race. He feels that the job of black writers is not to tell whites of black racial problems, that they should do more than work out their anger on paper. He prefers to show strength, pride, and humanity in his characters. *Miss Jane Pittman* has been criticized as being a novel of protest. If so, it is one of subtle protest.

Critics have suggested that with the writing of *Miss Jane Pittman* Gaines' own vision and distinct style really emerged, one which departed from Faulkner's sense of the past and Hemingway's sense of defeat. Gaines doubts that any of his characters really accept defeat, rather that they are able to somehow to rise above defeatism itself. If there was a noticeable change in style, it was because Miss Jane was so unlike his previous characters, with her own unique interpretation of life. Remnants of the Hemingway and Faulkner influence may always remain with him, just as the influences of different musical genres, the Russian writers, and the Greek tragedians have remained with him.

Gaines knows that critics often compare the female characters of Faulkner's Dilsey in *The Sound and the Fury* to his Miss Jane, though they are dissimilar. This does not displease him, but when complimented for being better than Faulkner at drawing black characters, Gaines remarked: "Well I *hope* I am. I *hope* I am." And continuing, he said:

> I want to write about my people. I happen to come from Louisiana and I happen to come from the land. My people did a lot of hunting, so I write about hunting, the same thing with fishing . . . and I try to write in the way that they spoke of the past . . . about a certain place

> because when I was a kid in the South my world was limited.[5]

Just as Faulkner wrote about his "place" in Mississippi, Gaines wrote about his in Louisiana. "There is no way that I *try* to imitate him. I know I am connected with my people here as much as he [Faulkner] was with his. . . . it is a major theme in most southern writers. . . . And there is always the past and present thing. . . . Your are constantly reminded of the past."[6]

Gaines applauds Faulkner's creation of believable black characters. He learned much from Faulkner's artful use of language for both black and whites in the South. Faulkner may have over-romanticized the peasantry, but from him Gaines learned to listen to dialogue—what and how to leave out. Unlike Faulkner, however, Gaines rarely uses long involved sentences. Though Gaines' and Faulkner's landscapes are similar with their small towns, courthouse squares, grocery stores, and small bars, in essence Faulkner clings to the past for the stability that social order offers; Gaines tries to escape the past's immobility by viewing change as necessary to sustaining life, realizing that this escape may result in alienation or even death.

Gaines has given an example of Faulkner's story about a mule. Knowing about a mule's erratic behavior, Gaines could also write a story about a mule, but it would be in a different locale, written from a black person's view point.

> You don't have to be in Mississippi. This kind of stuff is something that I have experienced myself. No, let's say I had never lived in the South, had never seen anything like this. Then you could say I was imitating Faulkner. . . . I think in my story 'Just Like a Tree' there is a definite influence of Faulkner's 'As I Lay Dying.' But as far as imitating him, intentionally imitating him, I don't do that. People have asked me if Hemingway has

[5]"An Interview with Ernest J. Gaines," 47.

[6]*Ibid.*, 47.

> had any influence on me. He definitely did. . . . Hemingway shows me how to put this [grace under pressure] on paper. . . . I suppose the reason I'm compared to Faulkner more than to anyone else is the Southern thing. . . . Most people feel that Faulkner has defined the South. Anyone else is imitating him. Just like anybody who writes about a bullfight is imitating Hemingway.[7]

Professor/editor William Decker said of Gaines' admiration for Hemingway (d. 1961) and Faulkner (d. 1962), "He never met either of them, but he often expressed appreciation of their writing skill."[8]

* * *

Except for *Miss Jane Pittman* Gaines uses only a short time period, as did the Greek tragedians. He cites Hemingway and Faulkner as other writers influenced similarly, saying, "Their stories did not go over a long period of time, they were usually confined to a few hours. So I was not only influenced directly by the Greeks, but also by the influence they had upon other writers whom I was reading."[9]

In expressing the concept of manhood, perhaps Gaines' most persistent theme, he mentions the Greek influence again. The black man's status as a man has been denied by the white race since he was brought to America as a slave in chains. Tradition demands that his attempts to be a man should be dangerous. Gaines says,

[7]*Ibid.*, 48.

[8]Letter to Anne Simpson from William Decker, April 3, 1990.

[9]John O'Brien, *Interviews with Black Writers* (New York, 1973), p. 83. Quotations from "Ernest J. Gaines," from *Interviews with Black Writers,* edited by John O'Brien, are reprinted with the permission of Liveright Publishing Corporation.

> The hoodoo lady and Joe Pittman [in *Miss Jane*] both say that man has come here to die. So whenever my men decide that they will be men regardless of how anyone else feels, they know that they will eventually die. But it's impossible for them to turn around. This is the sense of Greek tragedy that keeps coming back in my writing, that men are destined to do things and they cannot do anything but that one thing. Whatever that one thing is, it is to be done as well as the man can do it.[10]

Another of Gaines' characters who tries to assert his manhood is Jackson in *Catherine Carmier*. Catherine is caught inescapably between loyalty to her father and her love for Jackson. Gaines calls her a "tragic figure," who has no control over her condition. "We go right back to Greek tragedy again. People like Catherine Carmier cannot determine their way of living, it is fated that they must live a certain way," Gaines said in the O'Brien interview.

Jackson, too, is caught in the indecision of accepting the past or severing himself from it completely. Gaines knows that one can "go home again," and having done so could have written into Jackson some of his own feelings. "It was hard for me to go back and act the same way with my friends and people. Oh, I could drink and talk with them, but when it came down to accepting certain things as they did, it was just about impossible for me to do."[11]

* * *

Gaines does not concern himself with a writer's personal politics or philosophy, only his ability to write well and communicate. He has never allowed the political or philosophical views of his influencers to interfere with what he needed from them. He prefers to consider one's total

[10]*Ibid.*, p. 85.

[11]*Ibid.*, p. 86.

surroundings, knowing that men, he among them, "take what they need, whether from Louis [Armstrong], [T. S.] Eliot, or Jesus. And they leave the rest." Gaines never injects his own political views as such into his writing, assuming that the reader will get the feeling of his views from the story line. Some magazines have ignored or rejected pieces by him because he did not take a political stand. When asked by an interviewer in 1973 if he were political at all, he said, "I don't think I am. Oh, I vote. There's no point in not voting."

He has often been asked if the works of Ralph Ellison, author of *The Invisible Man*, influenced him. He has considered Ellison, along with James Baldwin, better essayists than writers of fiction. In an interview with Gregory Fitzgerald for The *New Orleans Review* Gaines said:

> No. . . . I didn't read anything at all by Ralph Ellison until I had formed my own style of writing. . . . I knew very early what it was I wanted to write about. I just had to find a way to do it, and the white writers . . . showed me this way better. I looked at Hemingway as a man who can really construct paragraphs; when I want to construct a good paragraph, I read a little Hemingway. You can look at Turgenev's structure of his *Fathers and Sons* for a perfectly constructed little novel, or at F. Scott Fitzgerald's construction of *The Great Gatsby*.
>
> You look at everything in Tolstoy, who I think is the greatest of them all, the greatest man to write a novel. So you learn from all these people; I've learned from all of them. I learned how to get what was in me onto the paper. As I said about the story 'A Long Day in November,' I had to get it from Faulkner and from Joyce, but not from Richard Wright or Ellison or Baldwin, or anybody like that. They showed me how to get it much better than the black writers had done because so many of them really dealt with style, whereas I think the black writers are

much more interested in content—you know, putting it down like it is—and the style is sort of secondary.[12]

Admitting to Fitzgerald that he was only an occasional reader of contemporary fiction, Gaines still reads Hemingway. "I'll pick up a Hemingway book any time to read a story or a novel. I'll pick up Faulkner, too. Someone like this I'll read all the time."[13]

MUSICAL INFLUENCES

In Gaines' address to the Modern Language Association in 1981 he recalled German philosopher Nietzsche's remark, "Without music life would be a mistake," and elaborated further.

> Well, music makes my writing go, and I know that for sure. The most wonderful musical instrument is the human voice. My characters must speak musically. My narrator must have a sense of rhythm. The great thing about listening to a story teller is not only what he says, but the way that he says it. In writing, I try to make you hear that story teller. Not only read descriptions, or dialogue, or follow the narrative, but hear it. People have asked me was it hard to write *The Autobiography of Miss Jane Pittman*. No, it was not, once I caught the rhythm of her speech.

He continued,

> Music is as much an assistant in my writing as anything else is. Lester Young with his saxophone teaches as much about understanding as does Hemingway on his typewriter. Lester, or Prez, shows

[12]Fitzgerald, "An Interview: Ernest J. Gaines," 333, 335.

[13]*Ibid.*, 333-334.

> you how to play round the note of the ballad, rather than the note itself, and still tell the story as truly as if he was playing the ballad word for word.

Gaines took example from the "Massacre" scene in *Miss Jane Pittman*:

> We hear the blows of the sticks, we hear the cries of the people, we hear the swearing, the cursing of the killers as they crack the skulls, the bones of men, women, and children, we hear the silence of death when it is all over. We don't see what goes on, we hear it. We hear the silence, or do not hear birds. You know, birds don't hang around where there is death, especially where there's death of man. So Prez teaches us much and Basie teaches us much, and so does Billie Holiday and Bessie Smith, and Muddy Waters and Leadbelly, and so does Lightin' Hopkins, and Louis Armstrong and Jelly Roll Morton.

In the previously cited Fitzgerald interview Gaines talked about the influence of jazz on his works.

> I think jazz is basically folk music. Originally it was, though I'm not sure what they're doing with it now. And folk music is a very simple thing. All folk music is very, very simple. Listening to jazz I find simple rhythms, simple repetitions. In order to communicate jazz to the layman it has to be simple, and of course these musicians were playing to people just like themselves, uneducated people. I wish to reach the same sort of thing in my fiction, to use the simplest terms in the world, you know, terms like 'Jesus wept; ' I think that's. . . . the most beautiful two-word sentence that has ever been written. It has all the meanings in the world in it. Another thing about jazz is that to be impressive it has to be repetitive. You get hooked upon a phrase and you stay

> with that phrase until you have really convinced the people.[14]

Gaines achieves a certain "mental rhythm" from the absorption of music.

Gaines' previously mentioned record collection includes not only jazz, blues, spirituals, European classics, but African and American Indian folk music as well. In the speech at Southern University Gaines said:

> I think I have learned as much about writing about my people by listening to blues and jazz and spirituals as I have learned by reading novels. The songs of Billie Holiday and Bessie Smith I find superior to the poetry of Gwendolyn Brooks and Nikki Giovanni. The blues of Leadbelly, Muddy Waters, B. B. King, and spirituals of Paul Robeson and Marian Anderson, I find far superior to the writing of Don L. Lee and the rest of that Chicago crowd. The understatements in the tenor saxophone of Lester Young, the crying, haunting, forever searching sounds of Coltrane, and the softness and violence of Basie's big band, all have fired my imagination as much as anything in literature. But the rural blues, maybe because of my background, is my choice in music.

Gaines enlarged on music's impact on his own writing in reply to New Orleans author Jason Berry, who had asked his opinion of an article "Jazz Literature." After praising Berry's basic research and writing skills, Gaines wrote to Berry (ca. March, 1971):

> Yes, there's definitely a Jazz Language, which we fiction writers are trying to use. But I think in my case that I've been just as much influenced by the great blues singers as the Jazz players. Remember, I come from the deep South—the plantation South. Rural blues music was

[14]Fitzgerald, "An Interview: Ernest J. Gaines," 334.

> our music. but the jazz language is with us all. There's not a day go [*sic*] by when we're not using it, Presidents, business men, advertisers, housewives, ministers, athletes—you name them. I always have music in the background while I'm writing and play music anytime when I have nothing else to do. When I travel in my car, and I travel a lot, I'm forever listening to music. Prez is quite possibly my favorite, but I listen to all of them. And I have records by most. No, I have not done the reading and research that you've obviously done, but I listen, listen, listen.

In Berry's article, "Jazz Literature," Berry, like Gaines, notes how the flow of words carries a rhythm of its own and in turn the rhythm carries those words, how "the voice of music weaves its way into rhythms of prose and verse." According to Berry, author Ralph Ellison (*The Invisible Man*) was a trained trumpet player who aspired to symphonic composition. Continuing the letter to Berry, Gaines comments on Ellison:

> And Ellison's [works], though I can agree with much of his definition of the blues, etc., just as much confuses the living hell out of me. I wish he could state things much simpler—as simple as those jazz and bluesmen he's always talking about. (Remember the Lord's prayer, Chief Joseph's farewell speech, and the Gettysburg address. Three fantastic pieces of work—simple, simple, simple.)
>
> This leads into *Invisible Man*, which I consider a great book, but not a great novel. Too controlled. Great novels must flow. Somewhere the characters must take over. Ellison never let his characters take over. He gives them just so much rope, then he jerks them back into place. Writers are gods over their characters, but even God lets us go astray at times. Ellison never does. They can only do what he wishes. Jazz spreads out, flows, is free. Ellison's characters are never free. He's

> always there telling them what to do. And you know that must not be so in Jazz.
>
> Billy Holiday, my favorite female singer, said she could not sing the same song the same way twice. Now, that's what I call Jazz. Have you ever heard Louis, or Bird, or Coltrane play the same thing the same way twice? No.! I have several takes of Louis blowing Stardust and Parker doing What is This Thing Called Love, and each take is different. Now, *that's* Jazz.
>
> But to get away from Mr. Ellison and get to Mr. Toomer. *Cane* is my favorite novel by an American black writer. Now, if you want to hear music, that's music. No one has done it better. Surely, none of the younger blacks who are constantly screaming Black is Beautiful. That book is the greatest compliment to our language that I know of. No other book I can think of has that combination of prose, poetry—music. If you run across one, please send it to me.

LOUISIANA INFLUENCES

The most profound influence on Gaines' writing has been neither the literary nor the musical one. The contour of his works may in larger part be attributed to his early life in South Louisiana. Without this particular background, backlog, there would be no Ernest J. Gaines as we know him.

Probably the strongest recurring theme which emerges in Gaines' works, as well as in Hemingway's, is the struggle of his characters to live with grace, courage and dignity under social and racial stress. Without detracting from Hemingway's influence on the subject, it is obvious that Gaines' South Louisiana background has heavily contributed to his need to probe this theme so thoroughly. After the publication of *Miss Jane Pittman* in 1971 Gaines said:

> That [grace under pressure] might be a good description of my work. I hope it is; it is such a beautiful description that any writer should be proud of it. I know

> that my characters are usually poor, mostly uneducated, and almost always very independent. The conflict in which they usually find themselves is *how to live as a man* in that short period of time.[15]

Speaking of his native Louisiana as a writing source Gaines said:

> It is something I have never tried to forget. I never hated things so much that I tried to blank them out. I love my people and I love the land. I don't love the politics, of course. If you had that hate you couldn't be a receptacle. You couldn't be open to do things. My use of narrative and dialogue are the strongest parts of my writing and I can bring in things because I am open. I can bring in the smells, the weeds, the roads, the houses, the trees. There are people who write about an oak tree and when you read it you feel they don't really know about it. They don't know an oak can be used for shade; can be used for shelter; that the old people used its moss to stuff their mattresses. My receptacles get out and capture things—old women complaining, men talking about dreams, even what my characters are thinking. I ask myself, how would they say, what they *don't* say?[16]

Gaines avoids using a heavy-handed pen because there is something he *likes* in all of his characters, both black and white, no matter their imperfections. If he does happen to write with hatred of a character, he realizes that he has lost control, and ultimately deletes such passages. Comparing the artist to a heart surgeon, Gaines says that both must have sympathy, but stay removed enough to achieve perfection.

Alvin Aubert's entry on Gaines in *Contemporary Novelists*, 1972, recognizes the cultural uniqueness of south Louisiana as distinguishable from the "state's Anglo-Saxon north, thus from

[15]Alvin Aubert, "Ernest Gaines," in James Vinson, ed., *Contemporary Novelists* (New York, 1972), p. 445.

[16]*Peninsula Times Tribune*, January 24, 1984.

the nation as a whole." Of the Gaines-Faulkner comparison/contrast he praises Gaines for generating a "more complex social vision than Faulkner's, an advantage Gaines has utilized with increasing dramatic force and artistic promise. The society of which he writes consists of whites, blacks, and Creoles, a traditionally more favored class (shade) of Afro-American given to fantasies of racial superiority."[17] Gaines' counterparts to Faulkner's Sartorises and Snopses are the south Louisiana plantation owners and their Cajun sharecroppers.

* * *

Just as the Russian writers incorporated their special touches of nostalgia, Gaines said in his 1971 Southern University speech,

> I wanted to smell that Louisiana earth, feel that Louisiana sun, sit under the shade of one of those Louisiana oaks, search for pecans in the Louisiana grass in one of those Louisiana yards, next to one of those Louisiana bayous, not far from a Louisiana river. I wanted to see on paper those Louisiana black children walking to school on cold days while yellow Louisiana busses passed them by; to see on paper those black parents going to work before the sun came up and came back home to look after their children after the sun went down; to see on paper the true reason why those fathers left home—not because they were trifling, shiftless—but because they were tired of putting up with certain conditions. I wanted to see on paper the small country churches (schools during the week), and I wanted to hear those simple religious songs, those simple prayers—that true devotion. (It was Faulkner, I think who said that if God were to stay alive in the country, the blacks would have to keep Him so.)

[17]Aubert, "Ernest Gaines," pp. 445-446.

> And I wanted to hear that Louisiana dialect—that combination of English, Creole, Cajun, black. For me there's no more beautiful sound anywhere—unless, of course you take exceptional pride in proper French or proper English. I wanted to read about the true relationship between whites and blacks—the people that I had known.

Gaines knew that he *must* write about the true relationship between these people, one that showed something other than hostility between the white and black.

> I still don't know what a black writer is supposed to write about unless it is the same thing that a Frenchman writes about—and that is what he feels deeply enough inside of him to write about. When I first started writing I wanted to write a simple little novel about people at home.

He *did*, but it was no simple little novel. It was the long aborning *Catherine Carmier*.[18]

* * *

Most of Gaines' stronger male characters are built around his step-father, Mr. Colar. Understandably, one of Gaines' strongest recurring themes is the search of the young man for the missing father, or the absence of the father, since his own father remained on the plantation only a few years after he was born. Gaines expressed his use of the theme in *Black Creation*, joking in "A Long Day in November" about the father's involvement with mechanical things and other diversions, not pertinent to a real education of his son. As a symbol of the mechanized world, the father seeks changes in ridiculous ways to regain his wife and child's affections. The search for a father is evident as well in "The Sky Is Gray," and clearly things

[18]A typed manuscript of the "Miss Jane and I" speech is in Gaines' papers.

would be better if the father were there. The agony of the painful tooth forces the boy to become a man in the father's place.

And continuing, Gaines does not follow the theory of some of the younger writers, that the fathers were jailed for being revolutionaries. He rather feels that because of the situation in which the black father lived, he became irresponsible, thereby unable to hold the family together. He agrees that in some cases the son becomes the father. "The son was separated from the father on the auction block and they have been looking for each other since. So it is not a revolutionary thing. I think that it is just that they have never been close together."[19]

Gaines clarified the "auction block" reference in "This Louisiana Thing that Drives Me," an interview with Charles H. Rowell in Baton Rouge in 1978, shortly before the publication of *In My Father's House*. "Blacks were taken out of Africa and separated traditionally and then physically here in this country. . . . Wherever the slave ships docked, families were separated."[20] Gaines feels that the erosion of thc authority of the black father, due to this separation, will possibly never be reversed.

Examples of the father searching for the son can be found in "A Long Day in November" and *In My Father's House*. In "The Sky is Gray" the situation is reversed. Gaines explained: "If the father was there maybe it wouldn't be so cold." "Three Men" presents a similar situation, in which a man cannot find his father, so be becomes the father to a younger man. In "Bloodline" Frank Laurent denies his son Copper, who declares, "This is my father's place and it belongs to me. This is it. This is my place."

When asked by Rowell about the son and mother relationship Gaines said,

> Son and mother have always sort of been there. Because let us take for example the white father who rapes the Black woman. No matter what happens, the

[19]*Ibid.*

[20]Rowell, "This Louisiana Thing," 40.

> child was the product of the mother. The father never had to look after the child. The mother had to look after that child. So that the child would always be with the mother. That is why the boy and the mother are always together in my books.[21]

* * *

Another of Gaines' themes is the control of life within a framework of society, one often entwined with the law; the concept of slow change and the black person's reaction to it and his role in it—change in society, in attitudes, and in material and emotional values. He is saddened that today's children would value an expensive Christmas gift more than the old-time apple, some marbles, and firecrackers that he used to receive, which at the time were given with love and respect. "I wish children could put the feeling before the gift," he told a *San Francisco Chronicle* reporter in 1978.

Alvin Aubert wrote that all of Gaines' works

> reflect the inherent socio-economic intricacy of this quadruplex humanity [white aristocracy, 'poor white trash,' blacks, and Creoles], though we are never allowed to lose sight of its basic element of black and white. In . . . *Catherine Carmier* we see the sickly proscribed love of Jackson, who is black, and Catherine, daughter of an infernally proud Creole farmer, as a perverted issue of the miscegenation that resulted from the white male's sexual exploitation of black people. This mode of victimization assumes metaphoric force in Gaines' works, figuring forth in historical perspective the oppression of black people generally. The fictive plantation world then is uniquely microcosmic. It is south Louisiana, the south, the nation as a whole.

Aubert cites the story "Bloodline" as an example.[22]

[21]Beauford, "Conversation," 18.

[22]Aubert, "Ernest Gaines," 446.

Michel Fabre's essay, "Bayonne or the Yoknapatawpha of Ernest Gaines" points out the difference between Faulkner's and Gaines' handling of such change. Bayonne is a world unto itself. In it Gaines fully explores speech patterns, social structures, multiplied here particularly because of the influences of Catholicism, Cajuns and Creoles. The pace is slow. The characters, each in his own way, have insight and thoughtfulness, but not necessarily compassion. They are rarely dummies, however, when Gaines does choose to convey their thoughts. Whatever takes place is within a framework of law, where the races must live together. Silence often gives permission for forbidden relationships, but along with it goes the idea that nobody will get away with anything, that either God or the law will punish him.

Fabre contends that Faulkner's blacks "attached themselves to former values in order to immobilize history," whereas Gaines' began to change the social structure little by little, hoping that the future would belong to his race.

> Faulkner had not refused them these same qualities of endurance, of dignity, of compassion, but he inscribed them within the hierarchy of white domination, often as a tool for its service . . . as an instrument for its redemption. . . . Gaines' character is marked by his immutability; he pursues his goal until the end, sufficiently conscious to know how little he will be able to change himself.[23]

Gaines does not actually commit himself to saying that his noblest, most dignified characters are on the right track, that they can definitely better themselves and make the world better. But in all the writings there seems to be one character who tries. Gaines' more dramatic scenes seem to culminate in the slow confrontations of two groups, precipitated by the actions of two individuals, for example Creole and white (Robert Carmier and

[23]Michel Fabre, "Bayonne or the Yoknapatawpha of Ernest Gaines," *Callaloo #3*, I (May 1978), 118, 120.

Marc Grover in *Catherine Carmier*), between convict and foreman (Marcus and Bonbon in *Of Love and Dust*), between young black and planter (Marcus and Hebert in *Of Love and Dust*, and Cooper and Frank in "Bloodline"). Blacks have largely asserted their maleness with rebellion. Movement in Gaines' works is carried by those who stand for change and openness, but critics wonder if he truly believes there is potential for real change.

* * *

A strong theme in Gaines' writing is the inability, especially for the artist, to escape the past, though living in the past and trying to escape it are different things.

> If you do nothing but worship the past you are quite dead, I believe. But if you start running and trying to get away from the past you will, I think, eventually run yourself out of whatever it does to you. It will run you mad, or kill you in some way or the other. So you really don't get away. It's there, and you live it.[24]

This conflict between change and stasis is evident in many of Gaines' characters. Some are victims of the past who are willing to change but who cannot overcome their racial and cultural past. Others sacrifice integrity by allowing the past to control them (Tee Bob in *Miss Jane Pittman* and Jackson in *Catherine Carmier*). Gaines says this problem will always be present in his writing, because one person alone cannot endure the burden of cleanly breaking away from the past. Each hands it on to another. He has no answer for resolving the conflict.

In an interview titled "On the Verge," published in *New Orleans Review* in 1973, Gaines was asked whether he still sees the black man as "on the verge," since in black people's history the black woman, in particular the mother, has acted as the dominant family member. Gaines replied,

[24]Rowell, "This Louisiana Thing," p. 42.

> I think that at the moment, right now, the black man is on the verge, like they say Rap Brown is, because these guys are not going to do what they talk about doing. In the title story of *Bloodline*, Copper comes home and he's mad; he's seen a lot of things and he's gone mad . . . or rather he's on the verge of madness. And he will not free people, but somebody else might do it. Someone else will pick it up and carry it a little bit farther.[25]

Emmanuel in "Just Like a Tree" was similarly "on the verge." Gaines, neither pessimist or optimist, could only hope that the black man's role as he sees it could change for the better.

* * *

Asked if he has any bitterness, Gaines says he is concerned about humanity rather than bitterness. He does not like racism, bigotry, or war. He wants his works to be considered the best art that he can produce, and above all to show that it is possible for an individual, black or white, to face a given situation alone, bravely. Gaines especially appreciates praise from Louisianians, because then he knows that they recognize him for being himself, for writing about them without florid language, and because they are proud to see themselves in his writings.

Of his respect for Louisiana ties, he told interviewer Ruth Laney that he feels good when people he has known at False River compliment his work. He mentioned, in particular, the Parlange family, owners of the oldest house in Louisiana, several of whom had read his work and commented favorably upon it. Appreciation from such people means more to him than compliments from the New York critics. He expressed a desire to Laney to be buried on River Lake Plantation.[26]

[25]Ingram and Steinberg, "On the Verge," 339.

[26]Ruth Laney, "A Conversation with Ernest Gaines," *The Southern Review*, X (January, 1974), 11, 13.

DIALOGUE, DIALECT, AND DESCRIPTION

In September of 1983 Gaines told a Lafayette interviewer:

> I believe in form and language—not only content—and that's what makes writing an art. Most of my characters have a dialect. But I create the dialect through syntax and the placement of words, not through misspelling. I also want my characters to be psychologically true so they'll be as real as real people.[27]

Gaines has an uncanny ability to string out a story with dialogue, and make use of repeated words or phrases within the dialogue, typical of black storytellers and words in blues tunes. He usually builds small incidents with it, using description sparingly. Drawing generously from his memories of radio shows, such as one favorite, "Gunsmoke," he likens conversation heard through a wall to radio talk. As an unseen voice, radio talk resembles somebody listening through a wall to someone else talking whom he cannot see.

Gaines feels that in conversational situations people understate things by leaving out words. Though he has no problem with dialogue, his best weapon, he always has a need to refine it, rewrite it, and add a little description. In recent years he has preferred to refine it as he goes, rather than fill in the whole story and then redo it.

He sometimes refers to a gesture, a look or expression in someone's eye, a look passing from one character to another, or a smile or lack thereof. Gaines says, "Tolstoy did things with the eyes, you know, the batting of the eyelashes, which other writers could not do, so I look to see how Anna Karenina bats an eyelash, that kind of thing." Even in his grimmest scenes there is such nuance that the reader can detect varying shades of grey and other of his subtleties, a reflection of the influences Gaines absorbed through his attention to other authors. He does not

[27]Lafayette *Daily Advertiser,* September 25, 1983.

hesitate to obtain information from others, in order to better describe some detail about which he is uncertain. He has asked women for input on house decor, confessing that he does not know "these things."

Gaines' use of dialect, appealing to most Southern readers, is masterful. Anne Price, Baton Rouge journalist, wrote: "He has a fantastic flair for dialogue. His word choices are accurate, his regional language incredibly right. And subtle differences in the speech patterns of each character establish individual viewpoints and goals with beautiful clarity."[28] Gaines says he purposefully does not write dialogue exactly the way it sounds, because if he did no reader could read it, not even himself.

The Negro dialect is highly humorous, accurate, and always expressive, especially to any reader raised in the South. Gaines rarely punctuates questions with questions marks, a habit also noticeable in his written speeches. Prepositions such as "to" and "of" are often omitted in Gaines" dialogue, as are the "ed" for a past tense, an "ing," or an "s", though he sometimes might add these for humor. Some of Gaines' choice words are: they (used for their); some (as in "it's some cold"); jugg (stick out, as in one's tongue); make water (use the toilet); right smart (quite a bit); Done, Jesus or Done, Master (I've finished my task, or have done what you asked, Lord); corn corb pipe (corn cob pipe); China ball trees (China berry trees, a species not particularly respected in the South); gived (gave); yer of corn (ear of corn); 'termination songs (determination songs, used in church); setting chair (comfortable or favorite chair); didn't want bring (didn't want to bring); tobacco color thing (tobacco colored thing); go'n do (going to do); jecking (jerking); when you killed hog (when you are killing hogs); patient (patience); drawers (underpants); move out your way (move out of your way); y'all (you all, singular or plural); strain of wire (strand of wire); usself (ourselves); munks (among); swole (swollen); had ate (had eaten); stension cord (extension cord); scawling (scalding); frizzly (frizzy); draw (drawer or compartment); beef meat (beef); bo' (both); 'thout (without); smelt (smelled);

[28] Baton Rouge *Morning Advocate*, February 22, 1974.

true (truth); rest her hat (take it off and set it somewhere); neighbo (navel); and hoodoo (Voodoo). And Gaines' character, little Tite in *Of Love and Dust*, who speaks French says such things as wee (oui); kess-cou-sey (qu'est-ce que c'est); maa-cee boo-coo (merci beaucoup); Monshoo (Monsieur); Bon-Swa (Bonsoir).

GAINES ON GAINES

Gaines told interviewer Paul Desruisseaux that writing a novel is like taking a train somewhere—you know the general route, but not all the major happenings which might occur, such as "What the conductor's going to look like." If a book has no *form*, "then damn, it ain't no novel," Gaines said. The content should make up forty percent. When a story takes form, "that's writing." This desire for form is immediately evident when one notices that Gaines' books are in small sections, sometimes designated as chapters, usually grouped to form three or four large parts. Plot, Gaines says, is what makes readers turn the page. His basic requirements are plot, characters, and action.[29]

In an undated lecture found among Gaines papers (one given to aspiring writers, sometime after the publication of *Miss Jane Pittman*), he said that he likes to write in long hand, because he likes the

> feel of something; it's like chopping or working the earth or building a house or something . . . I don't like lines. I want freedom in my writing. If I want to spread a line out, I do it. If I want to put 10 words on a page, okay. If the thing is going fast I might space my lines farther, farther apart, and if the thing is going slowly, I might writer closer. I might put 15 lines on one page and maybe 25 lines on another.

[29]Paul Desruisseaux, "Ernest Gaines: A Conversation," *New York Times Book Review,* June 11, 1978.

Gaines has never denied that his books always include characters on a road, that there is always a road. This is one of his techniques for getting action. In the lecture he told the audience,

> If they're standing in a road long enough, somebody's going to make a move or a truck will run over them if they don't. They're going to have to decide to go one way or the other. They got to do something. That's what I mean about the plot. You're going to have something to do.

Continuing, he advised writers to be honest about their characters—white or black.

> I never try to make the black characters angels and the white character a devil. I just try to get men caught up in some kind of problem—not only his country's problem but a universal problem. And, try to make him come through or make him fail or whatever happens—as long as he's failing or coming through truthfully and I'm not faking.

Even if there is failure, the situation or condition should always be a human one.

Gaines continues to hope that his books will gain a following from children and adults in foreign countries, but perhaps more importantly, from both black and white American youth, since he feels that in recent years the two groups have intermingled with a growing understanding.

> I think I have some things to say that not every one else says. I want everyone to read it, especially the Black kids in the South, because I think so much of the stuff being written today doesn't touch the Black kids' life in the South. You never read a book on the black ghetto in a Southern city. You always read about Chicago, New York, Watts, or Detroit. Many of your

> black writers are in the North now and they usually don't write about the South.

Speaking of the advantage black writers writing about the white have over white writers writing about the black Gaines said in the same lecture:

> When the white man is writing about the black, he's always sort of looking down . . . he doesn't have to fit into the black man's world . . . he can just pass by . . . look at it objectively and write about it. Whereas the black, since he is the minority in this country, he must always try to fit into something. . . . So I think I'm in a [better] position to write about the white man than, say, Truman Capote or William Styron is to write about the black man, because I've always had to be on guard, you know, a thing Baldwin always talked about. Whereas, the white doesn't have to do these things. He can look down on things where I must not look up to things, because there's not a thing in the world that I, Ernie Gaines, has to look up to, because I think I'm in a competitive world.
>
> You have to write as honestly as you can, as truthfully as you can, [with] all kinds of pressure on you . . . by one group who says that every damn thing must lead toward the revolution . . . [by] those who don't want to say anything bad about Blacks, and I, Ernie Gaines, say that Blacks do awful things too. Now if you can stand up under that pressure then you can be a writer. My world is as tough as anybody's world to compete in and I think I'm doing a pretty decent job as of right now.

Most readers and critics agree that the job Gaines is doing is more than decently. Some interesting comments were found in an unsigned term paper which discussed Gaines' works frankly. The writer described a typical Gaines work as having

> an attractive antique quality, as if it descended from the classical epic or medieval romance rather than the

> modern novel. . . . Gaines seems to view everything from the outside, and to present it with the detachment of the traditional folk singer or old minstrel. His narratives, therefore, have a kind of remoteness, and move with a slow, colloquial dignity, externalized and intense, but cool, controlled, austere. Sometimes the slowness turns to blandness, and the austerity leads to washed out characters. And sometimes the remoteness short-circuits the passions that are so important to him. But on the whole, when we read even his weakest material, we know that we're in the hands of a skilled writer and an acutely sensitive human being.

* * *

The majority of Gaines' works are written in first person. Gaines relates his ability to *listen* to the speech of others to writing in first person. He has listened well to what his people have said and the way they said it, especially to their interpretation of history. His definition of history is "something that happened a moment ago or a million years ago, told by anybody in his own ways." So, from differing points of view, history could well be truth or lies. His reasons for writing in first person are that it is easier, and because he likes the language of his people, one that does not lend itself to the omniscient point of view. He says that the language he wishes to capture is the "most beautiful sound to come from the mouth—as long as you don't know that they're trying to speak English, trying to interpret history as they see it." After some of his works were translated into Russian and German, neither of which he has mastered, he was anxious to hear them read aloud, just to see hear how these languages flowed.

This first person technique also seems related to the fact that Gaines' works are written to be read aloud effectively, as a story teller or actor would present them. How does Gaines choose his narrator? He creates a person who can relate to the other characters and communicate with them; believable, likeable characters, as opposed to those too angry or vindictive. For example, Jim was the logical communicator in *Of Love and Dust*. Marcus could never have been, for he was too angry and inarticulate.

A whole bag of subtle tricks can be used if properly manipulated by the narrator. Since the narrator cannot be in all places at once, believable incidents and believable minor characters must be created who contribute information. Often the conversation of others, which may be veiled or incomplete, allows the narrator, and also the reader, to read between the lines, from sounds, gestures and facial expressions. Gaines is well aware that the most skillful writers use tricks; certainly Shakespeare did in the many intrigues of his dramas. The narrator must never control, must not be a "puppeteer," as Gaines labels Ellison.

Gaines speaks of "disappearing" when he uses the first person approach. He, as author, must disappear and make the narrator the entire person. Writing in third person is more difficult, he explains:

> I know that I'm not nearly as in control in the third-person omniscient as I am in the first-person. If I get a character too close to me, I can't work with him. I'm having to deal with a character in this book I'm working on now [*A Lesson Before Dying*]. He's too damned close to me, and I'm having all kinds of problems. He's one of the reasons I'm not working as fast. He's too much like me. He's cynical at times. He hates things. He wants to say, 'Goddamnit all. The hell with this stuff.'[30]

His problem with the character, he says, is not making the distinction between the character and himself (the writer) who are so alike, but rather,

> It's the voice, not the person himself. . . . He speaks too much like me. You know you shouldn't let yourself think too much. It's good to just go on and do the work and stop all the damned thinking. When I come to the

[30]Wooton and Gaudet, "Talking with Ernest Gaines," 240.

> omniscient point of view and I create a character, a narrator who's much like myself, I do too much thinking. I don't have the freedom. There's too much thinking going on. . . . You don't think. Let the thing flow. Let it go.[31]

The voice of Gaines' narrator becomes omniscient, once a situation is presented and discussed, as if the narrator is sitting back to view the scene. An example is found in *Of Love and Dust* when Jim suspects that God is "up there" playing solitaire alone, having removed himself from the conflict below.

* * *

In a novel Gaines sets up immediate action which grabs the reader from the start. Rather than description, he most enjoys writing dialogue, when he has begun to "hear" his characters. "Of course when it's not going well, I don't like hearing them at all," he said. but he is always eager to write, even when things do not go easily. He is able to discipline himself to sit, waiting until something comes to him.

He has said numerous times that he does not lose sleep over the critics' favorable or unfavorable remarks about his writing. *Time*, May 10, 1971, commented: "He [Gaines] sets down a story as if he were planting, spreading the roots deep, wide and firm. His stories grow organically, at their own rhythm. When they ripen at last, they do so inevitably, arriving at a climax with the absolute rightness of a folk tale."

Time has called Gaines the "best black writer in the United States." But Gaines told journalist Ruth Laney this was almost meaningless to him, even if *Time* had called him the best *writer,* regardless of race. Rather than maintain a peak, his philosophy is to do his work as well as possible.[32]

[31] *Ibid.*

[32] Laney, "A Conversation with Ernest Gaines," 8-9.

He usually feels good after completing a work, while also feeling like he has not said everything he meant to say, a state of mind leading to the next book. Recalling Faulkner's philosophy on the subject, he told interviewer Desruisseaux, "Once you're satisfied with everything you've done, you might as well break the pencil and cut your throat . . . the whole damn thing is over with. So you never really finish. Not if you're a writer. And it never gets any easier."[33]

Gaines is interested only in writing fiction, as long as he considers it "honest work." One interviewer asked him why he had not written more short stories. Gaines replied that once he finished a novel, he always seemed to have another in mind, but that usually no interesting short stories had taken shape. In an undated, unnamed news item in Gaines files he addressed the situation frankly: "The problem isn't creating a story. It's getting it published." He constantly collects fragments from everyday experiences and lets them simmer and shift until he can use them. In the same news item he said, "I saw a lady in a bar, a small lady with a plump mouth, and she would sort of squint her eyes when she smiled and she would smile all the time. Watching her, I knew I'd use that smile in a story sometime."

* * *

Numerous offers to write for television have come to Gaines, and despite their financial rewards, that style of writing does not appeal to him. He writes slowly, realizing that one can write for a year with no money coming in, but he prefers building his work solidly, to endure. *Miss Jane Pittman* took two years, and *In My Father's House* seven. "There are so few of us black writers and we have so much to do. I feel I have to do my share and I put that before things, people, family. Even sometimes before myself," Gaines told *Los Angeles Times* interviewer Blake Green in December, 1983. The following month he said: "The actual time of writing a book is not the actual time of

[33]Desruisseaux, "Ernest Gaines," *New York Times Book Review,* June 11, 1978.

creating a book. You are writing all the time. Sometimes you are driving and you forget how you got to a place because you are 'writing.' Writing could kill you."[34]

Gaines told an interviewer for the *San Francisco Examiner*, June 20, 1978, that he is continually challenged with the transfer of the "images of the mind" to the "words on paper." Feeling that his thoughts are usually greater than what is said on paper, he estimates that abour forty percent of his thoughts reach paper, compared with his idol Tolstoy's eighty-five percent. He does not want the perfection of transferring 100 percent of his thoughts to paper, for there would be nowhere left to go. He prefers the on-going struggle, which may not place him on top of the mountain.

[34]Interview with *Peninsula Times Tribune*, January 24, 1984.

PART III

GAINES' WORKS: AN OVERVIEW

To date the published works of Ernest J. Gaines number nine short stories, three of which are a part of the *Bloodline* collection of stories, and five novels. Among Gaines' papers in Dupré Library, however, are several folders containing unpublished stories, fragments of stories and notes for stories. These materials are restricted and available only with Gaines' permission.

Each of Gaines' works is worthy and thought provoking. The following section, including literary criticism and analysis, is intended as a point of departure for the reader who wishes to further probe Gaines' writing. The comments are based entirely on research and do not reflect the personal opinion of the author of *A Gathering of Gaines*.

SHORT STORIES

"The Turtles"

"The Turtles," written while Gaines was a student at San Francisco State, was published in 1956 in the first issue of *Transfer*, the school's literary magazine, which sold for thirty-five cents a copy. The story deals with a young boy's sexual awakenings. As mentioned in Part I, Professor Stanley Anderson's title suggestion, "The Voice of the Turtle," was rejected by Gaines. Though this was Gaines' first published piece, evidences of his inimitable style are multiple.

In first person Gaines relates a fishing trip from the viewpoint of Max, a teenage boy. His father and Mr. James are more serious fishermen than Max and his friend Benny, who succeed only in catching several turtles. On the way home from the lake the foursome stops by Mrs. Diana Brown's who, Max says, "walked prouder than any other lady that I had ever seen." In the Widow Brown's absence the two older men are determined that Max and Benny display their manhood to Amy, her prurient niece, who says to Max, "Your pa want you to come where I'm at." Benny resisted, crying, but Max, afraid of losing his father's esteem, went into Amy's room.

His father says as they walk home, "I guess you think you're a man now?"

"No, Sir," I said. "I didn't think I'm a man."

"Well, you are," my old man said.[1]

* * *

"The Boy in the Double-Breasted Suit"

The following year, 1957, Gaines' eight-page "The Boy in the Double-Breasted Suit" was published in another issue of *Transfer*. In this clever piece Oscar, the widowed father of Max, a perceptive young man, is dallying with the idea of taking for his new wife a widow, Miss Adele. Miss Adele gives Max a double-breasted suit, finery to which he is unaccustomed but which pleases him. The minister, Reverend Johnson, pompously plays God. He tries to dissuade the marriage by verbally and physically abusing the father, at least temporarily achieving his aim. Oscar decides to leave, taking Max, who is allowed to keep the cherished double-breasted suit as a reminder of Miss Adele.

As the story begins, a confrontation is set up immediately between the minister and the boy's father. The minister strikes the father at the dinner table, determined to make him feel guilty, first for starting to eat the meal before the blessing has been said, and then for not being ashamed of his sins, real or imaginary. Miss Adele, out of "christianship," bows to the minister's dominance throughout the story, but is hopeful at the end that the father will return, for she wants to be his wife and the boy's step-mother.

[1]Ernest Gaines, "The Turtles," *Transfer*, San Francisco University, I (1956), 9.

The story is in first person, told by the boy Max. Relative to Gaines' later works this story has noticeably longer sentences. Proportionately there is more description than dialogue in this story, and more "proper" English than dialect, perhaps because Miss Adele was a "proper" lady, certainly in the eyes of the minister.

Gaines' description of the minister, perceived through the boy's eyes, reads:

> The preacher was a tall man, and wore a black suit with a long black coat and always had a wide rim black hat, and carried a gold chain over his chest, hooked into a button hole and the other end in his vest pocket, hooked onto a big watch that you could hear ticking if you sat ten feet away from him. He had very big wrinkled hands, and you could see the big veins on back of his hands and up his arms. He had eyes that set far back in his face, close together eyes, gray eyes, and his teeth that looked almost like horse teeth were very strong, and it was said around Wakeville that he could pick up a fifty-pound sack of rice with his teeth and swing it like a pendulum for a minute every week-day, and go to church on Sunday and preach two full hours without stopping as long as the sisters of the church kept wiping his face with the towel and supplying him with ice water.[2]

There is no description as such of Miss Adele, a lady of whom Max was genuinely fond. But through her actions and conversation, the reader assumes that she is a rather refined, "nice lady" who is sympathetic to the boy's needs and who defers to the preacher.

* * *

[2]Ernest Gaines, "The Boy in the Double Breasted Suit," *ibid.*, II (1957), 3.

"Mary Louise"

"Mary Louise," a story published in *Stanford Short Stories 1960*, was originally a chapter in Gaines' novel *Catherine Carmier*, but was omitted through revisions. In first person, told by Mary Louise, it presents two incidents between Mary Louise and her boyhood sweetheart, Jackson. In the first one she relates a harmless, near-sexual encounter with Jackson when they were very young. They were both beaten for "sinning," though whatever intimacy they achieved was in innocence. Mary Louise's love for Jackson never waned, even when he was away for ten years. She stayed at home, taking care of her father and working as a white woman's housemaid.

When Jackson returns as an adult, she describes her fear that he loves a pretty neighbor, Lillian, though he has not *said* that he does. Neither has he told Mary Louise that he loves *her*. He has thought that by now she would be married. When he asks her to meet for a talk, hopefully she fantasizes that he is going to propose marriage. Now she can be the envy of all the other girls, especially if he should take her into Bayonne to buy a ring.

But their meeting is a far cry from a marriage proposal. They walk through a pasture and sit under a tree. Once they reach the tree Jackson offers her his pocket handkerchief to sit on. She is shy. Their conversation is hesitant, formally old-timey, almost naive for two adults. Mary Louise narrates:

> I sat on the handkerchief and spread out my dress. I was wearing a white dress with lots of big flowers in it. I think it was Miss Charlotte who had give me the cloth. And I had made the dress myself.
>
> When I sat down, Jackson moved back and sat against the tree.
>
> 'Watch for ants, there,' I said.
>
> Jackson leaned forward and looked at the tree, and then he leaned back 'gainst it again.
>
> 'None,' he said, stretching out his legs and looking at me. I looked over at him, and then I looked down the field like I saw something down there I was interested in. There wasn't nothing down there, but I just couldn't

> look at him when he was looking at me like that. If he wasn't I could look at him all day, 'cause I like to look at him. But I couldn't look at him at all if he was looking at me at the same time.

So Mary Louise managed by what she said and did *not* say to tell Jackson that she had waited for him ever since he had been away, that there had never been anyone else for her, that she hoped he would come back for her. He told her that though they had loved each other as ten- and twelve-year-olds she should not have expected things to stay the same, that nothing can ever stay the same. Angered and hurt, sensing his pity for her as the undesired one, she tells him:

> 'I don't need your pity. . . . Take it to somebody else. Take it to them yellow bitches you like to go round. Just don't bring it to me.'
>
> I got to my feet and stood right over him. I hoped there was something close by I could hit him with. I couldn't see a thing, and I drawed back and hit him with my fist hard as I could. I hit him again, and I hit him again, and he didn't even try to get out my way. He just sat there with his head down, not even flinching. . . .
>
> When I got home I went to my room and locked the door. I just wanted to be by myself so I could think what a fool I had been. All my life I had been nothing but a fool for people.[3]

* * *

In 1963 "The Sky is Gray" was published in *Negro Digest*, (August) and "Just Like a Tree" was published in the Autumn issue of *Sewanee Review*. "A Long Day in November" was printed in *Texas Quarterly*, Summer, 1964, and was also published separately as a children's book by Dial Press in 1971.

[3]Ernest J. Gaines, "Mary Louise," *Stanford Short Stories 1960* (Stanford, Calif., 1960) 38, 42.

These stories will be discussed with the others in the *Bloodline* collection.

* * *

"My Grandpa and the Haint"

"My Grandpa and the Haint" was published in the Summer, 1966 issue of The *New Mexico Quarterly*. It is a funny story, punctuated with more dialect than was "The Boy in the Double-Breasted Suit," and told in first person by Bobby, a twelve-year-old boy, who often goes fishing with Pap, his grandpa. Pap foolishly allows himself to be seduced by Molly Bee, a light skinned Negro woman of dubious reputation who lives in a pasture en route to his favorite fishing area. During Pap's visits to Molly Bee, Bobby is always sent out to gather eggs. After curiosity forces him to spy a few times on their "foot washing," grunting, and giggling, Bobby begins to disapprove of such behavior and enlists his friend Lucius's help in subtly letting Mom, his grandma, know what Pap has been doing. The well-rehearsed Lucius effectively does his part to plant the seed of suspicion, as planned.

Mom then goes to Madame Toussaint, the hoodoo (Voodoo) woman, who contrives the ploy of a fake snake that scares Pap into a barbed wire fence near Molly Bee's house. Pap is totally shaken with superstition, suspecting that Madame Toussaint has devised the snake, thereby putting a hex upon him. His lesson is learned. He begins fishing in a different part of the river.

Pap tells of his bout with the snake, which he calls a haint that goes "Ciss-ciss."

> Faster I run, faster that haint run. Haint right behind me, going 'Ciss-ciss.' Then I see that haint making me run cross the pasture—towards the fence. Come to the fence, didn't even think, just went in. Haint knowed what he was doing. Got me all tangled up and tried to beat me to death. Lord, have mercy. Lord, have

> mercy. You ain't been beaten by a haint, you ain't been beaten. When I woke up, I was home. Don't know nothing. Don't know nothing. Nothing but that haint.
>
> Bobby further describes Pap's fear of the haint, even after he has supposedly recuperated from the ordeal. When Bobby relayed Miss Molly Bee's "get well" wishes, 'Pap didn't say a word. He just gazed at the ceiling. Then he started talking about the haint again. That haint just stayed in Pap's mind. Nothing else. Just the haint. And everything led up to the haint. If you said berry, Pap would put berry with bush, bush with pasture, and pasture with haint. If you said post, Pap would put post with fence, fence with pasture, and pasture with haint. If you said dirt, water, sky—anything; it all added up to haint.[4]

BOOKS

CATHERINE CARMIER

Originally titled *A Little Stream*, Gaines' first novel, actually begun as early as 1949-50, ultimately emerged in 1964 as *Catherine Carmier*. In a speech in Baton Rouge in 1971 Gaines said:

> I think the first title I gave it was "A Little Stream" because it dealt with two families, one very fair, one dark—separated from each other by a stream of water. But I gave the novel at least a dozen different titles before I was finished with it. Whenever the plot took a sudden change—a direction beyond my control—I erased the original title and gave the manuscript one that was more fitting. I had changed the title so many times in those fifteen years that even when it came time for publication the book was simply called *Catherine*.

[4]Ernest Gaines, "My Grandpa and the Haint," *New Mexico Quarterly*, XXXVI (1966), 159.

Gaines' editor suggested that another title would be better, but Gaines wanted to keep *Catherine* for two reasons. He had once been in love with a girl named Catherine, and he had just finished reading Hemingway's *A Farewell to Arms*, whose heroine was Catherine.

> I figured what was good enough for Hemingway was good enough for Ernie Gaines, so I said, 'What's wrong with Catherine?' My editor said he thought something else ought to go with it. All right, her last name is Carmier; call her that. Call her anything—as long as I don't have to think up another title.

Two other titles found on the reworked manuscripts were *The Barren Summer* and *The Comeback*, the latter being the title of his short-story submission which won the Joseph Henry Jackson Award in 1959. Gaines admits to anywhere from fifteen to twenty revisions as the novel grew. A look at Gaines' pages of manuscript reveals that many small scenes were omitted from the final book, and that some names of characters were changed, *i. e.* Mary Louisie was originally Mae Louise and Brother was Li'l Bud. In the early drafts the minor characters had more conversation. In an undated, unnamed news item found in Gaines' papers, he says, "You cannot rewrite a character fifteen times and emerge with the same person you based him on; you emerge with an authentic person of your own."

In writing Gaines omits all obvious messages and esoteric literary terms, figuring if his work is skillful his message will come through. Always interested in racial and social problems, he added, "If I write a very good book it will mean much more than carrying a placard. That *is* my placard."

Gaines told interviewer Ruth Laney that, using *Fathers and Sons* as his Bible, *Catherine Carmier* was written along the same structure. *Catherine Carmier* became the novel he had begun when he was sixteen.[5] The book was published seven

[5]Laney, "A Conversation with Ernest Gaines," 6.

years after Gaines had given himself ten years to become a writer. Meanwhile, the few stories discussed above had been published in journals.

In undated speeches found in Gaines papers, he recalls his agony while writing *Catherine Carmier*.

> My first book, *Catherine Carmier* took me so long because I was trying to write it the way Turgeniff [*sic*], Hemingway, Fitzgerald and others wrote their books. I haven't made that error since, and I doubt that I shall ever make it again. From now on it must be done Gaines' way, and Gaines' way is the way those people talk down there. And I don't mean only Black Louisianians. I mean Black White Brown Tan Gray Louisianians,

he said to an audience in Chapel Hill, c. 1969.

On another occasion he said,

> I tried every point of view you can imagine. I probably invented some points of view. But I didn't know how to write a novel, so I kept writing, sending it to my agent—sending it to Viking in New York. And they would send it back, say it wasn't ready, and I would rewrite it. And I did that several times from several different points of view, so many points of view, changing the plot, doing everything and changing again and for five years I did it. I must have written that book two or three times a year. My agent, my editors, they've told me, 'Why don't you try something else when one project is giving you a lot of hell—try something else.' But I usually try to stick to one project. I can't jump all over the place. I stick to one thing. I wish I could write the whole Goddamn thing the first draft, but I can't do it. It's just like building a house.

* * *

More than one editor suggested to Gaines that the manuscript was too long, that there was too much material, and that its title should be something other than *Catherine*. About the length of his manuscript Gaines said:

> I had put everything into those seven hundred pages that I could think of. I wanted everything that I had experienced, knew, and had heard about Louisiana. There were house fairs, with gumbos and fried fish, soft drinks and beer; there was much love making, and of course, there had to be illegitimate children; there were deaths, wakes, funerals, baptisms, even threats of race violence.

Two interesting letters were found in Gaines' papers, both written a few months before *Catherine Carmier* was published in October of 1964. The first, from Gaines to editor Hiram Haydn of Atheneum Publishers, concerned the book's revisions and content. (Haydn, who died in 1973, authored and co-authored numerous books and anthologies, and was a co-founder of Atheneum in 1959.)

> April 11, 1964
>
> My Dear Mr. Haydn:
>
> I received you letter, dated April third, concerning characters in the book. The characters are all fictional. The place is real—though I've changed the name, put in extra houses (the Carmier's for example) shifted trees, fences and roads. There's only one Negro farmer on the place now, but he's black instead of mulatto, he's a baptist instead of a catholic, and he's nothing at all like Raoul. I was talking to a mulatto girl about six months ago who believes she's very much like Catherine. But I'm pretty safe there, since the girl lives in Fresno, California, and has only visited the South twice in her life. She stayed only a week or two each time.

Furthermore, this girl's father has never killed a stepson (as far as I know) though her mother who looks a little like Molly Picou does flirt with her eyes a little bit.

About the Carmier's house: Yes, there was a house there once, but it was torn down about five years ago—about the same time I started this novel. I had to rebuild the house again (that was one of the reasons why I had to go South in sixty-three) and I hope I have done a pretty good job. If there are any loose boards or squeaking doors, then I'm less a carpenter than I thought.

The plantation is owned by a family called Major. They are Major and his two sisters-in-law. Major and one of his sisters-in-law own one side of the plantation (the quarters in which the Negroes live divides the plantation into halves) and the other sister-in-law and her family own the other half. However in the book I have it all under the one name of Grover. I think I'm pretty safe there since I don't mention anyone's name, nor do I describe any of them.

On Major's side of the place, the Cajuns farm all of the land. They have pushed the Negro sharecroppers off the land in one way or another. The lone Negro farmer, Johnny Hall, lives on the other side. As of now, the in-laws on that side will have nothing to do with Major's Cajuns. Only God knows how long this will go on. I'm afraid that like Faulkner's Snopes, the Cajuns will eventually take over everything.

There are a few changes about the Cajuns that I'd like to make. For example, I want to give them a last name, which I don't think I have done; second, I want to make them brothers and first cousins instead of brothers only. (In real life they're all brothers).

The rest of the characters are of no worry at all. There are no such persons as Madame Bayonne, Lillian, Catherine, Brother, Mary Louise, Charlotte, Della, Jeanette or Raoul. I suppose Jackson is a little bit of me—but only a little—and the rest of him was created out of my imagination. There's a river that runs along the highway—False River, it's called—but there are many plantations along this river. There are also many general stores—the one I write about in the book was closed down about ten years ago, and like the Carmier's house I tried to put life in it again. There was no drinking room to the side for Negroes when the store was opened, though in many of the stores along the river you will find these dirty little side rooms. My town, Bayonne, in real life, is a little place called New Roads. Bayonne is the maiden name of my stepfather's mother. I like the sound of it, and since many of the people I write about are of French descent or speak the language, I think the name is quite appropriate.

I hope I have cleared up some if not all the questions you had in mind. If there are more, please let me know. As for a lawyer, I don't think one is necessary, but I'm sure you know much more about this than I.

I remain yours sincerely,

Ernest J. Gaines

The other letter, dated May 9, 1964, suggests that Gaines had been questioned further, at Haydn's suggestion, by Alan U. Schwartz. Though Mr. Schwartz could have been a consulting lawyer, Gaines does not say so in the letter which reads:

Dear Mr. Schwartz:

In regard to your letter dated May 1, 1964, concerning characters in the manuscript, *Catherine Carmier*, I cannot see in any way how any of these characters can be identified with anyone living or dead. I know this sounds strange (people just naturally look like other people) but if this is so in the manuscript, then it is only by accident. When I conceived the idea of the novel—about fifteen years ago—many of my minor characters were modeled on real people. Since then, and after making several trips South, I'm sure there is no similarity between them whatsoever. It is only coincident that there is only one Negro farmer left on the plantation and only one Negro (mulatto) farmer in the book. I had put Raoul into this situation even before I knew of the situation in the South. Raoul is there to show the man's character. Raoul's great grandfather, grandfather, and father would have stood there. So Raoul must. He's a man alone. Because of his color—because he's neither white nor black (both in color of skin and conviction) he will always be alone. This is the only reason I have Raoul bucking the pressure of the Cajuns when all the time the rest of the Negroes have given up. The only reason why Johnny Hall is still farming is because he works for the other side of the plantation (please see the letter I wrote Mr. Haydn April 11). If he were on the same side as the Cajuns, where they could pressure him, he would have given up along with all the others. These two men, Raoul and J. Hall, definitely have nothing in common. As a matter of fact I've heard that Johnny Hall's wife beats him. Beside that she can handle a pair of mules, drive a truck, drive a tractor, ride a horse bareback, shoot a shotgun, and she also sets traps for wild animals. Poor Della, the lady in my book, could never do any of these things. Can you imagine anybody in his right mind trying to have an affair with a woman like Johnny Hall's wife?

The only question I have in mind about my book is about the place. Though my characters are all fictional, the place in the book is pretty much like Oscar, Louisiana. (By the way, I think the state in which the story takes place is quite obvious. Several times I mention Baton Rouge, New Orleans, and other places near there.) I mentioned to Mr. Haydn in my other letter that I had built houses, torn down houses, opened a general store, and shifted fences and trees. But before reading the dust jack of the novel and knowing anything about Oscar, Louisiana, they could easily compare the place in the book to the real place. As I said before, I don't know if this is necessary to __________ [word unintelligible, revision in pen] but it has been in my mind.

Respectfully yours,

Ernest J. Gaines

P.S. About that mulatto girl in Fresno. I tried to make a date with the girl one night, so I told her the plot of my novel. (Othello to Desdemona). Immediately, the girl loved Catherine, the heroine of the novel, and identified herself with Catherine. But unlike the tragedy by Shakespeare, she did not go for the teller of the story. She had already made a date.

* * *

After its publication by Atheneum in 1964, *Catherine Carmier* was reissued by Secker and Warburg in London (1966); by Scherz-Verlag in both Munich (1970) and Bern (1971) under the title *Es war die Nachtigall* (*It Was the Nightingale*), translated from the English by Hans Hermann; and by North Point Press in 1981, after having been out of print for a few years in the 1970s. Gaines' enigmatic dedication is "For S—."

When Atheneum's 1,500 copies were printed in October, 1964, the book got adequate but far from overwhelming attention, and soon, as one journalist put it, this first novel "faded into the twilight." By Gaines' own admission royalties were slim. *Catherine Carmier* actually got more attention after *Of Love and Dust* (1967) was published than it did in 1964.

Catherine Carmier has been called an "apprentice first novel" and a "simple little story." Because of the simplicity of its style and theme Hoyt W. Fuller, writing for the *Southwest Review* (Autumn, 1965), called it "one of the most promising of the contemporary crop," whose author had been neglected in "the clamor over the more colorful writers." One California journalist noted that "more than a trace of Hemingway appears in the clean, compressed prose . . . but Hemingway would not have got that dialect right."

* * *

Catherine Carmier is written in third person and in a less personal style than Gaines' later novels. For the most part the characters speak more formally, though some speak in dialect. Descriptions, though not expansive, are from an omniscient viewpoint, one which Gaines admitted was uncomfortable for him as the writer. When he uses this technique, rather than telling the story in first person, description and dialogue must be handled differently.

The novel concerns a returning Louisiana plantation native, Jackson Guerin, who has been away to California for an education. He visits his Aunt Charlotte who is hopeful, as is his childhood friend, Mary Louise, that he will remain in the area to teach. Jackson knows that he cannot stay, and is tortured in telling Aunt Charlotte that he cannot, for she does not want to understand nor to let him go again. Mary Louise hopes that Jackson will choose her, an unlikely situation to fit into his own plans.

Jackson finds himself in love with Catherine Carmier, daughter of Creole plantation manager Raoul Carmier and his wife Della. Catherine, who has a small son by a Creole man whom Raoul would not accept as her husband, also loves Jackson, but will not leave her emotionally dependent, overly doting father for him. Raoul is driven by competition with white Cajun farmers, his obsession for Catherine, his dislike for the darker skinned Jackson, and by Della's earlier indiscretion, one which led to the "accidental" death of a son he claims was not his.

Lillian, Catherine's younger sister, is home on a temporary visit. Unlike Catherine, as an infant Lillian was sent away to live with relatives in New Orleans, formally educated and groomed to "pass" as a white person in society. She is tortured by her own non-identity, and though she loves Catherine and encourages the affair with Jackson, she is hostile and sullen toward her parents.

Shortly before the book ends, Catherine has decided to leave with Jackson, but Raoul and Jackson have a brutal fight in which Raoul is bested. Much to Jackson's disappointment Catherine refuses to leave her father and go with him. Though she knows it is Della's turn to take her rightful place as mother and wife, Catherine knows that her father, whom she now pities, needs her, for Raoul is understandably humiliated at having lost face.

* * *

Jackson describes history as a wall, a symbol applicable to his own predicament, since he is unable to escape cleanly from personal or racial history. "So the struggle went on," he thinks.

> The little incidents, the little indirect incidents, like slivers from a stick. But they continued to mount until they had formed a wall. Not a wall of slivers that could be blown down with the least wind. But a wall of bricks, of stones. A wall that had gotten so high by now that he had to stand on tiptoe to look over it.[6]

Jackson is not only imprisoned by his unacceptability to Raoul, but also because of being an educated man in an uneducated community, "thrown back on his own scant internal devices," forced to make do within his racial and community confines. He hopes for a bloodline, or love, contact. He knows that the ossified past must be escaped, but he also knows that peace must be made between himself and the past in order to be really free. Instead he is a "freedman," realizing that "if racial and personal history are prisons, any hope of community is also dead." Gaines uses "dust" in *Catherine*

[6]Ernest J. Gaines, *Catherine Carmier* (1964, reprint ed., San Francisco, 1988), p. 94.

Carmier to signify what remains of a dead past—a dust that stifles Jackson.[7]

Interviewer John O'Brien asked Gaines if Jackson, like Catherine, should have been willing to sacrifice his life for the dying Louisiana culture. Gaines explained that Jackson, having been away, expected to come back and teach others the things that he had learned. But "Jackson does not have that kind of feeling about others at that time in his life. He was still searching for himself. And though he did not find himself in California, he knew that he could not do it back home, even with someone as beautiful and who loved him as much as Catherine Carmier."

O'Brien asked, "Do you think that Catherine's decision to stay with her defeated father is noble or cowardly?" Gaines replied:

> I don't know whether it's one or the other. It was fated that she stay there; I don't think she could decide her fate. Even if she had gone with Jackson, which she really wanted to do, she probably would have turned around and come back. It's almost impossible for Catherine to have left the South, especially at that time.[8]

Even if she had, she would have found that she could not exist permanently outside the South. She was trapped in her family conflict, in their dependency on her, and her color and the parents' color. Gaines, having known many such cases, is certain of this.

Gaines always manages to be inside his characters' heads. He is definitely inside Jackson's when Jackson is confused, thinking or questioning himself. Once when Jackson was undecided about meeting Catherine, Gaines wrote:

> That evening he [Jackson] sat on the porch, looking at the house. The sun was just going down, giving ev-

[7]Jack Hicks, "To Make These Bones Live: History and Community in Ernest Gaines' Fiction," *Black American Literature Forum,* XI (1977), 11.

[8]O'Brien, *Interviews,* p. 88.

> erything an orange and purplish color. He felt lonelier than ever before. It is like this with people who are in love. The setting of the sun is the worst time of day.[9]

The scenes between Jackson and Aunt Charlotte, and with the perceptive Madame Bayonne, also describe Jackson's malaise and indecision.

Gaines' picture of Mack Grover, one of the white landowners, is incisive:

> He was forty-five or forty-six, still a bachelor, and both winter and summer he could be seen in a seersucker suit. Every morning he stuck a match stem in his mouth, took it out at mealtime, then put it back again. . . . When the match stem moved to the other corner of Mack Grover's mouth, he would give his answer.[10]

* * *

The scenes in this book are not unlike those of a drama. Their dynamic emotional contrasts, from extreme tenseness with raised voices to total silence, would lend themselves well to a stage play. The following two incidents involving Della and Lillian bear quoting. There was noticeable lack of conversation at the table on Lillian's first night home. Gaines writes:

> Supper was eaten in near silence. Della asked questions every now and then, but Lillian's answers were so dry and abrupt that Della would be silent several minutes before saying anything else. Lillian kept her head down throughout the meal. Everyone at the table could see how uncomfortable she was, and this made everyone else feel uncomfortable also. Catherine asked Raoul questions about the field, but his answers were as

[9]Gaines, *Catherine Carmier*, p. 127.

[10]*Ibid.*, pp. 9-10.

> dry and abrupt as Lillian's answers were to Della. . . . Lillian chewed her food slowly and did not say any more. When she was through eating, she nodded her head—to no one in particular, but to everyone at the same time—and went out of the kitchen.[11]

The other incident shows Lillian's unchanging attitude toward Della, when she and Catherine are dressing for the dance. Della, starved for Lillian's love, approval, or merely the slightest physical touch, has made it a point to be in the room. When Catherine refuses to help Lillian with a zipper, she is responding to Della's need to be physically close to Lillian. Gaines' draws the touching scene well with fine detail:

> The zipper had caught in the seam of the dress and could go up only a few inches. Della drew it back down a couple of times and pulled it up again, but each time it stopped in the same place. She drew it all the way down, and Catherine noticed her working with the seam. She could see the side of Lillian's face, too, and Lillian looked as though she was becoming more irritable by the second. Catherine looked at Della as Della drew the zipper up again. It moved much more freely this time, and Catherine could see that Della had worked it loose from the seam. But just as she passed the original place where the zipper had gotten stuck, it stopped again.
>
> 'Don't look like it want pass that spot.'
>
> The zipper was not stuck, and Catherine could see that it was not. But Della had stopped it there in order for Lillian to stand before her a few minutes longer. This was the nearest she had gotten to Lillian since Lillian had come back there—the nearest she had gotten to Lillian since she had started coming back there six years ago. Was it only six? It seemed more like sixty. Della remembered how she had thrown her arms around Lillian, and Lillian had broken away from her as if she were some kind of wild animal trying to attack her.

[11]*Ibid.*, pp. 54-55.

> Catherine saw Della's hand move toward Lillian's shoulders, then toward her hair. But each time she made an attempt to touch her, she drew back again. Any other time she might have taken the girl in her arms, but she did not want to spoil this evening for her. Lillian already knew that the zipper was free, and she was waiting impatiently for Della to pull it farther up.
>
> 'You all right now,' Della said.
>
> 'Thanks, Mama,' Lillian said, and went back up the hall without looking at Della or Catherine.[12]

* * *

Literary scholars have continued to delve deep into Gaines' works, examining them with care. Thadious M. Davis' essay "Headlands and Quarters: Louisiana in *Catherine Carmier,*" goes into great detail on how the cultural and racial customs and plantation hierarchy influenced Gaines' writing of this novel. The Louisiana plantation with its inhabitants of white Cajuns, blacks, and Creoles so intricately entwined, was a perfect background for what Gaines wanted to convey—elements that make the book a "literary work attuned to the dynamic interaction of spatial boundaries, agrarian traditions, temporal suspension, and racial identity."

Jackson's attainment of Catherine was a means of escaping the unwanted legacies of the past and making a new beginning, as Jackson says, "one individual cannot endure alone" the breaking away from the past. Catherine, however, is actually an embodiment of the past from which he wishes to escape. Davis sees three basic patterns in the novel: 1) encounters, confrontations, meetings; 2) replacement or change; then 3) death, from the standpoint of the deteriorating Louisiana world and the psychological impact of racial traditions.[13]

James L. Green called *Catherine Carmier* a

[12] *Ibid.*, pp. 200-201.

[13] Thadious M. Davis, "Headlands and Quarters: Louisiana in *Catherine Carmier*," *Callaloo*, VII (1984), 12-13.

> deceptively simple novel. . . . Except for atmospheric symbols, notably heat and dust, Gaines relies on the repetition of key words, for example 'something' and 'nothing,' to provide texture and a poetic undercurrent for his realistic surface narrative. Unadorned simple and compound sentences are Gaines' chief stylistic instruments for mirroring the apparently simple and barren lives of his characters. Gaines generates a tension between the simplicity of his style and the complexity and intensity of his characters' underlying emotions and feelings, needs and desires. Ernest Gaines is an accomplished craftsman and a sensitive and compassionate artist.[14]

Gaines' friend Professor Alvin Aubert states his opinions on the "truly tragic mulatto." The collective fate or destiny of Gaines' characters as people delineates the "broader socio-political contours of his fiction." South Louisiana is distinct because of its cultural and ethnic diversity; French, African, black, white, Creole, Cajun, Catholic, and Protestant, for example.

Aubert interprets Raoul Carmier as an "over-reacher," one who is still "within his rights as a human being." He has a good opinion of himself, which in the end he loses, tragically. His is a self-imposed isolation; the land becomes for him a surrogate for humanity. He cannot bring himself to call on either blacks or whites for help. Aubert compares Raoul to the mulatto protagonist in James Weldon Johnson's *The Autobiography of an Ex-Coloured Man* who "persisted in living as a white man because of his shame at being included among a people who permitted themselves to be lynched." Raoul creates impossible conditions for his family, such having Catherine displace Della in the kitchen, sending Lillian away, and treating Della badly for bearing the dark child; yet he is not without appeal and deserves some pity.

[14]Unnamed, undated, incomplete, but published essay found in Gaines' papers.

The theme of determination is strong, Aubert maintains. Raoul could not change his life style nor his attitudes—they were already cut out for him.

> The overall effect is an indefiniteness that is in keeping with Gaines' frequent use of ambiguity, including his apparent reluctance to employ absolute racial designations. Nothing is absolute, final; all value lies in process, in the potentiality of process to produce viable human options—or, in religious terms, good seems to be Gaines' position. . . . Generally, Gaines posits a humanistic datum for religion.

An example is cited of Jackson's impossibility of telling Aunt Charlotte he had to leave and her unwillingness to accept her own Christian responsibility: that of ceasing to *possess* him and simply *love* him. Their understanding comes to pass "through the efficacy of the church he [Jackson] had nearly rejected."[15]

In another essay Winifred L. Stoelting is concerned with those of Gaines' characters who exhibit human dignity and pride in handling decisions in the face of polarization. She names these examples in *Catherine Carmier*: Raoul's standing in Catherine's way with Jackson because he is proud, hard-headed and determined; Raoul's turning away of Catherine's first lover, the Creole father of her child, Nelson, because he was just a farmhand; Raoul's pride for the land, which he values even above his family, even above Catherine; Catherine's dignity at the end in choosing Raoul over Jackson; Jackson's pride and dignity shown in the way he seeks truth for himself; the hurt pride which motivated Raoul in dealing with Della's misbehavior, thereby depriving him of a son, who could have been Mark, Della's dark child, or Jackson, also dark, except that neither forgiveness of Della's sin nor love for Mark or Jackson was possible, due to Raoul's consuming agony, his wounded pride. Raoul's near loss of dignity and pride when Jackson defeats him in the fight; and finally, Della's dignity

[15]Alvin Aubert, "Ernest J. Gaines's Truly Tragic Mulatto," *Callaloo #3,* I (May 1978), 69, 71, 73, 74.

when she finally understands Raoul's feelings, knowing that he needs her now whether Catherine stays or not. Each of the four must function in the situation he has created for himself without losing dignity.[16]

In 1989 Doris White, graduate student at the University of Southwestern Louisiana, made an in depth, insightful study of Gaines' various manuscripts of *Catherine Carmier*, as well as of the finished novel. White comments that some of the clarity written into the early drafts of the novel is lacking in the final version. Societal structure, according to White, is the basis for all of Gaines' writings. In this particular novel, the white man, present only by implication, is the ominous presence, "a perpetual shadow which stalks his characters, denying them not only freedom of movement but also freedom of self." The Carmiers were "Creoles of color," a unique segment of society. They were the upper class blacks who got the best of what was available to blacks.

White also sees Raoul as a tragic figure, who has no control over his position as a farmer, a position handed on by his father, Robert. Raoul had neither worked for the white man, nor alongside the blacks. He is filled with complexities, evident in his sending Lillian away to "think" white, and in his knowledge that Della is a Creole who "thinks" black. Raoul's obsession with the Creole status drives him to murder Mark, Della's dark son by a darker Negro lover. Her unfaithfulness was not as important to him as her "intimacy with a black man." In his obsession he puts the guilt of his crime on Della because she can never "think" Creole; therefore his position is threatened.

Catherine is his only hope, for she is like him in attitude, despite her love for Jackson. The conflict within Catherine is shown when she takes as long styling her hair as whites would, then abandons the idea. In a sense, then, Catherine no less tragic than her father and, being a Creole, is locked into conformity. Her fate is beyond her control. She regards Jackson's defeat of Raoul in the fight as a "bittersweet, empty"

[16]Winifred L. Stoelting, "Human Dignity and Pride in the Novels of Ernest Gaines," *CLA Journal*, XIV (1971), 340, 343.

victory at best, for the lovers can never "rise above the dictates of racism." She believes that Gaines' emphasis is "not on what the white man has done or is doing, but on how blacks respond to these actions and struggle to survive with dignity in spite of them."[17]

* * *

Dozens of critics reviewed *Catherine Carmier*, after each of its three printings. Excerpts from a few of them follow, though some of the dates and names of newspapers or journals found in Gaines' papers are incomplete.

An early reviewer for the *Virginia Kirkus Bulletin*, a book review service, August 15, 1964, called the book

> a curiously withdrawn novel of involuted passion. . . . Despair, torment and frustration overhang the scene like a static and oppressive high noon, but the mood is furthered, unfortunately, by the uniform dreariness of the characters. Still a promising first try.

More positive comment came from the *San Francisco Chronicle*, October 30, 1964:

> I realize that most readers do not rush out and purchase copies of first novels. But do yourself a favor in this case. Enjoy it; and also enjoy witnessing the emergence of that rare phenomenon—an under-publicized and honest literary talent. *Catherine Carmier* is a first-rate achievement in every sense.

Baton Rouge's *Sunday Advocate*, November 8, 1964, said:

> It is when the characters discuss the matter of color and the conflicts involved that the reader finds the most

[17]Doris White, "A Strain in the Blood: The Ominous Presence in the Society of *Catherine Carmier*," unpublished manuscript in USL's Louisiana Room.

> moving parts of the book. . . . Perhaps what Mr. Gaines is looking for is not so much the truth as the answer—and not necessarily from The Man, but from, and for, all men.

A writer for the *Baltimore Sunday Sun*, November 8, 1964, called Catherine and Jackson "sensitive young lovers," and said that the book is totally without bitterness toward the older generation or toward racial matters.

> So high is Mr. Gaines' hopefulness for reconciliation of people and situations that his characters seem sometimes less than real in their sympathy with one another. Because he represents a generation still maturing, because as a Negro he has experienced the parochialism of the Deep South and the cosmopolitanism of the West Coast, Mr. Gaines is an interesting person. Because his viewpoint is grounded in reasonableness, and his workmanship, although sometimes tedious, sometimes exciting, is always earnest, he is a promising writer.

From *The Fresno Bee*, November 23, 1964:

> This is an extraordinary novel in many ways. The author uses scenes and dialogue so effectively that the feeling of stage is often present. And his simplicity of style complements the heavy, life-giving force of the story. But the characters (all except marvelous Aunt Charlotte, who is a near classic) cannot quite seem to bridge the human chasm between what is personal and what is universal, any more than they can bridge the invisible chasm between what is color and what is boundary. Although not entirely the achievement it might have been, the novel marks the author as having sizable talent.

Stanley Gilliam wrote in The *Sacramento Bee*, November 29, 1964:

> There is here that timeless quality which marks first class characterization, and Jackson and Catherine could be the offspring of plantation owner and overseer in antebellum days, the children of the mill hand and mill owner during the reconstruction era or a dirt poor young Negro couple in 1964. . . . This is a novel of proximity and intimacy, and race, whether the author intended it that way or not becomes strictly a secondary factor to the reader. Ernest Gaines, after a shaky start in which characters come tumbling at the reader from all sides, has written a tight little novel with, among its other virtues, some noteworthy dialogue.

Reviewer Donald Stanley, in an unidentified review, compared the handling of the prodigal son's return as a theme in *Catherine Carmier* to James Baldwin's stage play of 1964, "Blues for Mr. Charlie," saying:

> *Catherine Carmier* is far more sophisticated, more ambitious, less dogmatic than Baldwin's impassioned misfire. . . . His [Gaines'] concern is . . . with the gulf that exists within the Negro community itself. Jackson's entire educative process—the thing his aunt sent him to California for—alienates him. A Jesus calendar hung on his wall by his aunt as 'inspirational' oppresses his taste. He is a stranger, united with his one-time friends only by the color of his skin, which, Gaines emphasizes, makes for a very tenuous unity. . . . The past of innocence and familiarity is symbolized for Jackson by houses and farms that have been plowed under, their occupants dispersed and now living anonymously in the cities. . . . His [Gaines'] concern is with people, rather than issues. If in these supercharged times this makes for writing that seems surprisingly mild, one can be confident that though issues burn out and lose their emotional charge, the residue that remains is the need of one heart to speak to another. When that time comes, it will be discovered that people

> like Ernest Gaines have been trying to cross the language barrier all the time.

The undated *San Francisco Examiner* commented that Gaines skillfully used his "Negroness" in *Catherine Carmier* to provide insight into the overall human condition, and not as a lesson the betterment of people through interjection of a racial situation.

An undated review by Patricia MacManus in *Book Week* titled "Solid, Jackson," said:

> What Mr. Gaines has subtly achieved . . . is to draw the reader into a sense of personal, not just sociologically 'sympathetic,' alliance with Jackson Guerin, the Negro protagonist. Enhancing this thrust towards personal identification is Gaines' effectively spare, non-dress-parade prose. . . . Mr. Gaines' voice is a new one worth attention.

From *Negro Digest*, January 1965:

> *Catherine Carmier* is a superior novel . . . brief, simple, sure, rich in characterization and meaning. It is a joy to read a book by a writer intent on telling a story and on investing it with a genuine sense of reality. But Ernest J. Gaines is a writer with artistry in his touch; he has the fight of perception and an affinity for that truth which is larger than the lives he creates. . . . With a minimum of description, the author evokes the steamy, cypress-marked countryside, recreates the deep, pervasive tensions among the races, and captures the essence of the gentle, deprived lives of the plain people in the Louisiana backwaters. On another level, he is concerned with the impact of the new and the vital on that which is accepted, which has been shaped into rigid patterns and gone dry. Here is a fine first novel by a 31-year-old writer who can only grow. Watch Ernest J. Gaines; he has something to say worth listening to, and he has the talent to say it well.

Some months later *Catherine Carmier* was described by the London *Evening Standard*, February 8, 1966, as "Romeo and Juliet in Louisiana. . . . This is a quiet, beautifully modulated story, a very good first novel."

* * *

After *Catherine Carmier* was published by Secker and Warburg in London in 1966, there were numerous reviews in London papers. Feelings were mixed. The *Daily Telegraph* said:

> We are used to sickly-sweet decay in Southern novels. It is often factitious, self-indulgent, but not here. Mr. Gaines' is himself a Negro from Louisiana. He does not reduce human complexities to moral simplicity. He does not judge: he presents. The result is more powerful than any preachment.

The London *Sunday Telegraph*, February 6, 1966, said: "Mr. Gaines, without overdoing it, has written a sad picture of some of the misunderstandings which burn across Faulkner's landscape."

The Times Literary Supplement, February 10, 1966, carried a review:

> He [Gaines] deals with the South in its subtler influences—not in it poisonous immediacy, but in the way in which its history has changed, shaped and destroyed families slowly, by a kind of corrosion. The white man is present mainly by implication, a ghostly but perpetual enemy at the gates, a stain in the blood. . . . In those passages that register shifts of feeling within the two hermetic families, Mr. Gaines reveals a genuine sensibility; but in many of the set-piece descriptions he is inhibited by a curious literalness, a fear of letting the drama develop freely. But if Mr. Gaines sometimes

> freezes his characters into unconvincing postures, it is only because he is clumsy before their mysteries—not because he is confidently in charge of their inner lives.

The London *Sunday Times*, February 13, 1966, called the book "a good idea . . . but the novel is crudely set up with a first half squandered on the punily-soul-searching Jackson." The *New Statesman*, February 18, 1966, said the book was

> serious, unsensational. Very effectively Ernest Gaines evokes the colour problem in Louisiana by depicting it in a situation where it seems no more than a nuance. . . . I don't think Mr. Gaines has got himself such solid material, but his writing—in plantation dialogue and in his own voice—is the more remarkable.

The *Spectator*, February 11, 1966, called it

> a love story [whose] racial problems are approached obliquely and with remarkable detachment. . . . The strange triangle of Catherine, her lover and her father is presented with objective sympathy, but under the simple texture of the prose throbs a baffled anguish which explodes in a final scene of inevitable and quite uncontrived violence.

* * *

Some reviews of *Catherine Carmier* under its German title *Es war die Nachtigall* were found in Gaines' papers. (Translations have been provided by Ebba Schoonover of the USL Department of Foreign Languages). A review from the German edition of the *New York Herald Tribune* (undated) called it a "wonderful honest book of amazing classical simplicity whose admirable people remain unforgettable," though the novel's content and construction are nothing unusual. It is an old love story, with the opposites of passion and sense of duty, which has some criticism of the social structure of society and some eroticism. It is not overpowering but flows smoothly.

Another, dated December 21, 1970, from the daily *Mittelbayerische Zeitung Regensburg* also refers to its old love theme.

> The novel portrays the passion and suffering of two young people who love each other. Their happiness clashes against the opposing forces of family and prejudices of the environment. It is narrated in a genuine, fascinating and contemporary way, keeping the reader's intense interest. The author's simple, unpretentious and straight forward style enables him to portray the story in a vivid and forceful way.

The *Freier Aargauer*, from southern Germany, carried a similar review, calling *Catherine Carmier* "a moving, passionate story of two people who love each other," and whose happiness seems threatened because of irreconcilable family conflicts and the environment. In this book an ancient yet always new story repeats itself. "It could have only been written with such intensity and passion by a very great writer."

In *Book Overview* from Vienna, January-March, 1971, it was seen

> along the lines of Romeo and Juliet, taking place among colored people of the United States in a world which is unfortunately still a real one. It is the attempt of a likeable young Creole couple to break away from the racist devil's circle of discrimination and hate. But this attempt fails because of prejudice and intolerance. The family tie makes it impossible for the novel's protagonist Catherine to follow the voice of her heart without reservation, to leave the American South and go with her beloved to California. The Creole nightingale sings the final stanza of a great love song which succumbs to the timeless law of insurmountable fate, against which she is powerless.

In an undated, unnamed paper in Bern a reviewer wrote: "This wonderful novel reminds us that there are people of mixed blood who hate whites and show contempt for blacks. Because of this deep impassable gap, Raoul was separated from neighbors and Catherine was unable to marry Jackson, a darker Negro."

Another undated, unnamed paper from Austria commented:

> The ancient theme of conflict between man and fate, man and love has been moved to the miserable restricted world of a small place in the South of the US, in which the black people living there barely manage to survive because existence is restricted by the whites. It is understandable that Jackson, after his education, returns there to take Catherine away to a more hopeful, distant place. Yet she is the only support of her father who was beaten by fate. A serious fight over Catherine results in brute force. Jackson is victorious, but Catherine cannot find the strength to leave her father and follow him at this time. The work is constructed by simple narrative means and well portrays the characters. The fate that follows is true to life. It is recommended to readers interested in such a milieu.

* * *

After the 1981 edition of *Catherine Carmier* a reviewer for The *Oakland Tribune* (undated) wrote:

> While *Catherine Carmier* is structured around timeless themes of exile and star-crossed love, it is set in a specific locale that vibrates with authenticity. . . . Catherine's young sister like Jackson, is in permanent exile even when she returns for a visit. Their mother is isolated within her own family because of an ancient adultery. And their father is enclosed within pathological pride and his own old but terrible guilt. These classically tragic pressures are contained within a spare, controlled narrative and given life by Gaines'

sensitive ear for the southern Louisiana speech rhythms that establish the individuality of his characters.

A reviewer for the *Los Angeles Weekly Examiner Book Week* (June 14, 1981) said:

> Catherine is light-complected; Jackson is dark. She's of and about her family; he's an educated orphan ready to break all ties in order to fulfill his quests and desires. She's blood knowledge; he's book learning. She's home, to parish, the soil, farm; he's exile, California, restlessness, uncertainty. . . . Thanks to Ernest Gaines' certain but quiet labors we follow the winding rows of Catherine Carmier's heart and discover the way her time is—modern boiling, backward sizzling, Southern Louisiana country time—and sweat and suffer in the heat of a perfectly controlled book about place, race, work and reckless love.

Professor/writer Walter van Tilburg Clark, noted for his succinct and careful comments on promising writers, called the novel

> a beautiful book—simple, direct, quiet, steadily and unfailingly moving. Its people remain with me, every one of them as individuals, and there is none who does not win my sympathy in his plight and my admiration for his courage and honesty and tenacity. . . . They act with tragic dignity and a constant, profound awareness of one another, even across the terrible divisions [which] despair, degree of color, and differences in faith, education, and experience have begotten among them.

Dr. Clark was a judge in the 1959 Joseph Henry Jackson competition. His comments on *Catherine Carmier* are on the book jacket of the 1981 edition by North Point Press.

A reviewer for *Essence*, January, 1982, said that some novels about Louisiana can "make writers pound their typewriters in despair" but *Catherine Carmier* "is something quite different."

OF LOVE AND DUST

Gaines' second novel, *Of Love and Dust*, was written in a little over a year's time, quite a different labor from that of *Catherine Carmier*. Gaines dedicated the book to LeVell Holmes and Alice Ryan Holmes, who are as yet unidentified. *Of Love and Dust* was published in 1967 by Dial Press, by Secker and Warburg in London in 1968, by Bantam Books in 1969, and reprinted in 1979 by W. W. Norton. Initially Dial Press printed 10,000 copies, of which 4,477 had been sold by mid-May of 1968, according to a letter to Gaines from agent Dorothea Oppenheimer, dated May 29, 1968. Gaines' picture was on the dust jacket, which also contained advance reviews by John A. Williams and Hoyt W. Fuller.

Sometime later, after the publication of *Miss Jane Pittman*, Gaines said in an undated speech that *Of Love and Dust* was "the first thing that made any kind of money—and since then I have been living on my writing. Before that I went through hell. I don't have the rejection slips, but I wish I had all the God damn pork 'n bean cans and cracker boxes and the hot dog wrappers. I'd have a whole room full of them."

In another undated speech for an unidentified Friends of the Library group, Gaines prefaced his reading from this new novel by a synopsis:

> The story takes place in 1948 on a Louisiana plantation. A young Negro, Marcus Payne, had just been bonded out of jail after killing another Negro youth in a bar fight over a woman. Marcus has been put on the plantation to work until his trial comes up. The overseer of the plantation is a Cajun by the name of Sidney Bonbon. Bonbon's job is to break Marcus. Marcus is proud, he's tough, he rebels against the system, the role a black man is supposed to play in the South. To break him, Bonbon works him like a slave from morning till night. They're pulling corn in the field now, and Bonbon has the habit of riding a horse only a step behind Marcus's back.

> Bonbon has a mistress in the quarters, a black woman by the name of Pauline. Pauline is the cook at the Big House. Marcus tries to make love to Pauline—first because he finds her extremely beautiful, and secondly because she's Bonbon's mistress. When Pauline turns him down, Marcus really wants revenge on Bonbon now, and he turns his attention towards Bonbon's little unhappy wife, Louise. What Marcus does not know is that Louise has been waiting a long time for something like this to happen. Because, she too, wants revenge on her husband for what he has done to her. She, too, wants to break away from that plantation.
>
> Other characters in the book are Jim Kelly [a black who works for Bonbon] who tells the story; Aunt Margaret who works for Bonbon and Louise; Tite, Bonbon and Louise's little daughter; Marshall Hebert, who owns the plantation; and Miss Julie Rand, Marcus's godmother, or his nan-nan, as we call them in Louisiana. Miss Julie Rand who had cooked for the Hebert family over forty years, but who now lives in Baton Rouge, got Marshall Hebert to bond Marcus out of jail. And she had asked Jim Kelly to look after Marcus while he's on the plantation, because she knows how brutal Sidney Bonbon can be, and she knows Marcus's temperament. And she knows that these two will never ever get along.

Pauline has twin boys by Bonbon. They are mischievous and healthy, unlike Louise's sickly little Tite, and in his way Bonbon loved them, though he could never tell them so. Gaines speculated that productive, strong, handsome children would have been born to Pauline and Bonbon, had they married. But Bonbon was hopelessly bound to Louise. Calling such melodrama "crap," Gaines admitted to interviewer Roger Hofheins in 1976 that he was hungry at the time he wrote the book, and he knew what would sell.[18]

[18]Dan Tooker and Roger Hofheins, *Fiction! Interviews with Northern California Novelists* (New York, 1976), p. 95.

The denouement of Marcus and Bonbon's hostility is Marcus's death. When Bonbon catches him trying to escape from the plantation with Louise a fight follows. Marcus's weapon is a piece of wood that he pulls from the fence. Bonbon comes after him with a scythe-blade and kills him. Though Louise's life is spared, her mind is ravaged. She is taken to a mental institution. From the beginning the reader realizes that Marcus and Louise's love affair is bound to result in disaster. Doom is inevitable for each of them.

* * *

Catherine Carmier and *Of Love and Dust* have been called by Noel Schrafnagel "two great works" by "probably the best black novelist of the decade." They stress the point that

> racism stems largely from sexual fears. While the white males consider the sexual exploitation of Negro women as their prerogative, the taboo against white women and black men mating is rigidly enforced—by the white men. Guilty of his own actions and fearful of the mythical sexual potency of blacks, the white males tend to place their women on a lofty pedestal. To the Negro males, then, she represents a challenge—a chance to prove their masculinity and to gain revenge on the white world.
>
> Meanwhile, the white women are curious about the sexuality of blacks and often willing to engage in amorous activities, especially if their husbands are doing the same. In this vicious sexual cycle everyone is hurt to some extent. If the Negro is discriminated against, it is the white woman who is often ignored, and who has to worry about the shame of bearing a black child if she does step over the color line. At the same time the fear of being cuckolded by a black man continually haunts the white male. This fear transcends the personal level as the white man, concerned with his possible sexual inferiority, tries to promote the problem to

> a level which encompasses the honor of the white race and the purity of white womanhood. Concomitant to this rationalization is the theory that the Negro is an animal who must keep submissive at all costs. The concept of white superiority is in the balance. . . . No novelist of the period explores sexual racism to the extent, or with the skill that Gaines does.[19]

* * *

In the speech which follows, another undated one found among Gaines' papers, Gaines explains about how he came to write *Of Love and Dust.* His construction becomes an intricate orchestration of the characters' motives, conscious or unconscious, and their manipulations in following such motives through. Gaines gives an important discussion of men's attitude toward both black and white women, and the woman's role in their lives. He began in good humor.

> If what I'm going to talk about here tonight doesn't make much sense to you, then our feeling about it is mutual. I wrote it in a bar on Divisadero Street, and I've titled it, 'Writing done under the Influence of Jim Bean' with the subtitle of 'Of Love and Dust.'
>
> I suppose every writer has been asked, sometime or other, how did he happen to write that novel or that story? . . . . I don't know when the idea of 'Of Love and Dust' came into my mind—I really don't know. But here are a couple of things which led up to my writing it. My hobby is collecting records, when I have the money. I collect jazz records, popular music, folk music—and blues—especially the rural blues by the Negro. I was listening to one of Lightnin' Hopkins records one day, titled, 'Mr. Tim Moore's Farm.' (By the way, Lightnin' Hopkins is one of the great folk and blues singers of this country—

[19]Noel Schraufnagel, ***From Apology to Protest: The Black American Novel*** (Deland, Fla., 1973), 163.

and whom I consider a great poet. Many of our young black poets, as well as the white ones, can learn from him.) I remember one of the verses going something like this: 'The worse thing this black man ever done, when I moved my wife and family to Mr. Tim Moore's farm; Mr. Tim Moore's man never stands and grin—say if you keep out the graveyard, nigger, I'll keep you out the pen.' (Lightnin' Hopkins is from Texas, and he was singing about a farm he knew in Texas.) Now a period of about ten years passed between the time I first heard that record and the time I started writing my novel 'Of Love and Dust.'

Here is another thing that happened to me about that same time, give or take a couple of years. I was visiting some relatives in Baton Rouge, Louisiana, I think about 1958, and a friend of mine and I went to a bar out in the country. This is the same Parish in Louisiana that Rap Brown comes from, this is the same Parish in Louisiana that James Farmer, in 1963, had to escape from a lynch mob by riding in the back of a hearse as a dead man.

My friend and I went to this bar, and in this bar I saw a fight between two young men. This bar is surrounded by sugar cane fields, and most of the people who come to this bar are from the country or from small towns not very far away. They come to dance, they come to drink, they come to gamble, they come to fight, they come to steal your woman—if you're a woman, to steal your man. Some of them come, knowing they'll probably end up in jail that night; they come, knowing they might get cut or even shot at. But they come. They come to forget the drudgery of working in the field all week. They come to forget that cheap mechanic job, their shoeshine job, their janitor's job, their dishwasher's job; they come to forget, to forget and to forget. And they will accept whatever fate is waiting them. If nothing terrible happens, then the night has been somewhat of a success; if something awful happens, then these things are expected in a bar such as this one. So it was here that I saw the knife fight between the two young men. Fortunately for both, the fight was stopped before either was fatally wounded.

Now, when I saw this fight, just as when I heard the record by Lightnin' Hopkins, I had no idea that either event would lead me into writing 'Of Love and Dust' or writing anything else. As I said, it was a period of eight or ten years between those events and the time I wrote one word of the book. During that time, I wrote at least four other novels—only one, '*Catherine Carmier*'—was published. I wrote at least two dozen short stories—of which six were published. Now, it was Spring, 1966. I had very little money, I had practically no money at all. I had been sponging off my friends for drinks, and I had not bought one drink for them in over a year. I had not given my poor mother a birthday present, a Christmas present, or a Mother's Day present in over two years. And neither had I given my girl anything in about that same amount of time. I needed money badly, but I didn't want to go out on an eight-hour-a-day job that would take me from my writing; I wanted to get money from my writing, my writing only. Now, if that was the case, I had to get something done. There had to be another novel in me somewhere that a publisher would accept.

I don't know how the idea from the Lightnin' Hopkins record got back into my mind. Maybe I heard it played again—I really don't know. Or maybe I remembered the incident in that bar when I went back to Louisiana for Christmas, 1965. But in early Spring of 1966 I got started working on the book. I started with these two ideas—[the Hopkins verse and the bar fight]. But where do I go from there? I started racking the brains again—where do you go? where do you go?

Then things began to fall into place. . . . I knew that Mr. Tim Moore's man . . . could be a Cajun overseer on a Louisiana plantation. I knew that my young man in the bar could have landed on that plantation if he had killed that other boy in the knife fight. So I had him kill the boy, and I had the owner of the plantation bond him out of jail. (I won't tell you why he did this, I want you to buy the book and find out.) But bonding a Negro out of jail after he's killed another Negro and putting him to work in your field was a normal thing in the forties. Some of our best Southern gentlemen did this. This sort of thing was still going on in the fifties—and as late as 1963 a friend of mine pointed out a black youth to me who had killed another black youth, and who had been bonded out only a few days later. . . . The only catch here, when the prisoner, the convict, found himself bonded out of jail, was that he usually spent almost twice as much time on the plantation than he would have spent in the penitentiary. Many times he found himself working just as hard, or maybe even harder. And there was nothing he could do about it—because the day he decided to run, the white man was going to put the sheriff on his trail again.

So, I brought my young killer to the plantation. I knew the kind of house he would have to live in—I had lived there fifteen years myself; I knew the kind of food he would eat, the kind of clothes he would wear in the field, the work he would have to do, the people he would come in contact with day in and day out. So I had a good starting point. But was that enough? Where would things go from there? What am I going to do with my young killer? He's no plantation worker, he's not even a country boy, he's from Baton Rouge. He's a playboy, he's a lover, and he hates authority—especially when this authority is given out by a Cajun—whom he considers White Trash.

So what am I going to do with these two people? I have two people on my hands who will never, can't ever get along with each other. . . . Well, let's see now, my young killer is going to be here five, seven, maybe ten years of his life. He will need a woman—yes, yes—he will need a woman—and *she* will be my third character. Now, he must start looking for that woman—but he doesn't want just *any* woman, not he, he wants the most beautiful woman on the plantation. But when he finds her, he finds that he can't have her. And why? Because she's the overseer's mistress.

'Oh, God,' my boy moans deep down inside of him. 'There's something rotten in the state of Louisiana. How can this be? What are they trying to do to me? I was born—no, not born, invented by this rotten society—the fathers of this society knowing all the time that when I grew up, I would end up in that bar among those cane fields, knowing all the time once I was there I was going to kill that other black boy, knowing once I did I would be slammed into a jail cell for a night, knowing that one or the other of them would bond me out, knowing that I would be put on one of their plantations, knowing that I'm a man of passion and will need a woman—and here, the only woman I want, the only woman that appeals to me at all, is owned by the man who dogs my trail day in and day out. What is a man of my passion to do—kill this man as I did the black boy? No, I can't kill him. To kill him will mean my own death—he is not that boy. That black boy was just another nigger—but this man is white and now all rules are different. . . . He has a wife, and what I've seen of her, she is lonely. Well, overseer, we'll both play the same game, because I know you would rather I slapped your face than look at your woman. Well, sir, I won't only look at her, but some way, somehow, I will take her, and take her with all the viciousness that *you* have forced in me.'

But what my young killer doesn't know is that this white woman wants him to take her. For she too wants revenge on that husband who sleeps with that black woman when he should be sleeping with her. She doesn't want herself a black love, now, that's not it at all—she wants trouble between her husband and the black man, and maybe her husband will be killed. But why does this particular white woman want this black man to help her destroy her husband? There are other white women of the South who know that their husbands have slept with and are sleeping with black women, and they *aren't* seeking revenge: why does this one want revenge?

When the first shipload of Africans were brought here 350 years ago, they were not looked upon as human beings but as animals to work the field. The white overseer in the Southern fields had the right to do whatever he wanted to do to the black or with the black woman. If he beat, crippled, or killed the black man, in many instances, little or nothing at all was done about it. He had as much freedom as he wanted with the black woman. She was not considered human (or if she was, at a very low level) so he used her as he willed. Rape?—No, it was not he raping her, but she raping him. Because his mind—the mind of those in power look at a situation and make that situation what they want it to be. So when the black woman gave birth to a half white child, it was said by White America that it was not the overseer who had raped the black woman, but that it was the black woman who could not resist the overseer—his charm—his straight nose, his blue eyes, his brown hair—and therefore she raped him. Raped this poor defenseless overseer while her husband stood by looking on.

In some cases the black husband helped her—and their reason was this—they wanted to lighten up their black race. Of course, now, this was the opinion of White America—never, never the opinion of blacks. *Their* opinion was quite different, but they were not in power. The power belonged to the Whites—and the Whites *had* to give this reason. Because once they admitted to themselves that the White man did find interest in the black woman, then they had to admit that the black woman was a human being and that slavery was wrong, and the sub-human position that they forced her race to be in was wrong.

So, let's say *she raped him*, they said. Let's say it and say it and say it—so much that we'll still believe it 350 years from now. For, how else could they possibly stand to see their half brothers walking pass [*sic*] the gate, hungry, half naked, and not offer them clothes or food? How else could they see their husbands' half black children and not hate their husbands?—Wouldn't they hate their husbands, even divorce their husbands, if those children were White and belonged to another *White* woman? How else could they look in the face of their half black cousins, half black nieces and nephews, every day of their lives and not feel pity? Their defense was this: it was not the black woman who was raped, it was the poor White man. Poor Papa, poor Brother, poor Uncle Clem who were raped—and it's just too bad that these little half black creatures are here as a result of the black woman's animal passion.

Now, let us say that one little White woman feels differently. Maybe she feels differently because she does not have it all up here—but still she feels differently. She knows for certain her husband not only looks at that black woman as a human being, but he looks upon the black woman as someone superior to her. Now, what does she do? She can't go out and tell the white world that she's jealous of a black woman. They would laugh her out of the community. They might even commit her to the insane asylum for suggesting such a thing could possibly happen. So what does she do? Well, according to Gaines, she runs away. But she does not get very far before the husband brings her back. She runs away again, several times, but each time the husband brings her back. Not because he loves her, mind you, and she knows this; he brings her back because he needs her in that house. He needs her there because he cannot bring that black woman to that house, because Society does not allow it. Society says no, never. . . . We *can't* let this kind of thing happen. If we let you and that black woman there live like two human beings in this country, we go'n have to let that nigger boy and your poor little old white sister live like humans, too.

So my little white woman knows why her husband keeps her there—not that he loves her, but because Society will not let him bring anyone else in. Now, since my little White woman can't get away, and since Society won't believe her if she told them that her husband has interest in the Black woman, then there's only one thing left for her to do, destroy him. Destroy this simple man who is controlled by this sick Society. And who does she seek to help her?—my young killer.

Now they come together—no love for each other at all—not even hatred. They come together to destroy that White man whom this Society has forced to hurt them. But then something unexpected happens when my two young villains meet. They find that there's something about each other which they have found in no one else. Both viciousness and revengeness [*sic*] have flown away and have been replaced by love.

But what about Society? Hasn't it warned my overseer over and over and over? Hasn't it told him what it would do to him if this did happen? My overseer says to Society, 'I could not help falling in love with her. I know you told me I was free to rape her—just as my father did her mother, my grandfather did her grandmother, my great grandfather did her great grandmother. . . . We do these things, have done these things, and shall continue to do these things because we have so much power, because we are so great. But, oh, God, how I wish that we could use our greatness some other way. How greater we would be if we were free to love anyone and everyone. . . . You have that power, Society, to control and destroy me. But you will not destroy what I've found in my heart—and that is love for her.

And because my overseer truly loved, he let the door open for the others to love, and because they loved, they were destroyed. Because we in this country are not ready for love yet. . . . But isn't it true that people who don't love at all are destroyed from the beginning? Isn't it true that nothing in this world is worth anything if there's no love with it? To me this is true. To me, Love is everything. Dust is the absence of Love.

* * *

Gaines' many references to different kinds of dust—grey, yellow, white, cloudy, dry, unsettled—frequently punctuate the story. He has said that dust is not only the absence of love but the absence of life, for man goes back to dust when he dies. A good part of *Of Love and Dust* takes place in the dust. Before Jim meets Marcus for the first time, he notices a cloud of dust; then Marcus walks away from the truck's dust which drifts slowly over the quarters. Gaines says,

> Each time Marshall Hebert, the man who owns the plantation, goes by the house in his car you will notice how much dust is flying all over the place. Because in the end it will be this man who will bring death. So this is the meaning of the story. . . . Eventually, death does separate—separates them all [the two pair of lovers]. . . . When Marcus falls dead, he falls dead in dust. . . . These people wanted to love, but because of the way the system is set up, it was impossible to love. Dust.[20]

(In *Miss Jane Pittman* dust reminds Miss Jane of the price paid by her ancestors for her own meager freedom and that of Ned. The "dust of the South" was on the river bank where Ned spoke).

* * *

Gaines always provides a *reason* for his characters' actions, especially if the actions are violent. He uses more "tricks" in writing the bedroom scene with Marcus and Louise. Aunt Margaret, the Bonbons' servant, tells what she hears without telling explicitly of the adultery that is taking place. Gaines says,

> She can't possibly tell Jim all that's going on. Jim has to interpolate what she's saying. . . . She's not giving him all the little, explicit details. Jim's watching her gestures; he's watching her face. But we take all that out. Jim is seeing beyond what she's saying, reading

[20] Rowell, "This Louisiana Thing," 43.

> between the lines. This is an old woman [who]. . . . is not going to explain these explicit sex sounds and all that kind of stuff. Jim has to read between all the things that she says and then he gives it to you.[21]

After Marcus had seduced Louise, Aunt Margaret said she could smell the "remnants of they [their] tussling."

Jim, the narrator, has been called by readers a "white mouthed nigger," but Gaines defends him as being able to fit into whatever the situation demands. His is the balance of the extremely opposite personalities of radical Marcus and conservative Aunt Margaret. They could never have understood each other, but Jim understands both of them. He acts as a sort of moral guide to the action. Jim preferred to be like Aunt Margaret, whereas Marcus could never have been. He could not mellow, so he could not live. Gaines knows that there will always be a few Marcuses, for they are needed. "We've *got* to have them," Gaines says. Jim, also, knew that there must be Marcuses, with their right to act, just as he had his right to act in his way. He could not change the system anymore than Marcus could. He was not completely like Aunt Margaret, but neither was he like Marcus. But in the end Marcus's influence, including the way that he died, motivated Jim to pack up and leave the plantation. He did realize that Marcus nobly maintained his own manhood by not running away, by staying and fighting Bonbon.

* * *

Gaines has compared the love story of Marcus and Louise to that of Romeo and Juliet.

> Marcus and Louise are in love, and with them anything is possible. . . . They feel that they can get away with it and there's nothing to harm them. Whereas the people who have lived longer cannot

[21]Wooton and Gaudet, "Talking with Ernest J. Gaines," 237.

> conceive of any other life than the one they have been living. But after the lovers have died, then—and only then—can the others see a future that permits change. There has to be this kind of tragic action before they can see things differently. This is why all the characters except Marcus and Louise feel that whatever is will continue to be.[22]

According to Gaines, Marcus has the attitude of a true rebel: that nothing will happen to him, that he believes only in himself and what *he* can do for *himself.* Gaines says that it was essential to the book that Marcus, as a pre-revolutionary, a pre-Civil Rightist, be totally ego-centric, Number One at all times.[23]

Gaines felt that *Of Love and Dust* would have made a good movie, and he was indeed approached by a screenwriter, as well as by CBS television. Negotiations were halted after Gaines learned that CBS might want to turn his book into a series, something he considered undesirable.

He purposefully picked the plantation on False River for the setting of the book, saying that he knew more about that place than about Baton Rouge, and because there were things he needed to say about his past that he had not said in *Catherine Carmier.* He said in a speech at Southern University in 1971,

> I wanted to talk about the fields a little bit more, the plantation store, the river, the church, house fairs, etc., etc., etc. And, yet, when that novel, *Of Love and Dust,* was finished, I realized that I had done only a small part of what I had intended to write. I still had not gone far enough back. Jim, my narrator, who was a man thirty-three years old, though good, kind to the old, and trying desperately to understand the young, still could not say all that I wanted him to say. Even when I brought in Aunt Margaret, someone twice his age, to help him out, they, both together, could not say it all.

[22]O'Brien, *Interviews,* p. 90.

[23]Tooker and Hofheins, *Fiction!,* p. 96.

* * *

In a critical essay found in Gaines' papers titled "Ernest J. Gaines—Change, Growth and History" the writer (unnamed) said that in Gaines' original version, Marcus and Louise actually escape the plantation, "and like two errant and fun-loving children go off to the city on a spree, thumbing their noses at the code." The publisher asked for another conclusion, and in supplying it Gaines did no harm to the novel's integrity,

> but the great difference between conclusions is instructive. Gaines' first inclination was not toward making Marcus a martyred revolutionary. It was toward creating a joyful and ironic triumph over a stifling system, which would have harmonized perfectly well with Marcus as a swaggerer and a dandy.

The first version has a "general tone of comic irony and it shows inertia being overcome by new and more vital forces, though not without pain and some sense of loss," the writer said.

Winifred L. Stoelting, in her essay "Human Dignity and Pride in the Novels of Ernest Gaines," cites specific examples of these attributes. Marcus maintains fierce pride in his own manhood, no matter how much Jim tries to persuade him that conformity is desirable, saying that any other behavior is unfeasable. He maintains his inner pride by wearing dress clothes for field work, though he suffers a great deal physically. He has already lost so much pride while being in prison, he is determined not to bow again. Working against unchangeable regulations, Marcus is determined to pull his load, but to also get revenge for his hurt pride after Pauline spurns him. But his own realization that he loves Louise, after all, helps him regain inner stature—his revenge turns to compassion.

Jim loses some of his dignity when asked by Bonbon to help him cover up his affair with Pauline, when he drives them to a bar for a few hours of intimacy. He feels he is playing the pimp. But Jim, like Aunt Margaret, finds dignity in deciding to survive in an ongoing confusion.

Bonbon takes on dignity in his devotion to Pauline, thus ostracizing himself from society. Pauline's acceptance of her own situation portrays dignity, according to Stoelting. Louise takes pride in re-establishing herself as a woman in her affair with Marcus, after Bonbon rejects her for Pauline.[24]

Jack Hicks in an essay for *Black American Literature Forum*, Spring, 1977, traces the part of history, sensed as a natural cycle, in Gaines' first four books. He suggests that Jim's responsibility for his own actions reflects existentialism. Even so, the other people are manipulative—everyone is another's tool to be used for personal desires. Other elements are cycles (Marcus is continually defeated, only to rise again fighting) or rituals (such as Jim talking several times with Aunt Margaret). Through Marcus, Jim see his own "face" more clearly: "that of a black individual whose features have been forgotten for a time, but can be reimagined in shaping a life with human dignity."[25]

John Wideman, in his essay "*Of Love and Dust:* A Reconsideration," compares Gaines to Faulkner, saying that *Of Love and Dust* succeeds as a "flirtation with melodrama," almost like a parody of the Southern novel. Jim as the narrator is "both an individual and a chorus. . . . He has the privilege of near omniscience, of the wisdom, experience and critical acuity of the entire community." His credibility as narrator is not important; he is a convention through which the reader enjoys the story. If there were several narrators the thoughts of the characters could not be conveyed so intimately. Repetitions are important in conveying the cyclical nature of farm life; mosquitoes, crops, stories told over and over, sitting on the gallery as witnesses to the same events, someone's comings and goings, and the like.

"Repetition," Wideman says, "establishes rhythms, the rhythms of the characters' speech, their movements, their sense of place, proportion and themselves." This repetition establishes a tableau of unifying episodes and commentary.

[24]Stoelting, "Human Dignity," 340-358.

[25]Hicks, "To Make These Bones Live," 13.

Setting the stage for Marcus and Louise is done by the repeated moving of furniture. Louise in her white dress is symbolic of innocence, an innocence later destroyed by things she cannot control. Each part of the tableau has some significance. "The repetitions fix the scene, reduce it to its basic constituents, and each repetition is a luminous projection of the meaning Gaines intends."

When the material digresses from the theme, it is all part of Gaines' plan to strengthen the theme, like the fitting together of a mosaic or montage. Jim Kelley is the orchestrator and he performs a dual role, a situation that Wideman feels is not altogether good. He is both a

> down-home speaker of Southern rural blackspeech . . . and a narrator whose syntax, grammar and vocabulary are usually standard English. . . . The loss of consistency and credibility and the opportunity for a *tour de force* display of blackspeech have to be weighed against the flexibility gained by Jim's inconsistent speech.[26]

Jim's solid and traditional ideas make him a 'carrier,' a preserver of the culture.

* * *

Gaines' descriptive passages in *Of Love and Dust* are priceless. The following quotes are taken from the 1979 Norton paperback. Of Miss Julie's house in Baton Rouge he says:

> I followed her into a small, ill-smelling room that had too much furniture. All old people who move from the country to the city live in rooms like these. They try to bring everything they had in the country and cram it into a little room that can't hold half of what they own. Miss Julie had an old sofa chair against the wall and

[26]John Wideman, "*Of Love and Dust:* A Reconsideration," *Callaloo #3,* (May 1978), 78, 79, 82.

> another little rocker by the bed. There was an old trunk by the window with a pile of quilts and blankets stacked on top of it. Against the other wall was an old armoire leaning to one side. There must have been a half dozen paste-board boxes stacked on top of the armoire. In the corner by the armoire were several paper bags packed full of clothes. The mantelpiece was cluttered with all kinds of nick-nacks, and there was an old coal oil lamp there, too, just in case the electric lights went out. No matter what wall you faced, you saw pictures of Jesus Christ. . . . Above the mantelpiece, stuck inside an old black wooden frame, was a picture of a man and a woman. The man was sitting; the woman was standing beside him. I figured that this was Miss Julie and her husband when she was much, much younger. . . . But the thing that hit me most about the room was the odor in there. It was the odor of old people, old clothes, old liniment bottles.[27]

Two descriptions of Miss Julie herself: "She was a very small old lady. . . . Her head was tied in an old pink rag, and her gray dress nearly touched the floor. The old brown slippers on her feet look pretty near old as she did." And: "She wore a purple dress. . . . It had a little bit of that odor. . . . The dress was long and pleated and came all the way to her shoes . . . old high-topped shoes with wooden heels . . . . they had buckles. Her skin had the color of a ripe prune. It was just as wrinkled as a ripe prune."[28]

Jim's observations and feelings about Marcus: "I wanted to feel sorry for Marcus, but God knows he didn't help you." After Marcus's first day of work Jim said, "When I came home I saw Marcus laying on the gallery. He looked like somebody had beat him with an eight-plait whip and left him there to die."[29]

[27]Ernest J. Gaines, *Of Love and Dust* (1967, reprint ed., New York 1978), pp. 9-10.

[28]*Ibid.*, pp. 10, 111, 112.

[29]*Ibid.*, pp. 31, 43.

> He had told me what a great lover he was. . . . He had told me how once he got after a woman she couldn't do a thing but fall for him. Marcus was a pretty handsome fellow and he knew it. He was about six feet tall, slim, but well-built; he had medium brown skin and a pile of curly black hair. He had light brown eyes, a kind of straight nose, thin lips, and a well-shaped mustache.[30]

And speaking of Marcus' going after Pauline, "How could a white man—no, not even a solid white man, but a bayou, catfish-eating Cajun—compete with him when it came down to loving."[31] After Marcus has explained his miserable life to Jim: "I looked at Marcus, and I felt empty inside. I felt empty because he could not believe in God or friendship: I felt empty because I doubted if I believed in anything, either."[32]

And more description: "Aunt Margaret was short and fat. Her face was round and black and oily. Her short nappy hair (you could even see her skull) was just starting to turn gray."[33]

> Bonbon was about six-four or -five, and I must say he was an impressive-looking man. He was handsome—I think very handsome—but nothing pretty or cute. Marcus, I think was pretty. Young gals would say that Marcus was 'dreamy.' Nobody would say Bonbon was dreamy, like nobody would say he was ugly. He was handsome in a rough way. He had a good build—maybe two hundred, two hundred and ten pounds. He had light gray eyes, a long, good-shaped nose, and a dry-shuck-color mustache. His mustache was lighter than his tan face and much lighter than his red neck.[34]

[30]*Ibid.*, p. 56-57.

[31]*Ibid.*, p. 57.

[32]*Ibid.*, p. 253.

[33]*Ibid.*, p. 137.

[34]*Ibid.*, p. 79.

> Louise was about twenty-five, but she was the size of the average twelve- or thirteen-year-old girl. Most of the time she wore the clothes of a thirteen-year-old girl—she wore skirts and blouses instead of dresses. She wore sandals instead of shoes. She never wore socks or stockings unless it was winter. Her hair was yellow (the same color with that hay in August) and her face was more cream-color than it was white. Her sad gray eyes were the only thing about her that made you feel Louise wasn't a child. They had seen too much sorrow, they had seen it much too long.[35]

* * *

Reviews of *Of Love and Dust* were not necessarily all favorable. Some were downright jaded. A few of them compared Gaines' novel to others published at the time. The comments of two advance reviewers were printed, in part, on the book's jacket. Author John A. Williams said: "This is a fascinating story, all the more so because it is set in the present. . . . I congratulate and envy Mr. Gaines." Hoyt Fuller's kudo was: "Ernest J. Gaines can write rings around dozens of American novelists with far more glittering reputations. . . . All the characters are vibrantly alive; they have been clearly and truly seen."

The *Library Journal*, January 15, 1968, said:

> This is a novel of many assets; it is simple, direct, uncomplicated, and in some instances, framed in believable terms. It is not, however, a successful novel. The most serious failure is the rigid, one-dimensional characters who never quite become real human beings. The most appealing character is the principal narrator, Jim Kelly, a Negro straw boss on a southern plantation. Set in the early 1940s, the thrust of the story centers on the inevitable, tragic destiny of the young Marcus, accused

[35] *Ibid.*, p. 119.

> Negro murderer, whose one simple ambition is to be free. The tragic impact of the story never quite achieves pathos, but instead is reduced to remote awfulness through unconvincing characters acting out predictable emotional conflicts. Mr. Gaines is a prominent young Negro author whose first novel, *Catherine Carmier*, was received with wide acclaim. He is clearly capable of fine writing and it is hoped that his third novel may repeat the quality of his first effort.

In the February 5, 1968, issue *The Nation*'s critic called it

> a serious, powerful novel. . . . Kelly's transition from cynical don't rock the boatism to something else takes place over a series of exciting and beautifully realized scenes, some of them funny. . . . [Mr. Gaines] is a writer of terrific energy; his characters have a dimension and authenticity that make us know and care about them. It takes a lot of nerve to write a novel like this today, and a lot of skill to bring it off. Mr. Gaines has plenty of both.

The *New York Times Book Review*, November 19, 1967, said:

> Aside from occasional technical awkwardness, the writing is clean, and Mr. Gaines paints some vivid scenes and fine portraits. The plantation . . . is convincing—the author was born on one himself and spent his childhood working in the fields. His 'presence' in the book remains modest, earnest and affirmative.
>
> Yet, despite these qualities, Mr. Gaines's second work is still an 'undergraduate' work, in which the author trusts craft formula too much, himself too little.

From *Saturday Review*, January 20, 1968, came these comments:

> The plot is mustily reminiscent of innumerable novels of the down-on-the-old-plantation variety, and the narrative style consists chiefly of stepping out, stumbling, halting, and retracting. Except for occasional flashes, the characters are either stereotypes . . . or are . . . unconvincing.
>
> Despite these weaknesses of technique Gaines . . . has succeeded where many others of his race and generation have failed; he has written a book about Negroes and whites as just plain people, sharing equally the blame for maintaining a worn-out tradition.

Kenneth Atchity of the *New Haven Register*, January 21, 1968, chose to compare it with William Styron's *The Confessions of Nat Turner*, also published in 1967. Atchity said: "Gaines is not so nearly a propagandist. . . . Gaines' is a more subtle brand, depending for its impact on straightforward presentation rather than rhetorical argument." His story is told well enough to draw us to his intended conclusion.

> With his natural, easy way of narrating precisely details and events, he shows that even the smallest human actions are important always—because they are human. . . . I find it [*Of Love and Dust*] more probable, both for its restraint and for its truer reflection of the nature of progress. It is the assurance that a common humanity is verified only man to man; that the Negro must be recognized as an individual—first to himself. As an author, Gaines is a promise fulfilled. *Of Love and Dust* suggests that personal action alone—and no amount of mass legislation—will make the Negro his own man. Real horses are the surest bet; losers bank on the wishes beggars ride.

Gaines' Stanford friend, writer Wendell Berry, expressed his approval of *Of Love and Dust* in a letter to Gaines, dated May 28, 1968:

> Dear Ernie, I've just read your book, Of Love and Dust, and want to tell you how much I like it. I admire everything about it: the attentiveness to the individuality of nearly every person in it, its clarity and quietness and strength, its great swiftness of movement. You give a fine full sense of the life and the people of the quarter, the dignity and wisdom of some of them, the work in the fields, the sadness and tragedy in racism. I think I'll remember it, and will want to read it again. . . . Tanya likes the book as well as I do, and she sends her regards.

Walter van Tilburg Clark gave Gaines another kudo in a letter to William Decker, senior editor at Dial in 1968. A copy of the letter, sent from Reno, but undated, was found in Gaines' papers.

> Dear Mr. Decker, Thanks for *Love and Dust*. If it lacks the memorable deep gentleness of *Catherine Carmier*, and though it does, it nonetheless took me straight through in one reading. An intense, slowly mounting drama of love, lust, pride, and racial and personal hostility, with no sense of the contrived about it. The inevitability of true tragedy.

After the Secker and Warburg publication of *Of Love and Dust* in London in 1968, the *New York Times Literary Supplement* provided this review: "The violence, perversity and end of the set-up are, of course, implicit in detail from the start. But the tale is so cunningly nurtured and the tenacious, diseased social network so richly dimensioned that even a much-tried story-line feels genuinely original."

BLOODLINE

Bloodline was published as a collection, containing five stories, by Dial Press in August of 1968, by Bantam Books in 1970, and in 1976 by W. W. Norton. The book's dedication to Gaines' agent Dorothea Oppenheimer reads, "To Dee with my deepest love."

Bloodline was part of a two-book contract with *Of Love and Dust* offered to Gaines by Dial Press, on the condition that the novel came first. The setting of the five stories is in the 1930s and 40s in rural southern Louisiana. Gaines and others have called *Bloodline* an "episodic novel," explaining that the "word" of each story begins on the plantation, goes to the town, and finally to the universal condition. "It's like planting a seed of grain that grows and spreads out a little more each time," Gaines said.[36]

William Decker, senior editor of Dial Press, wrote Gaines on April 1, 1968, regarding *Bloodline*. In part it reads:

> Dear Ernie:
>
> The people around the office who have read BLOODLINE like it a lot and that is an encouraging sign. You already know that Anne [Mrs. Decker] and I think it is just great. Now all we have to do is convince the rest of the world.
>
> All the best,
> Bill

Found in Gaines' papers also was a letter from mutual friend Walter van Tilburg Clark to William Decker, who had obviously sent Clark a copy of *Bloodline*. Dated April 22, 1968, the letter read in part:

> Thanks for Ernie Gaines' *Bloodline*. I read it straight through, a thing I seldom do with a collection of short stories, and I was strongly interested and deeply moved all the way. It has the same clarity, simplicity and vivid reality that marked his two memorable novels, *Catherine Carmier* and *Of Love and Dust*, and presents the plight of the southern rural negro through an

[36]*San Jose Mercury*, September 1, 1968.

> even greater range of people. And they are people, not symbols or propagandic caricatures.
>
> Not sure how long I can be quoted for Ernie Gaines without appearing to be in collusion, but I'll leave that to you, and of course you're free to use anything you wish from this note.

Decker sent bound galleys of *Bloodline* to writer John A. Williams, possibly for early review, as he had done for *Of Love and Dust*. Williams' letter acknowledging them reads:

> I like the stories very much. They represent to me a kind of black Populism which I find very important at a time when other writers are basing their stories in the cities, as though the farm scene was a thousand years ago. And in the plantation setting Gaines deals with humans as well as issues; sometimes we forget that from humans spring the issues. In fact, I believe I like the stories better than the last novel.
>
> While I know it is the practice to seek quotes for forthcoming books, it would be my feeling that Gaines perhaps would not like to have one from me this time around, and I can understand. Authors like to feel that their books are selling on their own merits. Between you and me, however, I've heard that Gaines is quite immodest about his work, and after this set of stories, he may well have reason to feel this way.

Preceding his review of *Bloodline* Donald Stanley of the *San Francisco Examiner* wrote to Gaines. His letter, dated August 12, 1968 reads:

> Dear Ernie:
>
> What a book! You really did it this time. It reads just like a novel and I hope people think of it that way—given the normal distribution of short story collections. The development is so certain. It comes right up to a climax in "Bloodline," you see the parting of the ways in

that story, and then that beautiful coda in "Just Like a Tree".

I did think "Long Day" was a hair long. Wasn't it longer than the Texas version? But "The Sky is Gray" is an absolute classic, best short story I've read since "Red-Dirt Marijuana"—not to make any comparisons.

Hell, they're all good and I wish I had had space to say more of the things you evoked for me. The review runs Thursday. I hope the New York crowd does something for it this time. I tried to interest Dave Scherman at *Life* a month ago, but he said the same old thing: Short stories? Nyet. That was before I had read them. Maybe my enthusiasm would have been more contagious. If there's anything I can do, let me know.

Regards,
Don

(Stanley's review is included toward the end of this section).

* * *

A letter to Gaines from Cyril Clemens, dated September 26, 1968, found in Gaines' papers, notified him that he had been unanimously elected as a "Knight of Mark Twain" by the International Mark Twain Society, "in recognition of your outstanding contribution to American fiction by your *Bloodline*." At this time Clemens was editor of the semi-annual *Mark Twain Journal*, which was established in 1936 and is still available. Its articles, in English, are largely about Mark Twain.

Gaines' reply, if any, on being elected as a "knight," was not found in the Mark Twain Society Archives. Information regarding the election of Gaines and other "knights" is quaint. Apparently Cyril Clemens "unanimously elected" the knights himself, copying names and addresses from *Who's Who* and sending out notes to those persons. This honor has not generally been considered prestigious. The eighty-seven-year-old

Clemens, though still active, no longer chooses to elect knights unanimously.[37]

* * *

"A Long Day in November"

"A Long Day in November" is the first and longest of the five *Bloodline* stories. It was published separately in *The Texas Quarterly*, Summer, 1964; in an anthology edited by Langston Hughes, *The Best Short Stories by Negro Writers: An Anthology from 1899 to the Present* (1967); and in 1971 as a children's book by Dial Press, illustrated by Don Bolognese.

Again, Gaines uses his favorite technique, that of telling a story in first person. The events are related by six-year-old Sonny in "A Long Day in November" and cover only part of one night and the next day. Gaines explains his own structure by comparing the confines of Greek tragedy to those on the plantation, as they limited every facet of life, including personal happiness. He feels that with such a background of confinement he is better able to write within any given time frame, whether it be a day, or longer. Gaines himself does not need to prolong a situation unnecessarily, but rather to tie up loose ends, as he did in "A Long Day in November."[38]

* * *

Late one night Sonny, in bed, overhears his parents squabbling. Mama has had enough of Daddy's addiction to his car and his habit of "rip and run up and down the road with his other nigger friends." She tells him she is taking Sonny with her to her mother's house. On this particular night Daddy comes in very late again and pleads with her to stay, but as soon as he is at work in the cane fields next day, she leaves for Gran'mon's.

[37]Letter to Anne Simpson from Dr. Thomas A Tenney, present editor of the *Mark Twain Journal*, February 9, 1990.

[38]Tooker and Hofheins, *Fiction!*, pp. 97-98.

Living at Gran'mon's is Sonny's uncle, who offers him more kindness and attention than the women do. A former beau who still has a yen for Mama complicates things by visiting at Gran'mon's. Gran'mon has no use for Daddy, and overtly tries to promote Mama's renewal with the old beau, Freddie Jackson.

Daddy comes to Gran'mon's after work for Mama and Sonny. Mama refuses to go with him but he persuades the confused Sonny to come outside with him. First they go for a talk with the minister, who makes a house visit to Mama in Daddy's behalf, but Mama still refuses to go back home with Daddy. Next Sonny is taken along when Daddy consults the highly recommended Madame Toussaint, a Voodoo fortune teller. Because he cannot meet her full fee of three dollars, she gives him only partial advice for his seventy-five cents, which is "Give it up." Not certain what she means, he borrows the rest of the money from a cane worker, to receive the rest of her wisdom, which is "Go set fire to your car." Unwillingly he burns the car with the whole neighborhood watching, thinking now that Mama will return. Mama and Gran'mon view his act with disbelief, and Mama is convinced that he really loves her more than his car. Symbolically, he may be demonstrating his readiness for intimacy by burning his car.

They return home and she persuades him against his will to beat her with a switch which she has fetched herself. In doing this Daddy will prove himself a real man, a conqueror who means business. Otherwise, he would remain the laughing stock of the community if his peers found out that he had only burned the car and not laid a hand on his wife.

As narrator of "A Long Day in November" Sonny's views of the family enigma, and his own miserable situation as a shy misfit at school who has not done his homework, make both a humorous and a pathetic story. The father-son relationship, or the lack thereof, is evident in this story. Daddy, having been somewhat immature and negligent in his role as father, needs an ally when the chips are down. Sonny, the only real pal he has, becomes that ally. He really loves Daddy, and does not like the way Gran'mon talks about him.

When Sonny returns to school, after the family reunites, he is more secure. He has done his homework, confident that he will not wet his pants again. Sonny is happiest and most secure when he is in a warm bed under the covers. His dread of the cold, a symptom of insecurity and loneliness, is almost heartbreaking. Gaines' use of repeated short phrases within the dialogue is frequent.

One interviewer said to Gaines: "I saw the child's returning to bed at the end of 'A Long Day in November' as a refusal to change, as an acceptance of defeat."

Gaines replied,

> I don't think it is the most significant thing about the story. The most important thing is his waking up in the morning and going outside because . . . he didn't want to get up. He had a hard time getting up. When he finally goes back to bed that night he feels quite good. He feels good being under the covers and he feels good that his mother and father are back together again. And he feels that tomorrow will be a better day for him.[39]

* * *

The following quotes are from "A Long Day in November" in the Norton edition of *Bloodline*. Sonny, thinking of his pig, Paul, said: "I bet you little old Paul is some cold out there in that back yard. I hope he ain't laying in that water like he always do. I bet you he'll freeze in that water in all this cold. I'm sure glad I ain't a pig. They ain't got no mama and no daddy and no house."[40]

Sonny's account of Gran'mon berating Daddy to Mama (Amy): "I told you," Gran'mon says. "I told you when that nigger got that car that was go'n happen. I told you. No—you wouldn't listen. I told you. Put a fool in a car and he becomes a bigger fool. Where that yellow thing at now? . . . I warned you 'bout that nigger. . . . I sung at you and sung at you. I said,

[39]O'Brien, *Interviews,* 91-92.

[40]Ernest J. Gaines, *Bloodline* (1968, reprint ed., New York, 1976), p. 9.

'Amy, that nigger ain't no good. A yellow nigger with a gap like that 'tween his front teeth ain't no good.' But you wouldn't listen."[41]

In school, Sonny, called Eddie by the teacher, is uneasy, unprepared for the day's lesson.

> Juanita's some pretty. I hope I was big so I could love her. But I better look at my lesson and don't think about other things. . . . I don't know my lesson. I don't know my lesson. I don't know my lesson. I feel warm. I'm wet. I hear the wee-wee dripping on the floor. I'm crying. I'm crying because I wee-wee on myself. My clothes's wet. Lucy and them go'n laugh at me. Billy Joe Martin and them go'n tease me. I don't know my lesson. I don't know my lesson. I don't know my lesson. . . . 'It's running under that bench there now,' Billy Joe Martin says. 'Look out for your feet back there, it's moving fast.' 'Juanita,' Miss Hebert says, 'get a mop, will you please?'[42]

Gran'mon takes a dim view of Daddy coming to her house, and says: "You just take one more step toward this door, and I bet you somebody'll be crying at your funeral. If you know anybody who care that much for you, you old yellow dog."[43] Gran'mon later took a shot at Daddy. Sonny thinks about it at meal time. He says:

> We having spaghetti for dinner. I pick up a string of spaghetti and suck it up in my mouth. I make it go loo-loo-loo-loo-loo-loo-loop. Uncle Al looks at me and laugh. I do it again, and Uncle Al laughs again. 'Don't play with my food,' Gran'mon says. 'Eat it right.' Gran'mon is standing 'side the stove looking at me. I

[41]*Ibid.*, p. 18.

[42]*Ibid.*, pp. 23, 24, 25.

[43]*Ibid.*, pp. 33-34.

> don't like old Gran'mon. Shooting at my daddy—I don't like her.[44]

Sonny uses the outside privy at night:

> I go round the house and go back to the toilet. The grass is dry like hay. There ain't no leaves on the trees. I see some birds in the tree. The wind's moving the birds feathers. I bet you them little birds's is some cold. I'm glad I'm not a bird. No daddy, no mama—I'm glad I'm not a bird. I open the door and go in the toilet. I get up on the seat and pull down my pants. I squat over the hole—but I better not slip and fall in there. I'll get all that poo-poo on my feet, and Gran'mon'll kill me if I tramp all that poo-poo in her house. I try hard and my poo-poo come. It's long. I like to poo-poo. Sometimes I poo-poo on my pot at night. Mama don't like for me to go back to the toilet when it's late. Scared a snake might bite me. I finish poo-poo-ing and I jump down from the seat and pull up my pants. I look in the hole and I see my poo-poo. I look in the top of the toilet, but I don't see any spiders. We got spiders in us toilet. Gran'mon must be done killed all her spiders with some Flit.[45]

About the minister, Sonny says: "Reverend Simmons is big and he can walk fast. He takes big old long steps and me and Daddy got to walk fast to keep up with him."[46]

Madame Toussaint is a bit more macabre:

> Madame Toussaint's a little bitty little old woman and her face is brown like cowhide. . . . Madame Toussaint's house don't smell good. It's too dark in here. It don't smell good at all. Madame Toussaint ought to have a window or something open in her house.

[44] *Ibid.*, p. 37.

[45] *Ibid.*, p. 38.

[46] *Ibid.*, p. 42.

> . . . Madame Toussaint ain't got but three old rotten teeth in her mouth. I bet you she can't peel no cane with them old rotten teeth. I bet you they'd break off in a hard piece of cane.[47]

Madame Toussaint gives Daddy some advice as reported by Sonny:

> Women like to be in their own house. That's their world. You men done messed up the outside world so bad that they feel lost and out of place in it. Her house is her world. Only there she can do what she want. She can't do that in anybody else house—mama or nobody else. But you men don't know any of this. Y'all never know how a woman feels, because you never ask how she feels. Long's she there when you get there you satisfied. Long's you give her two or three dollars every weekend you think she ought to be satisfied.[48]

In the very last paragraph of the story, Sonny presents his views of the day's events after his family is back home and in bed.

> I hear the spring. I hear Mama and Daddy talking love, but I don't know what they saying. I go to sleep some, but I open my eyes again. It's some dark in the room. I hear Mama and Daddy talking low. I like Mama and Daddy. I like uncle Al, but I don't like old Gran'mon too much. Gran'mon's always talking bad about Daddy. I don't like old Mr. Freddie Jackson, either. Mama say she didn't do her and Daddy's thing with Mr. Freddie Jackson. . . . I know my lesson. I ain't go'n wee-wee on myself no more. Daddy's going to school with me tomorrow. I'm go'n show him I can beat Billy Joe Martin shooting marbles. . . . Madame

[47]*Ibid.*, pp. 46-47.

[48]*Ibid.*, p. 61.

> Toussaint's old house don't smell good. Us house smell good. I hear the spring on Mama and Daddy's bed. I get 'way under the cover. I go to sleep little bit, but I wake up. I go to sleep some more. I hear the spring on Mama and Daddy's bed. I hear it plenty now. It's some dark under here. It's warm. I feel good 'way under here.[49]

* * *

William Peden in "The Black Explosion" calls "A Long Day in November" a "masterly novella." To him the most powerful scenes are when Daddy destroys his car and when Mama insists that he whip her. In any other writer's hands this might have been "either ludicrous or melodramatic." In the piece Gaines has avoided both the "Scylla [incomprehensiveness] and Charybdis [inaccuracy] of didacticism and heavy symbolism." It is a "memorable picture of family relationships."[50]

Essayist Barbara Puschmann-Nalenz, in "Ernest J. Gaines, A Long Day in November," calls Sonny's limited viewpoint a "specific narrative method" of Gaines'. The boy remains passive and is never in control of happenings. He is too young to understand all the intricacies of his family's troubles, certainly not his Daddy's tears. His problems are largely due to the squabbles of the parents which cause him to move without assurance. He is rather a peripheral figure to the drama between the parents and shows little emotion except negative feeling toward his Gran'mon.

His mind acts as a receptive and sensitive filter. Gaines' "consistent application of the child's perspective results in a paradoxically mixed effect of immediacy on one hand and detachment on the other," the writer says. What the boy sees and hears without fully understanding is handled ingenuously by Gaines. His intuition either makes him assume that things are

[49]*Ibid.*, pp. 78-79.

[50]William Peden, "The Black Explosion," *Studies in Short Fiction*, XII (1975), 238-239.

all right or not all right. His physical and emotional feelings are definitely connected. The adults do not give him credit for knowing what is happening, but neither do they care, for they are too taken up with their own woes.

Sonny becomes a "mirror reflecting his father's image," especially as the story unfolds and Sonny is alone with his father. The father begins to give him more attention, as a sort of ally, a second self. Sonny, after all is a *male* child. The father's behavior is almost childish, whining, self-pitying. He is incapable of dealing with the situation by himself and relies on the voodoo woman for answers. As immature as the father is, however, Gaines never ridicules him; rather he forces him to achieve pride and dignity. Gaines is able to present the average black person "from within," displaying a "microcosm of private life and personal relationships."[51]

In "*Bloodline*: A Man's Black South" William Burke sees Daddy as a stereotype of the black male. Gaines ameliorates his situation by allowing his wife to be less shrewish than Madame Toussaint or Gran'mon. She allows him to salvage his masculinity.[52]

The theme of confirming manhood is dominant in the first four *Bloodline* stories. Inevitably the black man in the United States is not supposed to be a man. His manhood has been suppressed by the white man. Gaines' black man strives to be a man toward family, woman, and friends. Essayist Frank W. Shelton says that Gaines' often ambiguous picture of black manhood implies its achievement not only as an obsession, but as a dangerous loss of something more humanly important.

"A Long Day in November," Shelton continues, is distinguished from the other stories by the fact that the boy has a father to whom he can relate. Madame Toussaint's lecture to Daddy is a definite downer, except to alert him to the fact that he has neglected his wife. Possibly the black man cannot find

[51]Barbara Puschmann-Nalenz, "Ernest J. Gaines: *A Long Day in November*," in Peter Bruck, ed., *The Black American Short Story in the Twentieth Century: A Collection of Critical Essays* (Amsterdam, 1977), pp. 161-163.

[52]William Burke, "Bloodline: A Man's Black South," *CLA Journal*, XIX (June, 1976), 548.

meaning for his personal life, in terms of manhood, within the home and family, an attitude exemplified in Daddy's obsession with his old car. But when Mama forces him to beat her, he supposedly will regain the community's respect, though he does not feel that his Manhood as such depends on this.[53]

* * *

The children's book, *A Long Day in November*, was dedicated "to all those children who have had One Long Day in their lives." It was supposedly intended for readers in the third grade and upwards. Of this children's version Gaines said in 1978 to an interviewer who asked about its success: "No, it was not very successful. They really didn't push that book at all. The girl who edited the book really wanted a children's book from me, but I don't think the Dial Press really cared about pushing it." The book did win a prize for its illustrations, which Gaines called "very good."[54]

Reviews after its publication in 1971 were varied. There were some changes in language from the story included with the *Bloodline* collection, though in length and essence it was not in any way "watered down." Generally no offense to the language or the story was taken by the critics. One particularly frank non-commendation, however, was found in Gaines' papers. Dated December, 1972, and signed "D. S.", it came from the Richardson, Texas, Independent School District:

> I am *not* recommending this book for elementary school libraries for many reasons, although the book is depicting a time, place and a people. The story undoubtedly took place and the author says that this is a story of his childhood.
>
> It is the story of a Negro family in the late 1930s or mid-1940s who worked on a cane plantation in the South.

[53]Frank W. Shelton, "Ambiguous Manhood in Ernest J. Gaines," *CLA Journal*, XIX (1975), 201, 202.

[54]"An Interview with Ernest J. Gaines," 42.

> Poverty is evident as well as futility on the part of the adults. However, through this, there is a strong faith and love of the family. . . .
>
> There are many implications in this book—morals are questionable. When the daughter returns to her mother's home, the mother has conveniently brought back a girlhood sweetheart whom she wants the daughter to go live with immediately. Implied in the story is the mother's hatred for the son-in-law who is evidently of mixed breed.
>
> I also question the lady who is supposedly knowledgeable in the ways of voodoo. She cheated the man of 75 cents and told him to burn his car if he wanted to win back his wife. I realize that in doing this he was to prove his love for his wife. He did burn his car . . . but I felt that the book would have been better for children had this element been omitted.
>
> I also question the vocabulary. It is an carthy vocabulary, probably a very common one among children of this time and place, but not one which will upgrade the feeling of people toward the Negro race at this time.
>
> This is a story which should be told. . . . But for children, I feel it should be told with more discretion and an upgrading of the people.

These sentiments were definitely in the minority of total reviews of *A Long Day in November* as a children's book. Most others, ranging from one short paragraph to several, found it highly suitable for young readers. A few of the non-critical reviews, such as those found in *Book Gleanings, Best Books of 1971* in *Library Journal*, and *St. Louis Post-Dispatch*, gave only the story without comments.

The *New York Times Book Review*, February 13, 1972, called it a

> wonderfully funny, . . . very satisfying book. Ernest Gaines includes those small, human details that so many authors neglect. The passions and humor in this

> story may climb to epic proportions, but the people stay little and for real. Don Bolognese's illustrations are fine and flavorful. . . . Ernest Gaines, maybe because he is black, can see people moving under their skins. . . . It [the book] treats of a vanished world, the author tells us, an insular, superstitious world of back-breaking work and near poverty. . . . That humor can rise out of such a setting makes it all the richer and more powerful.

The Hartford Star, February 5, 1972, called it a "warm and tender love story for children." The *Bulletin of the Center for Children's Books*, February, 1972, commented: "The book is written with flair and sensitivity, but it seems more an adult short novel than a children's story." *Children's Book World*, November 7, 1971, and the Washington, D. C., *Post-Times-Herald Book World* of the same date carried identical reviews. Included in them are compliments on Don Bolognese's illustrations, and high praise for Gaines' perfectly suited language. Enjoyable to both adults and children, though on different levels, the piece is highly logical, believable, tender, an portrays the gamut of emotions, ending in reconciliation and forgiveness.

Time, December 27, 1971, called Gaines "one of the best writers in America, of any color or persuasion. . . . Painful, hilarious and humane, it [Long Day] is so good a story that the illustrations, which are not bad, seem like a desecration." *The School Library Journal*, December, 1971, said: "The dialogue is sharp and believable and the Louisiana sugar cane plantation background is perfectly realized." From the *Virginia Kirkus Service*, December 15, 1971: "An affectionate and genuinely funny novel. . . . If the concerns are still essentially adult ones, it's warming and refreshing fun for whoever does tune in." The *NJEA Review* for September, 1972 considered it "best used with the youngster needing high-interest, low-reading level books, because of the mature subject and third-grade reading level."

A lengthier, more thoughtful review was carried by *The Horn Book*, April, 1972, which read in part:

A Long Day in November calls for a reader sufficiently sophisticated to appreciate the subtle nuances of characterization, the skilled uses of contrast, and the superbly realized setting of the rural, black Southland. Indeed, rather than a story about a child, it is about adult relationships and emotions as chronicled by a child observer who is sensitive to, and yet confused by, events which are beyond his level of experience. Thus, his reactions to the quarrel between his parents are of the most elemental nature—an ego-centered response, where his own bodily functions and needs are documented with as much attention as his mother's decision to leave his father. Consequently, what makes the book succeed from the adult's point of view may tend to limit its appeal for children: first, because the child narrator, a first-grader, is too young to interest the average adolescent; second, because he is acted upon rather than being the prime mover; third, because he senses the problems but plays no real part in their solution. Listing these points for consideration is not intended to discourage, but rather to encourage those working with young people to find the right audience for a well-wrought story which is very real and touchingly human.

* * *

"The Sky is Gray"

Second in the *Bloodline* collection is "The Sky is Gray", first published in *Negro Digest* in August, 1963, having suffered several rejections, according to an unnamed, undated news item in Gaines files. The editor of *Black World*, February, 1971, said that after its publication "a kind of literary lightning struck." It has been acknowledged as the most widely anthologized short story by a black American. By the time *Bloodline* was published, "The Sky is Gray" had come out in over two dozen anthologies. In 1980 it was televised.

The poignant story, set in the 1940s in rural South Louisiana, is told by James, an eight-year-old boy whose father has been drafted into military service. James lives with his mother, younger brothers Ty, Louis, Val, and Walker, and an aunt. For some days he has had an agonizing toothache, but will not admit it to his mother for he knows she does not tolerate complainers. As the oldest he must be the Man, now that the father is away. His mother even demands that he prove his manhood by killing one of his pet birds, a terrible deed that he does not understand at the time. James endures the hurting tooth (teef) for weeks, pretending ('tending) bravely that he is all right, until his mother realized that she must take him to the dentist. On the bus to Bayonne he and a little black girl have a comical flirtation.

James and his mother wait hours to see the dentist, during which time a confrontation takes place between a minister and an adult black student. The dentist puts James and his mother off until after lunch. In the interim they wander along the street in the cold. James becomes so cold that he cannot even think about the tooth. He tries reciting poetry to himself to avert his misery. He and his mother go inside a hardware store, where she pretends to purchase an ax handle, though she only wants him to be inside where it is warm. She prolongs looking at the ax handles, never intending to buy one. They then move on to a colored cafe across the track, where she gets James something to eat. There a pimp tries to pick her up, but she fights him.

Outside on the cold street, they head back for the dentist's office. On the way there they are spied by an elderly white woman bakery shop owner who needs help with chores. She gives them a meal in return for James' help, promising to telephone the dentist to be sure that he can see James. Before they leave, James' mother buys a small piece of salt meat, making sure that the white woman does not give her any extra out of pity. As they walk along the chilly street James is told to turn down his coat collar, despite the cold and sleet, for now he has proved himself to be a Man, not a bum. Gaines has etched their situation within the frame of their own unyielding pride.

* * *

Essayist Shelton mentions the mother as being the father symbol in this story, since the father is away, and she is responsible for the children. In order to make a man of James, she forces him into submission to do acts which he does not understand. He feels both love and fear for her, but cannot really express either—it would not be manly. She is in danger of causing James to lose his sensitivity, while at the same time expecting him to be a "man."[55] William Burke says that the theme of the story is the maintenance of manhood within the code's confines, causing the loss of compassion and gentleness. Suffering, both physical and emotional, is the story's keynote. James' courage and innocence are broken by both white society and his mother.[56]

Another writer says that the sufferings must precede any social change that is meaningful, and that a balance of non-violent black militancy, and human qualities of the whites contribute a certain warmth to the story's chilly scenario.[57]

* * *

The following excerpts from "The Sky is Gray" are quoted from the 1976 edition by W. W. Norton and Company.

James, the eight-year-old narrator, thinks:

> I look at my mama and I love my mama. She's wearing that black coat and that black hat and she's looking sad. I love my mama and I want put my arm round her and tell her. But I'm not supposed to do that. She say that's weakness and that's crybaby stuff, and she don't want no crybaby round her . . . I'm the oldest,

[55]Shelton, "Ambiguous Manhood," 203.

[56]Burke, "*Bloodline,*" pp. 545-558.

[57]James A. Emanuel and Theodore L. Gross, eds., *Dark Symphony* (New York, 1968), p. 428.

> and I got to set a good sample for the rest. I can't ever be scared and I can't ever cry. And that's why I never said nothing 'bout my teeth. It's been hurting me and hurting me close to a month now, but I never said it. . . . Look like it wouldn't start till at night when you was trying to get yourself little sleep. Then soon's you shut your eyes—ummm-ummm, Lord, look like it go right down to your heartstring.[58]

When James' mama made him kill the red bird, he did not understand at first, but later said: "I'm still young—I ain't no more than eight; but I know now; I know why I had to do it. . . . Suppose she had to go away like Daddy went away? Then who was go'n look after us? They had to be somebody left to carry on. I didn't know it then, but I know it now."[59]

Of the little girl on the bus James says:

> She got on a red overcoat and her hair's plaited in one big plait. . . . She got a cold, and every now and then she h'ist that little handkerchief to her nose. She ought to blow it, but she don't. Must think she's too much a lady or something. . . . When we get to Bayonne, she jugg her little old tongue out at me. I make 'tend I'm go'n hit her, and she duck down 'side her mama. And all the people laugh at us again.[60]

Gaines' description of the preacher in this story reminds the reader of those in "The Boy in the Double-Breasted Suit" and "A Long Day in November." James is thinking: "The man looks like a preacher. He's big and fat and he's got on a black suit. He's got a gold chain, too." And James describes the young student: "He looks like a teacher or somebody that goes to

[58]Ernest J. Gaines, *Bloodline* (1968, reprint ed., New York, 1976), p. 84.

[59]*Ibid.*, p. 90.

[60]*Ibid.*, pp. 91-92.

college. He's got on a suit, and he's got a book that he's been reading."[61] He also hears what the student tells the preacher:

> I'm not mad at the world. I'm questioning the world . . . [and] with cold logic, sir. What do words like Freedom, Liberty, God, White, Colored mean? I want to know. That's why *you* are sending us to school, to read and to ask questions. And because we ask these questions, you call us mad. No sir, it is not us who are mad. . . . You believe in God because a man told you to believe in God. . . . A white man told you to believe in God. And why? To keep you ignorant so he can keep his feet on your neck.[62]

Admiring the student for his forthrightness and for being a student, James says: "When I grow up I want be just like him. I want clothes like that and I want keep a book with me, too."[63]

Even more aware of his mother's struggle, James says: "I look up at mama. I love my mama. I love my mama. And when cotton come I'm go'n get her a new coat. And I ain't go'n get a black one, either. I think I'm go'n get her a red one." He is reticent to get close to her, thinking: "I look at Mama standing there. I want stand 'side her, but she don't like that. She say that's crybaby stuff. She say you got to stand for yourself, by yourself."[64]

Perhaps envisioning a slow but positive change, the student says:

> Things are changing because some black men have begun to think with their brains and not their hearts. . . . Unfortunately I was born too late to believe in your God. Let's hope that the ones who come after will have your

[61]*Ibid.*, pp. 94, 95.

[62]*Ibid.*, p. 97.

[63]*Ibid.*, p. 100.

[64]*Ibid.*, pp. 99, 105-106.

> faith—if not in your God, then in something else, something definitely that they can lean on. I haven't anything. For me, the wind is pink, the grass is black.[65]

James talks about the cold and his hunger:

> I ain't just hungry, but I'm cold, too. I'm so hungry and cold I want to cry. And look like I'm getting colder and colder. My feet done got numb. I try to work my toes, but I don't even feel them. Look like I'm go'n die. Look like I'm go'n stand right here and freeze to death. I think 'bout home. . . . Give anything in the world if I was home round the fire. . . . My feet so numb I can't hardly feel them. . . . Oh, Lord, oh Lord, I pray. Don't let me die, don't let me die, don't let me die, Lord. . . . I don't care if I don't eat. I been hungry before. I can stand it. But I can't stand the cold. . . . I hope they'd make it summer all the time. I'd be glad if it was summer all the time—but it ain't. We got to have winter, too. Lord, I hate the winter. . . . I can hear my teeth. I hope they don't knock together too hard and make that bad one hurt. Lord, that's all I need, for that bad one to start off.[66]

James misses his daddy: "I used to like to be with Mama and Daddy. We used to be happy. But they took him in the Army. Now, nobody happy no more. . . . I be glad when Daddy comes home."[67]

Still dreading the cold, James describes the white lady's place: "The kitchen is a little bitty little old thing, too. The table and the stove just 'bout fill it up. . . . We go out in the yard. Little old back yard ain't no bigger than the store or the kitchen. But it can sleet here just like it can sleet in any big back yard. And 'fore you know it, I'm trembling." The story's last lines are: "The sleet's coming down heavy, heavy now, and I turn up my

[65]*Ibid.*, p. 102.

[66]*Ibid.*, pp. 106-107.

[67]*Ibid.*, p. 108.

coat collar to keep my neck warm. My mama tells me turn it right back down. 'You not a bum,' she says. 'You a man.' "[68]

* * *

"The Sky is Gray" was filmed for the American Short Story Series under auspices of the National Endowment for the Arts and Humanities. Due to be seen on March 10, 1980, it was preempted by another movie during a fund raising pledge week, and was postponed until April 7. At that time PBS had been accused of ignoring minority-group audiences, so the preemption "left an unfortunate impression of calculated or benign neglect," according to The *New York Times*, April 7.

For the film version, the story was not in first person. James Bond III as James and Olivia Cole as his tall, slender mother gave outstanding performances. One critic called Cole's acting "riveting." Others in the cast included Cleavon Little, Clinton Derricks-Carroll, and Margaret Avery. The story's theme was not easily translated to the screen, but was adapted quite effectively by Charles Fuller. Director Stan Lathan "kept the production as beautifully stark and touching as the story," the *New York Times* review of April 8 stated. Original music for the film, incorporating blues, minimalism, and a honking saxophone, was composed by Webster Lewis.

The incidents were not connected except as a chain of conflicts, every one involving a struggle of some kind. Compared to the original story, the film moved fast, but nevertheless the viewer felt the excruciating cold and the whole pathetic situation. The story was spoken of as "full of struggle and pain, sharp, pointed objects, and muted violence," in an undated, unnamed review in Gaines' papers. Especially memorable are the scenes in the dentist's office, the cafe scene, and the buying of the salt meat.

* * *

"Three Men"

Gaines' idea for "Three Men" may very likely have been drawn from his recollections of a bar fight, as was *Of Love and*

[68] *Ibid.*, pp. 114, 117.

Dust. In the previously quoted speech at Southern University Gaines mentioned hearing about two particular incidents in which blacks had murdered blacks. He said,

> In one case, when the white lawyer offered his services for a small fee, the prisoner told him that he would rather go to the pen and pay for his crime. But in case two the prisoner left with his white employer. Remembering the first incident, I wrote the long story, 'Three Men.'

In 1972, when interviewer John O'Brien asked Gaines about the influence of Hemingway and Faulkner in this particular story, he said,

> I was not conscious of Hemingway as I was writing the story 'Three Men' or the novel *Of Love and Dust*. I should point out that Procter Lewis and Marcus Payne are the same character; I wanted to show what would have happened to Procter Lewis had he gotten out of prison, the chances he would have taken to attain his freedom. The stoicism in these two characters was not because of Hemingway's influence on me. I was writing these stories during the time when young blacks were standing up against the establishment. They were no longer doing what everyone thought they ought to do, whether it was the white man, or the law, or their own black people. So that was an influence. Then I also knew a guy on whom I based Procter Lewis.[69]

* * *

"Three Men" concerns a nineteen-year-old black man, Procter Lewis, who had provoked a fight in the Seven Spots Bar for trying to pick up the girlfriend of Bayou, an irascible black patron. Bayou comes at Procter with a knife. Procter's only

[69]O'Brien, *Interviews*, p. 81.

protective weapon is a broken bottle, which he finally jabs into Bayou's stomach. Afraid that he has killed him, he gives himself up to two white policemen. One of them, T. J., wants to make things tough, while the other shows as much sympathy as he dares to still appear dutiful, later giving Procter some cigarettes as he is taken to jail.

Procter's cellmates are Hattie, a male prostitute, and Munford, who cannot resist fighting and has become a "regular" at the jail. Munford, a real twit himself, has no intention of reforming. As a frequent offender, he is allowed some weekends out. While Munford is on such a pass a fourteen-year-old boy who stole something to eat was beaten by the police and put in the cell with Procter and Hattie. Hattie tries to comfort him, an action which Procter fears will lead to the boy's seduction. It does not, however. Both Hattie and Procter play the father by trying to comfort the boy.

Procter is torn with indecision: whether to stay in the jail to be beaten, then tried, in order to prove that he is a real man, at the risk of the death penalty, or let his uncle's plantation owner bail him out and forever play the obsequious Uncle Tom role of bowing and scraping.

Before being in jail Procter had attained his manhood by wenching, drinking, and fighting. But the grimness of the jail scene has given him some deeper thoughts. At the end, after Munford talks, Procter knows that if he follows Munford's way of getting in and out of jail, he will be a victim of the white man's whims. Hattie, the homosexual, perhaps represents less than a man, but at least has some human qualities, such as his concern for the beaten young boy. Since at the end the reader is left with Procter's indecision, total manhood is perhaps not found in any of this story's characters.

* * *

Procter's experience in jail helps him find out who he is, what he is capable of, and how he might react in certain situations. He struggles with his own integrity, debating over whether or not to reject the code. Vision is suggested when

Procter decides to forego physical for spiritual freedom, representing an "upward direction" in his aspirations. Munford acts as a catalyst. According to Todd Duncan in "Scene and Life Cycle in Ernest Gaines' *Bloodline,"* this story points up one of Gaines' more serious concerns, "the connection between generations and the acceptance of the responsibilities of literal or symbolic parenthood."[70]

Ronald G. Billingsley, in his "Forging New Definitions: The Burden of the Hero in Modern American Literature," sees Gaines as a writer who cuts through definitions confining the black man and wants to change them. The price of re-definition is either to suffer willingly or face possible death. The black man is worthless—if one black man kills another, who cares? Usually the penalty is small. Procter, however, did not feel this way. He demanded punishment by giving himself up. He wants to be responsible for his own acts, thereby keeping his sense of dignity and manhood.[71]

* * *

The following quotes from "Three Men" are particularly descriptive. Procter has just come to the police station and is being questioned by T. J. and his deputy: "They looked at me, but when they saw I was just a nigger they went back to talking like I wasn't even there. They talked like that two or three more minutes before the one behind the desk looked at me again." Procter describes T. J.:[72]

> He was a mean, evil sonofabitch. He was big and red and he didn't waste time kicking your ass if you gived him the wrong answers. You had to weigh every

[70]Todd Duncan, "Scene and Life Cycle in Ernest Gaines' *Bloodline*," *Callaloo #3*, I (May, 1978), 94.

[71]Ronald G. Billingsley, "Forging New Definitions: The Burden of the Hero in Modern American Literature," *Obsidian* (Winter, 1975), 15-17.

[72]Gaines, *Bloodline*, p. 121.

> word he said to you. Sometimes you answered, other times you kept your mouth shut. . . . He looked at me hard again. He didn't think I was crazy for turning myself in, he thought I was a smart aleck. I could tell from his big fat, red face he wanted to hit me with his fist. . . . Now he just sat there looking at me again. He wanted to hit me in the mouth with his fist. Not just hit me, he wanted to beat me. But he had to have a good excuse. And what excuse could he have when I had already turned myself in.[73]

Procter describes Munford:

> He must've been sixty; he had reddish-brown eyes, and a stubby gray beard. 'Cross his right jaw, from his cheekbone to his mouth, was big shiny scar where somebody had gotten him with a razor. He was wearing a derby hat, and he had it cocked a little to the back of his head.[74]

A few pages later Munford described the attitude of benevolent white men who get criminals off, one that he hates, but neither will he stay out of trouble in order not to fall into this trap. His words are:

> I kept on getting in trouble, and they kept on getting me off. Didn't wake up till I got to be nearly old as I'm is now. Then I realized they kept getting me off because they needed a Munford Bazille. They need me to prove they human. . . . they need us. Because without us, they don't know what they is—they don't know what they is out there. With us around they can see us and they know what they ain't. They ain't us. Do you see? Do you see how they think? . . . Cut them open; go 'head and cut one open—you see if you don't find Munford Bazille or

[73]*Ibid.*, pp. 122-123, 125.

[74]*Ibid.*, p. 133.

> Hattie Brown. Not a man one of them. . . . You know what I'm getting at? . . . Don't let Medlow get you out of here so you can kill again.[75]

Procter watches Munford and Hattie eating:

> The freak, Hattie, sat on his bunk, nibbling at his food. He wrapped one slice of bread round the slice of baloney and ate that, then he did the same thing with the other sandwich. The two extra slices of bread he dipped down in his coffee and ate it like that. All the time he was eating, he was looking at me like a sad woman looks at you. Munford stood between the two rows of bunks, eating and drinking his coffee. He pressed both of the sandwiches together and ate them like they were just one. Nobody said anything all the time we was eating. Even when I poured out the coffee, nobody said anything. The freak just looked at me like a sad woman. But Munford didn't look at me at all—he was looking up at the window all the time. When he got through eating, he wiped his mouth and throwed his cup on the bunk.[76]

Munford has given his theories on how gays become gay. "Hattie looked up at him just like a woman looks at a man she can't stand. . . . Hattie rolled his eyes at Munford the way a woman rolls her eyes at a man she can't stand."[77]

Procter notices more about Hattie's effeminateness which disgusts him: "Hattie started singing. He was singing a spiritual and he was singing it in a high-pitched voice like a woman. I wanted to tell him to shut up, but I didn't want have nothing to do with that freak." When Hattie wanted a cigarette, "He came over and got the pack out of my shirt pocket. His fingers went down in my pocket just like a woman's fingers go

[75]*Ibid.*, pp. 137-138.

[76]*Ibid.*, pp. 134-135.

[77]*Ibid.*, pp. 141-142.

in your pocket. 'May I? ' he said. I didn't say nothing to him. He lit his cigarette and laid the pack on my chest just like a woman'd do it."[78]

Thinking to himself, Procter asks,

> Where is my father? Why my mama had to die? I used to love my mama so much. Her skin was light brown; her hair was silky. I used to watch her powdering her face in the glass. I used to always cry when she went out—and be glad when she came back because she always brought me candy. But you gone for good now, Mama; and I got nothing in this world but me.[79]

About other people Procter thinks, "I never messed with a woman I didn't love. I always loved all these women I ever messed with. . . . No, I didn't love them. . . . Maybe I ain't never loved nobody since my mama died. Because I loved her, I know I loved her. But the rest—no, I never loved the rest. They don't let you love them. Some kind of way they keep you from loving them. . . . I wish I knowed a good person. I would be good if I knowed a good person. I swear to God, I would be good."[80]

* * *

"Bloodline"

Felix, a black maintenance man who has been on Frank Laurent's plantation for many years, is the logical character to narrate "Bloodline," due to his relatively placid nature, as compared with that of Frank or of his nephew, Copper (Christian), the story's protagonist. Gaines' other main character is Copper's aunt, 'Malia (Amalia), a seventy-two-

[78]*Ibid.*, pp. 143, 146.

[79]*Ibid.*, p. 147.

[80]*Ibid.*, pp. 148, 149.

year-old servant in Frank's house. Minor characters include J. W., Frank's head strong-arm, Stateman, his butler, and Dee-Dee, the young "yellow" black maid, for whom Stateman lusts.

Copper is Frank's only direct heir, his brother Walter's son by a Negress. Walter was killed by a stallion. Copper, obsessed with military procedure and attitude, has come back to claim his birthright, and will only appear at Frank's house if admitted by the front door. Though he has not actually served in the military, he has been a part of militant groups, and has been in jail more than once. He fancies himself as an officer, even calling himself "General." He sends a note to Frank, stressing the fact that he must be admitted by the front door. In reply to Frank's ultimatum that he appear at the house, Copper beats up the two black men hired to fetch him, and then ties them with chains. Frank then sends J. W. and his hit crew, all of whom Copper bests, forcing one to jump into a ditch teeming with yellow jackets.

Frank finally goes to the quarters in order to talk to Copper, but remains firm about not considering him an equal, or kin. He promises to do better by the black help, but will not give Copper a share of the property. Copper does not bow to Frank. He decides to leave the plantation instead, vowing to come back one day and claim his birthright and his share of the property.

* * *

In Gaines' address for the Modern Language Association in 1981, he recalled a prison story related to him by a friend ("a damned boogood mechanic who could hardly sign his name").

> He [the friend] told me one day that he found a long strand of brown hair on the leg strap of the electric chair. In Louisiana when they would execute somebody they would bring in this portable electric chair on the bed of a truck. They would go from one parish to another with this damned thing, anytime they had to execute somebody. . . . Now, I forget whether he told me he had to clean the chair, or help unload the chair, or help put it

> back on the truck. I forget exactly what he had to do, but I've used the story. I mean I've put that information in a story called 'Bloodline.' But I'm not satisfied, because, you see, there are at least two stories there—maybe even three. If the strand of hair was found when he was unloading the chair, then it was from a previous execution. And if he found it while helping them put the thing back onto the truck, then it could have been of the recent execution, a guy he probably knew. But I remember he telling me that for the first time, he realized that they also executed white boys too. One of these days I'm going to use that information again.

* * *

The following excerpts from the story "Bloodline" are from the 1976 edition of *Bloodline* issued by W. W. Norton and Company.

No matter how tragic or dramatic Gaines' story, he manages to punctuate it with humor. Felix, the narrator, remarks on 'Malia's decrepitness as she walks ever so slightly uphill to the house:

> It wasn't much of a incline. To them children who came to the yard to pick figs and pecans, it wasn't a incline at all. They could run it just like running on flat ground. but when you got old as she was—she was seventy-two, I was seventy—everything looked like a incline. Even walking downhill looked like a incline.[81]

Felix speaks of Walter's sexual exploits:

> That was one, that Walter. A black woman, no matter who she was, didn't have a chance if he wanted

[81]*Ibid.*, p. 160.

> her. He didn't care if it was in the field, in the quarters, the store or that house; when he got his dick up, he hopped on any of them. But them days are gone now, just like he's gone. That black stallion saw to that.[82]

Concerning the not so successful Stateman in pursuance of Dee-Dee, Felix says:

> 'He [Stateman] in there begging with his clean-head self,' she said. 'You ought to give Stateman what he want,' I said. 'Make yourself a little piece of change.' 'Huh,' she said. 'Bet he die 'fore I let him crawl on top of me.'[83]

Felix, as servant, understood Frank, as his master, perhaps better than most could have, due to respectful familiarity through longevity. Felix says:

> When something's too heavy, it makes most people wild animals or it breaks them. The land had broken Frank. It had aged him too fast. It had given him two heart attacks—and the next one was going to kill him. He knowed I knowed all of this. He knowed I knowed he wasn't hard, he was helpless. But he was still the authority there, and when he spoke I was supposed to move. . . . Me and 'Malia had been there almost long as Frank had been there, and he told us more than he ever told anybody else. And that's why he never scared me. I obeyed his orders because I respected him; not because I was scared of him.[84]

Later, when Felix needs to talk with Frank, he says, "I went to the chair in the other corner, and I brushed off my pants before I sat down. It was the first time I had ever sat in the library, but I

[82]*Ibid.*, p. 162.

[83]*Ibid.*, p. 163.

[84]*Ibid.*, pp. 165, 166.

had sat in the living room two or three times when they had wakes there."[85] Then later, while he was still talking with Frank, he continues:

> I rubbed my hand over my old black cap I had hanging on my knee. Then I just looked at my hands a while. I guess I never would 'a' done that if I was out in the shop or at my own house. But in here, with all these books and furnitures and fine things, I just, all of a sudden, looked at both of my hands. How rough they looked. Knotted, old, hard, and wrinkled.[86]

Felix describes Copper's physical appearance: "He looked more like Walter Laurent than Walter ever looked like himself. Tall, slim, with a long face just like Walter. Only difference was, he was brown with curly black hair; his paw was white with straight brown hair." And later he said: "Anybody in the world who had ever seen Walter Laurent and saw Copper could see that Walter Laurent was Copper's paw. But you wasn't supposed to ever say it."[87]

Copper's letter to Frank shows his resentment and the working of his military mind. It is almost humorous to the reader:

> If I thought you meant that invitation, I would tell you, without hesitation where to put that back door. But I am sure you did not mean it, therefore I have forgotten about it. If you wish to send me any other messages—an apology, or an invitation to speak to me as a General, as a Laurent, you can send the message to me in the quarters, I shall be there reconnoitering the area. Your respectful kin, General Christian Laurent.[88]

[85]*Ibid.*, p. 186.

[86]*Ibid.*, p. 189.

[87]*Ibid.*, pp. 167, 181.

[88]*Ibid.*, p. 170.

Copper tells Frank some powerful things about the injustice of whites to blacks and blacks to blacks. After he was born his mother married a black man, whose name Copper took. When she died the husband threw Copper out.

> He was not going to support any white man's child. He was tired supporting a white man's child. I was fourteen years old then. . . . Not a soul in the world to turn to, not one. . . . There're millions just like me. Maybe not my color, but without homes, without birthrights, just like me. And who is to blame? . . . Men like my father. . . . Rapists, murderers, plunderers—and they hide behind the law. The law they created themselves. . . . I used to pray and pray and pray. But the same God I was praying to was created by the same ones I was praying against. And Gods only listen to the people who create them. So I quit my praying—there would have to be another way. I remembered that I had a father who had property, and I remembered that I was his oldest son. I would take that property—my share of that property—and I would share it with those others who were like me. . . . Whether you like it or not, I'm a Laurent. I'm a Laurent, Uncle, and you better remember it.[89]

At the end Copper tells Frank that he is leaving: "Tell my aunt I've gone. But tell her I'll come back. And when I do she'll never have to go through your back door, ever again." Then, "He bowed and went inside—walking fast the way soldiers walk."[90]

* * *

Some analyses from previously cited essayists follow. Frank Shelton, in "Ambiguous Manhood in Ernest J. Gaines'

[89]*Ibid.*, pp. 212, 213, 214, 215.

[90]*Ibid.*, p. 217.

Bloodline," says that Copper's domineering, haughty, intolerant attitude actually makes him a "carbon copy" of the white men that he hates. He makes people afraid of him, and has few if any feelings for Uncle Frank. In a way, like Jim and Aunt Margaret in *Of Love and Dust*, Felix and 'Malia are caught between the Laurents and social change. Felix insists that human relationships be based on respect, not fear.

William Burke in "*Bloodline*: A Man's Black South" calls Copper a logical product of his inescapable tradition. He is of mixed blood, is bordering on madness, is certainly mysterious, and is determinedly militant. Frank denies his own humanity in not treating 'Malia as an equal, though he feels kindly toward her—a slave to tradition.[91]

Copper is seeking a sort of intimacy with both his black Aunt 'Malia and his white Uncle Frank, Copper is more into his own "ego integrity" than Frank, who is hopelessly bound up in tradition.

* * *

"Just Like a Tree"

The last of the *Bloodline* stories, "Just Like a Tree," was first published in *The Sewanee Review*, Autumn, 1963. More recently it was included in *A Century of the Short Story in Louisiana, 1880-1980* (published 1985), edited by Mary Dell Fletcher.

A letter from *Sewanee Review* editor Andrew Lytle to Gaines, dated June 19, 1963, suggested revision of one section, though the specific one is not named. (At the time Gaines was living in Baton Rouge). The letter reads:

> Dear Mr. Gaines:
>
> I did not mean for you to cut the entire episode. What I felt was that it was inert and reported, not an active

[91]Burke, "*Bloodline,*" 553, 555.

> dramatic incident. Don't you see that an anecdote is never clear in its being reported at second hand? The only way you can put an anecdote in fiction is to show its effect on the spectator who is being amused or moved by it.
>
> Sincerely yours,
>
> Andrew Lytle

Gaines has said that "Just Like a Tree" is possibly his favorite of the stories, and has read from it on numerous occasions. It is a series of sketches told by several people as things seem to them. They are gathered to say goodbye to Aunt Fe, who must leave her home of many years because of bombings in the area by anti-civil rights people.

Though Gaines is examining the impact of Aunt Fe's leaving on her family and neighbors, each character is to large extent occupied with his own smaller problems. Chuckkie, a small boy, the son of Emile, tries to help his father by guiding the wagon, but coming into Aunt Fe's yard he knocks part of her fence down. He is too young to understand Aunt Fe's sorrow in leaving her old home. Emile is frustrated by his balky old mule, "Mr. Bascom," whom he would like to replace with a horse who can work and help produce more crops for him. In frustration he whips the mule severely, then talks nicely to him. He thinks his own mother, Gran'mon, in the wagon with them, likes the mule better than she does him. She berates him for whipping the animal. Leola, Emile's wife, is concerned that Aunt Fe (no actual relation, but an old friend) is being moved by her niece, Louise, and Louise's husband, James. She had offered to take Aunt Fe into her own home.

Leola does not like James. James is an impatient, uncouth boozer, who at the gathering is taking orders for eggnog and sizing up the group sarcastically, calling them "country niggers." He is a real cool cat, up to no good, interested mainly in his bottle of "Mr. Harper" and in speciously petting his wife. He has no remorse about "hauling this old chick [Aunt Fe] away."

Ben O, a young boy, insists on having some eggnog. Gran'mon says no; his mama says yes; Gran'mon says she is spoiling him. Aunt Clo is the one who compares Aunt Fe (or anyone who is old and unwanted) to a tree that has been uprooted, painfully, slowly. There is no really good place for either the tree or the person. Chris, a peripheral kinfolk, hates the jokes that are being told. He only hopes that Aunt Fe will leave him her big iron pot.

Anne-Marie Duvall, a white lady for whose father Aunt Fe was a cook, comes to Aunt Fe's in the rain and sleet to bring her a small gift and to say goodbye. She has come against the wishes of her husband, who refused to come with her. She is just as discontent as the black characters, feeling a terrible sense of guilt for not having spent more time with Aunt Fe before she is forced out of her home. This visit was as important to Aunt Fe as to Anne-Marie.

In one segment of the story Etienne, a family friend, tries to explain why Aunt Fe has to go, and that Emmanuel, a young civil rights activist, has only done what he feel is right after the bombing. Having predicted the idea of change, Aunt Fe has psychologically prepared herself for death, and is now able to accept the imminent changes. She demands respect for the past while realizing the importance of growth as a form of change. Aunt Lou (Gran'mon) has been with Aunt Fe in her last few months. They sing their 'termination songs, then pray. When Aunt Fe dies, Gran'mon says: "Sleep on, Fe. When you get up there, tell 'em I ain't far behind."

* * *

Emmanuel, the civil rights activist, is no lost soul like Jackson in *Catherine Carmier* or a "cocky swaggerer" like Marcus in *Of Love and Dust*. Hoping for the change that his work will bring about he is totally committed and fearless. The writer of an unsigned, undated essay found in Gaines' papers sums up the situation well.

> He [Emmanuel] feels sad that his family and friends resent him and his work, but he understands their anxieties. Above all, he hates the pain he is causing old Aunt Fe, the epitome of black life in Louisiana since the Civil War, for he loves her deeply. Her niece wants to take her North, out of range of the white man's retaliation against the black activists. But it is impossible to save Aunt Fe. She can't go North, because she can't be torn away from her native South and survive. Nor can she continue to live her old life in the South, for a new world is replacing the old one. But Aunt Fe, unlike Aunt Charlotte and Aunt Margaret, knows that her time has come, and she accepts the inevitable, revealing a wisdom and grace that few of her relatives and friends have. She doesn't warn her young descendent to beware the wrath of the gods for his disobedience. She crawls into her bed the night before she is to leave and dies. We lament her passing but we can't tolerate any longer the conditions under which she lived. The young rebel has made a valid commitment, and sad as its consequences are, it looks forward hopefully to something better.

Essayist William Burke in "*Bloodline*: A Man's Black South" called Anne-Marie Duvall a stereotype of the Southern white woman. By not having Aunt Fe or Emmanuel speak in first person in the story, Gaines makes Aunt Fe's storehouse of past trials and Emmanuel's precarious future presently inaccessible. He says that Gaines' talent is balanced by an honest intelligence, since he detects an equal erosion of the centers of both blacks and whites, remnants of the imposition of an unfeasable code. There is potential for its destruction, and their transcendence.[92]

In "Ambiguous Manhood in Gaines's *Bloodline*" Shelton maintains that Aunt Fe's reaction to the inevitability of social changes does not deny her sympathy for others. (Copper in *Bloodline,* on the other hand, remains as merciless and

[92]Burke, "*Bloodline,*" 557, 558.

unyielding as ever. Anne-Marie Duval, the story's only white character, is aware of the impression she has made at the gathering by going out of her way to visit Aunt Fe, an old black lady. She is curious, perhaps resentful, that the black people will not allow her to feel as deeply about another human being as they would.[93]

Ironically, many whites, simply through their insensitive treatment of blacks, appear to have no human feelings. Thus, by meeting the white man on his own terms, the black man may preserve his dignity. Empathy and mutual sympathy between the two is sometimes construed as a frailty. Gaines, however, does not allow the black man's aspirations to dignity and manhood, nor his callousness toward whites, to exclude feelings of his heart. To do so would deny any freedom and harbor imprisonment of the soul.

In Gaines' Southern University speech (1971) in Baton Rouge he commented on the structure of "Just Like a Tree:"

> The story was told from multiple points of view—that is, several people telling a single story from different angles. Most of the people were her [Aunt Fe's] age, and while they were telling you the reason she had to leave, they were also telling you something about themselves. But they only touched on their [own] lives; they were not going into any great details. In the case of Aunt Fe, the protagonist, you only hear snatches of conversation about her life. You know that she must leave the South, because they are bombing near her home, and she might be killed. But you don't know her life—where she comes from, her children, her husband—her life, in general, before that particular day.

* * *

The following quotes from "Just Like a Tree" may illustrate some of the viewpoints which make up the plot of the story.

[93]*Ibid.*

Chuckkie talks about Gran'mon's "setting chair" and how she asserted her rights as a matriarch:

> Pa didn't want bring the setting chair, telling Gran'mon there was two boards in that wagon already and she could sit on one of 'em all by herself if she wanted to, but Gran'mon say she was taking her setting chair with her if Pa liked it or not. She say she didn't ride in no wagon on nobody board, and if Pa liked it or not that setting chair was going.[94]

Etienne, describes Mr. Bascom, the mule, as a

> little dried-up, long-eared, tobacco-color thing. . . . That mule know long's Mama's alive he go'n do just what he want to do. He know when Papa was dying he told Mama to look after him, and he know no matter what he do, no matter what he don't do, Mama ain't go'n never let me do him anything. Sometimes I even feel Mama care mo' for Mr. Bascom 'an she care for me her own son. When Mama die, I say to myself, Mr. Bascom, you going.[95]

Leola notices James' behavior with his wife Louise.

> Her husband come back in the kitchen and kiss her on the back o' the neck and then look at me and grin. Right from the start I can see I ain't go'n like that nigger. . . . He kiss her on the other ear. A nigger do all that front o' public got something to hide.[96]

James calls the country niggers "weird cats." "I can feel Mr. Harper [the whiskey] starting to massage my wig and I bat my eyes twice and look at the old girl [Aunt Fe] over there. . . . I

[94]Gaines, *Bloodline,* pp. 222-223.

[95]*Ibid.*, pp. 224-225.

[96]*Ibid.*, p. 228.

feel Mr. Harper touching my skull now." Speaking of Aunt Fe's insistence on taking her chair with her, James says,

> Wait, man, I mean like, you ever heard of anybody going to somebody else's house with a chair? I mean, wouldn't you call that an insult at the basest point? . . . . I mean—dig—here I am at my pad, and in you come with your own stool. . . . I mean that's an insult at the basest point. I mean, you know . . . you know, like way out. . . .

In a more playful mood, James says, "I go up to Baby [his wife] and kiss her on the back of the neck and give her a little pat where she likes for me to pat her when we're in bed. She say, 'Uh-uh,' but I know she likes it anyhow."[97]

Aunt Clo compares uprooting Aunt Fe to uprooting an old tree.

> Yes, you got the tree—least got it down on the ground, but did you get the taproot?. . . No, sir, you don't get the taproot. . . . You never get the taproot. But I tell you what you do get. You get a big hole in the ground, sir; and you get another big hole in the air where the lovely branches been all these years. . . . The holes . . . you can't never fill no matter how hard you try.

Like an old uprooted tree that can never be totally disposed of, "She kind o' stand in the way no matter where you set her. So finally, sir, you say, 'I just stand her up here a little while and see, and if it don't work out, if she keep getting in the way, I guess we'll just have to take her to the dump."[98]

Chris, concerned about getting Aunt Fe's iron pot says, "If they offer me anything, I'd like that big iron pot out there in the back yard. Good for boiling water when you killing hog, you know."[99]

[97]*Ibid.*, pp. 231, 232.

[98]*Ibid.*, pp. 236, 237.

[99]*Ibid.*, p. 238.

Anne-Marie, the white lady, is sure that her husband does not understand why she must go to Aunt Fe's, though he knows that Aunt Fe was her companion after her mother's death, and that she cooked for the family. He thinks she is being unreasonable. Anne-Marie says, "And I'm trying to pay her back with a seventy-nine-cents scarf. Is that too much?" She has mixed feelings about going.

> I wish I was a little nigger gal so I could pick pecans and eat them under the big old dead tree. . . . Can't I simply send the gift by someone tomorrow morning? But will there be someone tomorrow morning? Suppose she leaves without getting it, then what? What then? Father would never forgive me. Neither would grandfather or great-grandfather, either. No, they wouldn't. . . . I can hear the people laughing and talking. Sometimes I think niggers can laugh and joke even if they see somebody beaten to death.

When she presents the scarf, she relates:

> I take out the package and pass it to her. The other niggers gather around with all kinds of smiles on their faces. Just think of it—a white lady coming through all of this for one old darky . . . a white lady, a white lady. They must think we white people don't have their kind of feelings.

She is finally overcome with emotion: "I look into that wrinkled old face again . . . and I lay my head in that bony old lap, and I cry and I cry—I don't know how long. And I feel those old fingers, like death itself, passing over my hair and my neck. I don't know how long I kneel there crying, and when I stop, I get out of there as fast as I can."[100]

About Aunt Fe and Emmanuel, Etienne thinks to himself, "She ain't nothing but one little drop o' water laying on top of the

[100]*Ibid.*, pp. 239, 240-241, 242, 243.

sea, and what this boy's doing is called the wind . . . and she must be moved."[101]

* * *

In an interview for The *New Orleans Review*, Gaines was thoroughly quizzed on the *Bloodline* collection, allowing him to expand on the subject.

> NOR (*New Orleans Review*): Which of the characters do you like the most in *"Bloodline?"*
>
> GAINES: I think the two of them, Frank Laurent and Copper. I like someone who has to touch his chest every now and then to keep living. But I don't really thing Frank Laurent touched his chest *all* the time. I think what he's doing is sorta like making the sign of the cross, and I think at times he didn't have to touch it for God to keep his heart beating. But these things are the subtleties, you know. This is the kind of thing you lose out on in first person. From the omniscient point of view, the author can catch all these subtleties. He can indicate that Frank does not touch his chest all the time, and of course the author can reenter the mind and say exactly what is going on, whereas Felix [the narrator] cannot. He just sorta stands there and sees the physical things that are going on. And he thinks he can imagine what is happening, like when the guy is coming in from the field and tells him how Copper has been treating everybody, so Felix *thinks* he can imagine what's going on in this guy's mind, because he knows what would be going on in *his* mind if he was sitting there. But he doesn't know exactly what is going on. These are the kind of things you lose when you tell it from the first person point of view. You lose so much but you gain so much too.

[101]*Ibid.*, p. 245.

NOR: You expand your technique, I think, in the last story in *Bloodline* when you put together in one story many people's point of view and then you finally get, I think, the advantage of both the first person and the omniscient narrative.

GAINES: Yes, I think that is absolutely so. But even there you lose a little bit. You don't get it all.

NOR: Is the structure of "Just Like a Tree" derived primarily from Faulkner's *As I Lay Dying*?

GAINES: Oh, absolutely. Well, I read Chaucer's *The Canterbury Tales* and that has something to do with it. But I think Faulkner has influenced me more than any other writer, and of course, *As I Lay Dying* has influenced me. Definitely. Just as Eudora Welty's *Worn Path* has had definite influence on "The Sky is Gray." There's no plagiarism or anything involved. But since you can't write out of a void, you need some crutch somewhere; you need somebody to say ok this is one route you can take. . . .

NOR: What about the other two stories ["Three Men" and "Bloodline"]? Did you write them specifically for *Bloodline*?

GAINES: The other two, yes. [Gaines recalled that when he had written "A Long Day in November," "The Sky is Gray," and "Just Like a Tree" that he had planned the three as a volume.] I definitely wrote them for the book. When I was working on them, suddenly I wanted them to fit in with what was going on here. I think the next one was "Three Men" and the last one was "*Bloodline*" itself, the title story. But once I realized that I was writing a group of stories that had some similarities, I wanted them to have relationship with the other ones. . . . I mean the progression. [There's a progression] in age as well as experiences. . . . A six year old child would not experience what Procter . . . would experience. The six year old child—all his action is in the quarters, the eight year old child moves out of the quarters and he goes into a small Southern town, which gives him a feeling of much of what a small Southern town would be like. He meets whites, he finds there are certain areas where you cannot go. In the plantation, in the quarters, he could go almost anywhere, everybody knows him, so he can move around. . . . Then he moves out of that, just like the six year old boy, who doesn't want to come out from under the covers when the mother's trying to get him out because he knows it's cold out there. The eight year old kid begins to feel all these things when he moves out and stands on the road to catch the bus going to Bayonne Institute. He has to walk to the back of the bus. . . . He sees so much more than the six year old child can see. And in "Three Men" there's a murder; one has committed a murder. . . . When one takes a life, he's different from any man who's never taken a life.

NOR: You leave Procter with a difficult choice at the end. You leave it ambiguous, whether or not he's able to do what he hopes he will do.

GAINES: My men are always standing like they're waiting to go through a door.

NOR: In a way, Procter is facing the worst there is to face. . . . He's going to have to go through so much that's brutal, and so alone, with only his own integrity to maintain him. It's going to be total loneliness every day. I feel that he really has the hardest road to hoe of all the characters in the book. Is that why that's the central story in the book, or is the book really asymmetrical? Do you place a greater emphasis on "Bloodline" itself?

GAINES: In "Bloodline" you go beyond all that. In all the other stories you're centered around my little area of Bayonne, you're on the False River, of the Pointe Coupée Parish area. In "Bloodline" you go beyond, you go farther. For example, Copper in "Bloodline" finds a long string of brown hair on the electric chair. So he knows damn well that not only my people are being brutalized; somebody else is being brutalized too. And this is the kind of thing that might have really snapped his mind. He could have fought the rest of his life, or maybe he could have been like Procter, but then when they started putting white boys with brown hair in the goddamn chair, something else is happening in this world.

NOR: I thought that he was the kind of person that had just been touched by the casualties in Vietnam and that sort of thing. Everybody's death and pain bothered him; it's no longer racial.

GAINES: Yes, that's what he's going through, that's the point where Copper had reached.

NOR: When you get to "Just Like a Tree," do you try to draw a connective line with the other stories?

GAINES: Yes. I think that everything sort of came together at the end. All the characters' experiences, and the many points of view, and many side points . . . like the little boy Chuckie would come in on the scene, and Emmanuel will come in, and the white gal from the big house comes in on the scene, the dude from up North moves in. And you progress in time.[102]

* * *

The following material has been written about the *Bloodline* collection as a whole. Often referred to as a cycle, it has been called a "metaphor standing for Gaines' entire network of implied kinship," including the concepts of nurture and literal or symbolic parenthood.

Gaines himself explained in the previously cited interview with John O'Brien how each of the stories grew into the next, though he did not actually write them in the order that they appeared in *Bloodline*. "I definitely arranged these stories in this order because there is growth." Gaines restated to O'Brien much the same thing as he had told the *New Orleans Review* interviewer, tracing the progressive stages of growth. "By the time you come to the last story there is much more experience to interpret. You have both older women and older men. You have the point of view of the white woman. There are many different experiences coming into the story. So there is a constant growth from the first to the last story."[103]

[102]Ingram and Steinberg, "On the Verge," 339-344.

[103]O'Brien, *Interviews,* 91.

The author of an undated, unsigned essay found in Gaines' papers titled "Ernest J. Gaines—Change, Growth and History" wrote:

> It isn't the hopefulness per se of *Bloodline* that makes its stories generally strong fiction. It's that Gaines seems to feel more comfortable with the tone he establishes, and so produces sharper pictures and more satisfying characters. There's no tragic irony here, but there is pathos. And there's comedy—sometimes sad, sometimes funny. There are characters who can't be reduced to any scheme, political or otherwise. Some are as weak as Eddie . . . some as determined as Gran'mon. Some are slightly mad, some inflated with their own self importance. We laugh, but only a little, at Copper Laurent . . . when he proclaims himself the 'general' of a non-existent 'army.' We feel sorrow at the ridiculous scene in 'The Sky is Gray' when a preacher, whose religion commits him to love and non-violence, frustrated by a young man's revolutionary political ideas, knocks him to the floor. Gaines is in control here. He gives us events and characters that are vivid and richly meaningful. The meaning has its political side—that blacks can and do change their world as well as themselves, and in doing so acquire an intensity of experience that surpasses mere survival. But the political meaning carries conviction only because the human meaning is there, too.[104]

Jack Hicks, in "To Make These Bones Live: History and Community in Ernest Gaines's Fiction," speaks about the line from "Just Like a Tree," "History is the wind on the water." He says, "the vision of history as fate, as a cycle from which one cannot escape, is expanded." The focus of each story is individual growth. Hicks feels that "Bloodline" is the weakest of the stories, and calls "Three Men" a "hard-boiled and

[104]Unidentified essay found in Gaines' papers, pp. 8-9.

understated tale," which still has truth: that "true community, in its most supportive and nourishing aspects, is fragile and organic. . . . We see . . . that it *is* possible and can be birthed in the most unlikely places, that it is natural and tropistic," evolving from "a collective sense of dignity and personal and social past, just as surely as a plant turns to watch the sun and water evaporates to the upper airs."

Hicks continues that the emphasis in "Just Like a Tree" is on reconciliation rather than on conflict.

> Gaines's final comment on Aunt Fe's importance is an expression of his most sweeping historical vision. The language and rhythms of Etienne's testimony grow from the Bible and the folk sermon; this is a cosmic vision, simply and dramatically built, and it resolves all of the apparent conflicts and contradictions between people and races and eras. . . . It takes us further, suggests that like the vast natural turnings (as in the wind on the water), there is a pattern in the growth of peoples and communities, that a single human tragedy can nourish a greater communal birth. 'Three Men' signals the future way for young black manhood; 'Just Like a Tree' is an homage to the being of an old black woman. They are part of a larger process, as Etienne tells us, 'Cause that's what life is. . . . 'Cause tomorrow will he [*sic*] his time to be turned over just like it's hers today. And after that, be somebody else time to turn over. And it keep going like that till it ain't nothing left to turn—and nobody left to turn it.[105]

* * *

Approximately thirty separate reviews of *Bloodline*, as well as a compilation of excerpts from two dozen more, were found among Gaines' papers. There were few negative remarks among these reviews, most of which were offset by praise.

[105]Hicks, "To Make These Bones Live," 13-14, 16.

Granville Hicks in *Saturday Review*, August 17, 1968, said "Gaines has trouble in winding up [some] stories. In spite of my reservations about the ending, they are strong stories. . . . Gaines knows how to create living characters and to set them against a rich and vivid background."

Bookshelf's reviewer, August 15, 1968, said, " 'Just Like a Tree' is complicated by being told from ten different viewpoints, with each character involved taking his or her turn. Gaines nearly accomplishes his aim, but it is still an awkward device for telling a simple story."

Sam B. Girgus of the *Providence Journal*, August 25, 1968, was one of a few reviewers who liked "Bloodline" the least of the five stories. "The story, which is weak, contrived and annoyingly romantic, seems to have been written with the idea of giving the author the opportunity to criticize the Negro's white oppressors. However, such obvious criticism is not necessary because Gaines' strongest arguments come from his clear descriptions of Southern Negro life. When he superimposes polemics on top of his story the point gets muddled and lost." Of "Three Men" Girgus says:

> The story is rich with political and social overtones while the main character comes off as being symbolic of all Negro youth who are seeking both independence from and participation in modern society. Taken as a whole the book offers an effective panoramic view of the country Negro. . . . The author's style is simple and straightforward. He avoids unnecessary embellishment but sometimes settles for a superficial sketch when a deeper probing of his subject matter might be more exciting and interesting.

In The *New York Times Book Review*, September 29, 1968, Laurence Lafore calls Gaines a naturalist. "Mr. Gaines' understanding of the scene is brilliantly subtle and complex. He makes his narrative into handsome formal designs. . . . In the longest, the title story, the naturalism is touched with cliches and formulae."

Another critic who liked "Just Like a Tree" the least of the collection, said that "Gaines seemed to have sacrificed some literary fire to his technique in showing how 10 different people react when an old lady is forced to migrate from Mississippi to Chicago." More subtle in the other stories, "he writes in idiom, but without the Uncle Tomistic ellipses, apostrophes and dashes that once were part of black literature written for whites. To call Gaines a 'racial' writer, however, would be like calling Tolstoy a Russian dialect writer."[106]

Curiously, one reviewer was offended at the book's earthiness, saying

> only his [Gaines'] rare talent brought me back for a second look, but now, having had it, I'll cross him off my reading list. . . . Only ["Bloodline"] . . . leaves the reader with a sense of satisfaction, of having been glad he read it. This, at first, is puzzling, but then the answer slowly emerges. To the same dark skinned characters—uneducated, comic, subservient—the author has added a magic touch. Dignity.[107]

"Bloodline" was David Green's favorite of the five stories. He admitted in the *Detroit News*, September 22, 1968, that he had begun "reading in the center of the book." He called "Bloodline" both the weakest and the strongest of the stories. "It is weakest because it tends to be melodramatic, Uncle Tomish; one can hear the banjos softly strumming in the background. But it is also the meatiest of the pieces, for in it Gaines unleashes the only real fury he reveals in this collection." It "has the cohesion and drama of a one-act play. There are moments of humor, but there also is the constant building of a tension as the meeting of the Laurents looms."

William Hogan of the *San Francisco Chronicle*, in an undated item, called *Bloodline* "a remarkable performance, fresh, original, moving, not a false note in any of it. . . . He

[106]*St. Paul Sun*, October 13, 1968.

[107]*Kannapolis* [North Carolina] *Daily Independent*, September 8, 1968.

[Gaines] is a growing, underrated talent. . . . I hope he attracts an audience with this performance. It is worth more than dozens of novels by lesser talents."

Another reviewer says, "Here Gaines very skillfully raps the knuckles of two violently opposed extremes. While he knows the rules must and are being charged, he holds out for legal redress rather than bloodletting. . . . He writes a cracking good tale with subtle undertones that stay with you."[108]

The Nashville *Tennessean*, September 15, 1968, called "Three Men" "a strongly symbolical story, rather a fictive rendering of a Greek play in which a young tough relates the odd kind of education that the experience of being in jail means to him." Of "Just Like a Tree" the reviewer said,

> Here is the insinuating edge of the knife of militancy and dissent jabbing, cutting through the structure of the plot, adding a mood of immediacy and the spirit of urgency, but the real spark of the piece is the will of old Aunt Fe . . . who will not be uprooted 'by the rebellion of the young.' . . . Gaines' story-endings are psychologically false for the most part, but one cannot quarrel too firmly about these. His memory is long for the 'voices' functioning in the manner of the Greek chorus, who tell what happens according to their own consciousness and in the tradition of the best story-tellers, from Chaucer to Faulkner. . . . To this, Gaines adds his own style, the folk speech, sentiment, and belief of the Louisiana ruralite given vitality in the modern pattern of protest for manhood and independence.

In the *Sacramento Bee*, August 18, 1968, Stanley Gilliam wrote:

> There is no uncertainty in his characterizations; he knows his people (so well, indeed, does he know them that some of this has to be autobiographical) and he shows them deftly and surely and sympathetically—although

[108]*Charlotte Observer*, September 8, 1968.

> he is never maudlin. This, the reader feels sure, is truth; for the truth can hurt, and one aches for the people of Gaines' Louisiana.

The *Fresno Bee*'s review of August 18, 1969, was enthusiastic, calling *Bloodline*

> a collection of five stories that are pure soul, baby. Gaines demands classification as not a Negro who is a fine writer, nor a fine writer who is a Negro, but purely and simply as a fine writer. He has all of the tools—acumen, beautiful simplicity of style and a remarkable ear for dialogue.

Comparing Gaines' work to that of other contemporary black writers, the reviewer says, "some of it [their writing is] memorable and some of it so steeped in vitriol it makes you gag." Gaines

> puts his ax to the grindstone but he projects himself as a story-teller first and a crusader second. . . . He does not write in English, he writes in soul, preserving a wonderful sense of speech and thinking. . . . There is an honesty and a sense of deep-rooted dignity in all of Gaines' stories, and best of all, his characters are not one-dimensional—that is to say, all good or all bad. Gaines may be a city-slicker these days but he can be thankful he has not forgotten the smell of salt meat in a frying pan or the cool taste of a tall glass of clabber.

Donald Stanley, a pro-Gainesist, wrote in the *San Francisco Examiner* in mid-August of 1968 that *Bloodline* was perhaps Gaines' best work. Not only was it "a magnificently wrought odyssey," but it silenced Gaines' critics by asking hard questions and offering "tentative answers."

A lengthy review in *Freedomways*,[109] said of Gaines:

[109]Loyle Hairston, Review of *Bloodline, Freedomways,* IX (1969), 262, 264, 265.

> He is, to put it simply and without exaggeration, one of the best writers we have produced, a story-teller with creative power of genius. With economy and clarity, he writes about ordinary people whose behavior and passions are as universal as they are commonplace. His work is not mired in sentimentality, neither is it tendentious despite his strong feelings for his characters.

In criticism of the book, the reviewer says:

> 'Bloodline,' the title story, is less successful than the others because its statement . . . is too explicit and it lacks the sustained emotional intensity which makes the other pieces so compelling. . . . The characters are fascinating but they are two-dimensional and the way they are manipulated by the author undermines their plausibility. Despite these flaws, this is still a powerful and well-told story. Apart from being a writer of feeling, depth, and sensitivity, Ernest Gaines is one of the best craftsmen writing fiction today. . . . *Bloodline* is *soul* writing at the level of fine literature.[110]

According to the *St. Louis Dispatch* reviewer, David W. Read, "'Bloodline' is absolutely worth reading. Mr. Gaines writes with authority, insight, and compassion, making articulate at last a world that has seemed inarticulate—except for its suffering—for too long."[111]

A pre-publication review in the *New Haven Register*, July 21, 1968, said:

> The reader is constantly reminded that change is here, now, and out of it will emerge freedom. But what form will it take? he asks. Will it be violent or non-violent? Undertaken with reason or insanity? For the

[110] *Ibid.*

[111] *St. Louis Dispatch,* August 11, 1968.

good of all blacks or for just a few? Gaines has avoided some of the errors other Negro authors have made. He is not guilty of one-sidedism, nor is he a pragmatist. Deftly, almost gently, he makes his points, one by one. His message is not one of 'burn' or 'kill whitey,' although he does not seem to rule out the possibility that certain militants may take this course. Rather, it is a message of compassion and understanding. The Old Order—and some of what is good about it—is slowly crumbling. In its place is a New Order and leading it are sensitive men and women whose motivations and goals are understandably different. Gaines' writing is directed toward them as well as indifferent whites; he pleads for change, to be sure, but change guided by rationality, not brute callous force.

* * *

Citations for the remaining reviews are footnoted.

In *Bloodline*, Ernest J. Gaines turns the soil of his native Louisiana bayou country with a hand contoured to the ax helve, the cane knife and the trace chain. The tone . . . is an agrarianism of the heart. . . . Unlike the agrarianism of many white writers, Gaines' is not an intellectualized yearning for a lost way of life, lost values. As the cotton springs pure from the dying boll, so his people, Gaines believes, can embody even in Babylon values as vital and rich as the loam that gave them birth.[112]

The title story is the most powerful and (hopefully) forecasts a novel. . . . Few novelists of any complexion can handle the short story form with such compelling ease.[113]

[112]Winston-Salem, N. C., *Journal*, October 6, 1968.

[113]*The Kirkus Service*, July, 1968.

> There are five stories in this volume and they are like five sculptures in a setting; each is distinct, its own, but there is one unifying landscape. . . . He [Gaines] does not strain to create figures of mythic proportion, but several of the figures achieve this.[114]

> Gaines conveys the warm beauty of the illiterate, and as practitioner of the logical extension of an oral medium, he has trained his ears extremely well. All of the narratives are in the first person, and the author's feeling for dialect augments the relaxed tone of his writing. . . . 'Bloodline' is the strongest story in the book. . . . Each of its characters are archetypes, and are more three dimensional than the narrator himself. . . . It is full of symbols and metaphorical meanings. . . . Cooper's error, if we choose to hold it as such was this: he denied his own capability and omitted the possibility of creating his own God, or his own conceptual image of a God. Symbolically his words are a contradiction against even his own real name, Christian; yet Gaines has given us an honest portrait of a bitter angry young black which is deemed par for the course. *Bloodline* gives Afro-American folklore a shot in the arm. In literature we hope it is the beginning of a resourceful new trend.[115]

> He [Gaines] has a marvelous ear for speech rhythms, content, and dialect; a deep knowledge of the people, black and white, of the region; and a rich fund of humor, compassion, and understanding. This is a good book—one which cannot be skimmed—for short story collections.[116]

[114]*The New Orleans Review*, (n. d.); © 1970 by Loyola University, New Orleans. Reprinted by permission of the *New Orleans Review*.

[115]*Nickel Review*, October 23, 1968.

[116]*Library Journal*, (July, 1968).

He's [Gaines is] every good storyteller I've ever heard. But in the same way it took the elders years of telling to perfect, to shape the tale just right, Gaines too is not the 'natural' he appears to be. The seemingly unrehearsed, nonchalant, uninsistent weaving of the story is no improvisation; it is a very careful rendering of an experience. It's just that the agony of pulling the whole thing off is never felt, for Gaines does not inflict his reader with the writer's problems of craft. He does not exhibit his wares or call attention to the well-wrought line, the seductive truth, the witty dialogue, the precisioned insight in that self-conscious way that has become the hallmark of contemporary artists. Gaines simply does it without neon and trumpets. The pages show no sweat, no erasures. You have to love a writer behind that.[117]

The dominant sound in Gaines' folk-tales of plantation life is the pure melody of the talented story-teller, singing of the world he knows best. . . . Gaines . . . seemingly is more interested in telling a tight, well-planned short story than in generating black power literature. He has a sensitive ear for the colloquial, and the soft, lilting cadence of Southern speech rings true.[118]

He [Gaines] writes in the dialect that reflects only too clearly the apathy and the misery of a three-century bondage. His words are both appalling and appealing because they describe something living and capable of loving, but able to do them only mutely. If only his characters could get angry, it would absolve us of just a little guilt. Writing passionately with restraint is incredibly difficult, yet this relatively new author has a highly finished product. The title story is one of the

[117]*Liberator* (London), December, 1969.

[118]*Boston Sunday Globe*, November 3, 1968.

> finest short stories that I've ever reviewed. It is the battle of two bastards for the control of the future of the South. . . . Cooper is illegitimate by birth; Frank by our culture. . . . How does an author capture and express a mood so completely? Is it an art that can be learned?
>
> When it is done with the precision of this author, when it seems to be done so effortlessly, I think it is the token of native genius, or at least a touch of it. . . . This book should enjoy great circulation in public libraries and among serious college students.[121]

> Mr. Gaines' skill lies in his well-nigh perfect ear for dialog and his ability to recapture people and situations familiar to him. Each incident is forthright and dramatic; the people are honest, proud and above all, very real.[122]

In an undated item from *Book World* found in Gaines' papers writer Ralph Ellison (*The Invisible Man*) chose *Bloodline* as one of his three "Books I Liked Best in 1968."

THE AUTOBIOGRAPHY OF MISS JANE PITTMAN

Millions of words, mostly ones of praise, have been written about *The Autobiography of Miss Jane Pittman*, first published in 1971 by Dial Press, and about the television film made from it which aired in early 1974. Its audience of both readers and viewers has been vast.

In 1971 G. K. Hall issued a large print paperback of the novel. By mid-1975 850,000 copies in paperback and over 26,000 hardback copies had been sold, figures amply surpassing the total of Gaines' previous three books. By August of 1986 *Miss Jane* had been reprinted over twenty-eight times by Dial and Bantam Books, and had been translated into several foreign

[121] *Best Sellers*, August 15, 1968.

[122] *Publisher's Weekly*, June 3, 1968.

languages, including German, Dutch, Swedish, Japanese, Chinese, Spanish and Russian. It was the first of Gaines' novels to make substantial money for him, though its precedent of *Bloodline* firmly established him as one of the best contemporary writers.

Even with such success from *Miss Jane*, Gaines never intended that it be his peak novel for the rest of his writing career. He wanted to top it. Gaines' many honors and awards for *Miss Jane* have been mentioned in Part I, between the years 1971-78. There was disappointment, especially from agent Dorothea Oppenheimer, that it received neither a Pulitzer prize, for which it was nominated, nor a National Book Award. According to Gaines, she felt that Dial Press should have promoted more publicity for it. William Hogan of the *San Francisco Chronicle* (April 17, 1972) suggested constructively, "Give him [Gaines] your own award by reading *Miss Jane Pittman*."

Miss Jane is dedicated to the memory of Julia McVay, Gaines' grandmother, to his stepfather, Mr. Ralph Norbert Colar, Sr., and to the memory of "My beloved aunt, Miss Augusteen Jefferson, who did not walk a day in her life, but who taught me the importance of standing."

In 1970, when the manuscript of *Miss Jane* was finished, Gaines sent it to *Cosmopolitan* hoping that this magazine would choose to serialize it. Favorably excited, *Cosmopolitan* agreed. But through ensuing correspondence the editors discovered that the book was a novel, not an authentic autobiography, and they reneged. Many other readers of *Miss Jane*, including a representative of *Newsweek* who wanted a photo of Miss Jane, were also reluctant to accept her as a fictitious character. Gaines recalls an elderly woman's answer when asked who she thought Ernest Gaines was: "Well, I guess he edited the book for Miss Pittman," she said.

* * *

As mentioned in the preface of *A Gathering of Gaines*, the list of outstanding events which Gaines compiled with Alvin

Aubert provided a basic framework within which to structure *Miss Jane.* Miss Jane is her own narrator for the novel, set in 1962. At the age of 110 she tells her story to a school teacher, as chronologically as she can recollect, from the time she was a youngster of ten. Her name was not Jane, but Ticey, while she grew up as a plantation slave before and during the Civil War. Just as the war ended she took the name Jane Brown, suggested to her by "Mr. Brown," a kind Union soldier. As a freed Negro she naively heads for Ohio to gentler life, in hopes of finding Mr. Brown. She narrowly escapes the violent massacre of other freed black people by Klansmen and defeated Confederate soldiers just after she leaves the plantation. She and Ned, a small black boy whose mother was killed in the onslaught, are the only survivors. Ignorant of direction and terrain, Jane and Ned travel in circles on foot, encountering some kindness but mostly unpleasantness, finally to realize they are still in "Luzana" not too far from their former plantation.

Once established on another plantation Jane and Ned become a family. Ned gets some schooling, despite the havoc caused by Reconstruction. By the time he is seventeen he is already working to promote the civil rights movement. He urges Jane to leave for Kansas with him, but she will not. Soon she marries Joe Pittman, an excellent horse trainer and farm-hand. They remain on the plantation for ten years, laboring to pay off a debt. Miss Jane would like children, but cannot bear them, due to an old injury from a beating.

After they have moved to another plantation, Miss Jane has recurring premonitions of Joe's death while he is breaking a wild horse, a challenge which actually does cause his death. Ned comes back with his wife and begins teaching, hoping to build a new school for the blacks. He is not welcomed by the whites, namely devious Albert Cluveau, who pretends to be Jane's friend. Eventually Cluveau kills Ned, a blow for which Miss Jane has psychologically prepared herself, since she has never completely trusted Cluveau. In a short while Cluveau, who lives with his two daughters, goes berserk.

Miss Jane has now lost the two men that she loved, Jim and Ned. She joins the church, but would rather listen to a baseball game on the radio than attend services. Miss Jane can neither help knowing about nor help a young white man, Tee Bob, who finds himself hopelessly in love with a Creole school teacher who has not encouraged the affair, despite the claims of Tee Bob's family, friends, and his parrain (godfather), Jules Raynard. Tee Bob cannot fight the rules of white society, however, and in his loneliness and misery, he stabs himself.

Jimmy, a young black of Ned's caliber and aspiration, is looked up to as being The One, the person who will bring about change, as Ned had tried to. He fights for civil rights to his own detriment, and as Ned was killed, Jimmy is killed. However, he has had enough success with organizing a peaceful march into Bayonne that blacks can now drink from the public water fountain. Miss Jane is the silent spokesperson for the blacks as she walks proudly by Tee Bob's hostile father, Robert, without speaking. The reader is certain that she will continue to the fountain and drink from it, thus scoring a victory not only for herself, but for her people.

* * *

Author's note: Because every page of *Miss Jane* is rich in quotable dialogue and/or description, selected examples will not be included in this discussion. The reader would better profit from reading *Miss Jane* for himself.

* * *

Miss Jane has not only been called the story of a 110-year-old black woman, but an historical chronicle as well. Though Gaines did extensive historical research in preparing *Miss Jane*, history as such was never intended to upstage Miss Jane's story. Gaines rather meant to show the uneducated but natively astute Miss Jane's interpretation of the events of a century (1862-1962) and how they affected her own life and milieu. The idea for this novel had been brewing, off and on, in Gaines' mind for about ten years before it came to fruition, ever since his first trip back to South Louisiana in 1963.

A vast amount of reading, research, and interviewing older black people on the plantation to absorb the rhythm of their speech went into Miss Jane's narrative. Gaines' structural method has been compared to that of *Lay My Burden Down*, published as a WPA project in 1945, which recounted stories told by slaves. He freely admits that this book was invaluable to him, having read at least a hundred of its interviewed stories in order to get the Negro speech rhythms and pronounciations of other Southern areas. Then he fused these sounds and rhythms with those of his own people on River Lake into the voice of Miss Jane.

In *Miss Jane* Gaines aimed to create a folk autobiography, not a folk biography, which he said might carry too many lies by way of folk tales. When he began to think of the conversational procedure he knew that Miss Jane, never having been to school, must tell things solely from memory, things she herself remembered and things that other people told her. Miss Jane was not modeled physically after Gaines' Aunt Augusteen, but he did want her moral strength to show through Miss Jane, as "a black woman on her toes." From taking definite action in the first part of the book as a young woman, she later sits and observes. This is not a sign of weakness by any means, but rather because of her age, intuitiveness, wisdom, and vast experience she is emotionally able to undergo and transcend traumas that characters in Gaines' earlier books could not have handled.

Gaines has said that he did what he wanted to do in writing *Miss Jane*, that it did not happen accidentally, that it was carefully schemed out. When asked if he might have changed anything, or given emphasis in different ways, he mentioned Joe Pittman and the horse. He would have done more with this, and also with Miss Jane's travels, and with her conversion from "sinner" to religious person. Too, he would have done more reading on black folklore, religious interpretations, the ministry, voodoo, and general history.

A part of his scheme included the Introduction. As Gaines told John O'Brien,

> It [the introduction] was the first thing I wrote. I

> couldn't see the novel any other way. . . . I could not see how a person who is a-hundred-and-ten years old could actually tell the story, and I wanted to use the whole community to help. . . . I've seen this kind of story telling many times before. One person may be the main narrator but there were these other people around to help her along if she could not remember or if she got tired talking. I also used the Introduction because I wanted to explain some things about my writing. . . . The book covers a hundred years and I wanted the reader to know exactly how all this came to pass . . . As an explanation for when Miss Jane started rambling from one episode to the next. I suppose I also put it there to make the story seem credible. It is hard for people to believe somebody like Miss Jane really exists.[123]

The chapter in *Miss Jane* titled "The Hunter" was published in *Black World* (formerly *Negro Digest*), July, 1975, a few months before the book was issued. Gaines' skillful use of dynamics is exemplified in this scene, one of calm assurance as opposed to the swift violence of the massacre which preceded it.

Gaines wrote and rewrote the memorable massacre scene many times. He did not aim at violence alone, but more so at accuracy. He told interviewer Charles H. Rowell:

> I don't know of any other writer who has done a more violent scene than that. At the same time, my aim was to write well. . . . to get the dialogue that was going on at that time, as well as the swinging of the clubs, as well as the noises made in the bush, in the shrub, in the trees, and among the leaves. I wanted to get the sun coming down through the trees, on the ground where the men lay dead, and a woman lay dying with a child clutched in her arms. This is what I mean by doing it well no matter what you're doing—no matter what the politics or what

[123]O'Brien, *Interviews*, pp. 92-93.

> the violence is. . . . If you are going to use words, put them where they are going to have the greatest and most lasting effect. . . . My aim in writing will always be at perfecting a sentence, just as the aim of the great fighter (or any other athelete) is perfecting his style, making the right move at the right time.[124]

O'Brien asked Gaines about the naïveté of the history teacher, the interviewer who hopes to improve his teaching through listening to Miss Jane's narrative. "There is the suggestion that he may be missing the most important and subtle things about what Miss Jane tells him," in her ramblings. "He wants her to tell him about facts and events; she succeeds in explaining 'how' history works."

Gaines' reply was,

> Yes, I think he's naive in a way, just as we all are naive about the true history of blacks in this country . . . . We don't have the story of the average black who has lived to be that age. . . . He does see that she is not going in any definite direction . . . but Miss Jane has not read all these books on what a narrative should be and she could only narrate history the way she saw it.[125]

* * *

Gaines has said that collecting the information for *Miss Jane* was not as large a problem as using it through the voice of an illiterate person possessing tremendous common sense and intelligence—one who did not know how to speak about it in proper English. He has said,

> Even if the house was exploding around me, I was going to write *Miss Jane*. I always had faith in what I

[124]Rowell, "This Louisiana Thing," 45-46.

[125]O'Brien, *Interviews*, pp. 92-93.

> was writing about. . . . If I had to lose everything doing so, I would just have to lose it. . . . The difference in Faulkner and myself is that I ate in Miss Jane's kitchen, and Faulkner would have had her cooking in it. Miss Jane is feeding me now.

Since the publication of *Miss Jane*, when Gaines is in Oscar, Louisiana, he is invited to the "big house. We sit and have a little coffee, a little sherry. They act as though I've been in that room all my life. . . . If anyone stopped buying *Miss Jane* tomorrow, I might have to dig ditches maybe two years from now."[126]

Before writing about an unfamiliar subject, Gaines is very careful to explore it to the fullest. In an undated speech among his papers he said:

> I would have an idea for a scene and check it with an expert. Bill Decker [then senior editor at Dial Press] had written a book about a cowboy, TO BE A MAN, and he knew horses. 'Bill, I'm trying to write this God damn story here [*Miss Jane*] and I've got my man [Joe Pittman] getting killed on a horse. This guy's a damn good rider, man. He's one of the chief horse breakers. Suppose I have a horse, now, sort of like the Moby Dick of the ocean. I'm gonna have this horse—it's a horse that every man ain't supposed to break. What do I do? Listen, I have this guy go out to this horse without a saddle, because he's in a hurry—got to get out of here—he ropes the horse and the horse jerks him off of his own horse and because he hasn't got anything in the world to fight this horse with, the horse drags him off and drags him through the swamps—off through the trees and rocks and things like that. He keeps getting up, he keeps falling back down. Listen, could the horse kill this guy?' Bill said, 'Hell yes, he can kill him!' I said, 'O. K., Good, man, I got my story.'

[126]*Arkansas Gazette,* April 24, 1977.

In an article titled "Miss Pittman's Background" written by Gaines for The *New York Times Book Review*, he said more about his research for *Miss Jane*. Recalling the many-faceted conversation with Alvin Aubert, he recalled:

> For the past year or so I had been doing research in the San Francisco Public Library and also bought books for my own personal library. But there were still many gaps. I needed to know more about Louisiana history, myths and traditions. About Creoles and Cajuns and Mardi Gras, and La Toussaint and gumbo and jambalaya, and sugar cane fields and the bayous. And about Angola State Penitentiary and the state mental hospital in Jackson. I had already talked to many people in Baton Rouge and in Pointe Coupée Parish, where I come from. I had gone back to the River Lake Plantation, where I was born and raised. An old man called Walter Zeno—my model for Pap in *Miss Jane* — and I spent many hours talking about things that had happened in that part of Louisiana. Mr. Zeno could remember many things vividly by associating them with 'the last frost,' 'the last big storm' 'the time so and so was drowned in a certain bayou.' But he could not remember dates, years, distances, numbers. Now I went to the library to fill in what he and others like him could not remember and also to verify what these people had told me. The state librarian, Sallie Farrell, gave me all the information I asked for and even suggested things I might have overlooked. There was documented information about Angola and the Jackson mental hospital that Walter Zeno and other people in the field could never have known about. And after my return to San Francisco, she sent me copies of documents that I asked her for and suggested books that I was able to get from the Louisiana State Library through my branch of the San Francisco Public Library.
>
> Next to God, Huey Long is the most talked about subject in Louisiana. I had read books and articles about

> Long, but one thing I needed for my novel and could not find was how the weather was at the hour of his funeral. When I returned to Louisiana a year later to do more research, that was one of the questions I asked people. Some one would tell me that it had rained that day; someone else would say it *was raining*. Still someone else would say the sun was blazing hot because he was at the funeral and he could remember it burning the back of his neck.
>
> I went back to the library, this time to the LSU Library, to see Evangeline Lynch. Miss Lynch is in charge of the Louisiana Room of the LSU Library. She and I had a cup of coffee together, and I told her what I needed. . . . Every paper in the country had written about the death of the Kingfish [Long], and every article was right there. But only one of them had anything about the weather—a three-inch story in an Arkansas paper. 'Intermittent showers', it said. So the information I had gotten in the field was right. In September it rains in Louisiana all the time. Five minutes after the rain ceases, the sun can burn the back of your neck.

Gaines used much of his research, but noticed that he had neglected some minor points. He continued,

> Twain once said to Rudyard Kipling: 'Know your subject well, then distort.' Lester Young might have said the same thing when playing all around the note and seldom touching on it. And of course Count Basie at the piano is a genius at leaving out everything except what is absolutely necessary.[127]

Gaines talked more about the process of writing *Miss Jane* in the previously mentioned speech at Southern University. Since he had used the narrative technique in "Just Like a Tree" he felt it would be easy, but

[127]*New York Times Book Review,* August 10, 1975.

> what in the world would these people talk about that could possibly fill five hundred pages? . . . The things I found in common, both while talking to people and reading books, was that to a point I would get the same answer, and then personal opinions would come in. When I talked to an educated black man and an uneducated black man about Huey Long I got different interpretations. The same results when reading the papers of the North and the papers of the South, or reading history books by black historians and by white historians.
>
> I started writing . . . with this idea of narration in mind: that different characters would tell the story of her life in their own way. . . . I followed this multiple point of view technique for a year, then I discarded it.

Originally it was titled *A Short Biography of Miss Jane Pittman*, but was changed when he decided that Miss Jane should tell it herself.

> I had fallen in love with my little character, and I thought she could tell the story of her life much better than anyone. . . . Who is Miss Jane—and what does she represent? . . . Miss Jane is Miss Jane. she is not my aunt, she is not any one person. . . . She knows much—she has lived long. . . . Sometimes she's impatient, but most times she's just the opposite. If you take time to ask her a question you will find her to be quite dogmatic. You will say, 'But that's not it, that's not it, that's not it.' But she will stick to her beliefs. Truth to Miss Jane is what she remembered. Truth to me is what people like Miss Jane remember. . . . I try in some way to get the answer. But I'm afraid I have not gotten it yet. Maybe in the next book, or the one after, or the one after. Maybe!

In an interview with Ruth Laney, he said of the courageous Miss Jane that he admired her small size, her individuality, her frank preference of hearing a baseball game on the radio to a live church service (especially a game between the Giants and the Dodgers). This has nothing to do, however, with her basic pholosophy of living.[128]

About the character of Tee Bob, Gaines said: "He was an innocent person caught up in something he had no control over. . . . Tee Bob was a victim. He had no strength, he was not tough and hard. He *loved*, you know, but you can't just make it on love. You got to be able to do other things." Gaines felt that Jules Raynard, Tee Bob's parrain (godfather) might have been more communicative, closer, with Miss Jane had she been white.[129]

Speaking of Miss Jane as a "representative" as opposed to a "real" personage Gaines told an interviewer for *New Wings*: "She represents something universal. Southerners, white and black, have told me 'This could be *my* grandmother.'" Comparing Miss Jane's ability to elicit response from others to that quality in Huck Finn, Gaines considered both chaacters appealing to readers of any nationality. In particular, he thought Southerners would like their subbornness, a quality also possessed by Scarlett O'Hara.[130]

The *Shreveport Times* (undated) quoted Gaines as saying: "Black writers are said not to be universal, but I have my doubts about that. A German critic said of Miss Jane that she was one of the greatest characters in literature. There must have been something universal about her."

After Gaines had read from *Miss Jane* in Baton Rouge at the YWCA on March 6, 1976, someone asked him why Miss Jane was important. He replied,

> Anyone who had lived 110 years in a country like this, under the conditions she lived and could love God, could still love baseball, and ice cream, was worth

[128]Laney, "A Conversation with Ernest Gaines," 8.

[129]*Ibid.*, 7.

[130]Reid and Contis, "Searching for Miss Jane,"11, 20.

> writing about. . . . If she could come out as a whole human being after living 110 years with the kind of life she had to live, she is worth writing about. Survival with sanity and love and a sense of responsibility, and getting up and trying all over again not only for one's self but for mankind—those achievements I find worth writing about. Miss Jane, not generals who had killed thousands of people . . . Miss Jane, who loved humankind so much she did not have to kill one person to continue life.

Gaines really felt that Miss Jane was a "little old lady" who had done something for other people's lives.[131]

Regarding the matter of Miss Jane's reality, John F. Callahan said in a Marshall-Woods lecture at Lewis and Clark College (December, 1973):

> Gaines' triumph is that his novel convinced these editors that Miss Jane Pittman was an authentic historical person. The response [to the book] reveals a continuing color line of culture which Gaines' growing audience is dissolving reader by reader. So this novel's journey parallels that of its character. Gaines' risks, stamina, vision, and achievement are in the heroic tradition. Slowly, his novel has begun a journey, against setbacks, toward a terrain where freedom is a national matter of consciousness and action.[132]

* * *

Miss Jane has been required course reading for English students, as well as the focus of numerous term papers and critical essays ever since its publication. (Oddly enough, no dissertations on Gaines or *Miss Jane* are listed in *Dissertation*

[131]Unidentified news item found in Gaines' papers.

[132]The Callahan lecture is among Gaines' papers.

Abstracts International). *Miss Jane* charms, instructs, provokes thought, and invites discussion and analysis. The essayists who have written on the book's many facets, have found much in it to ponder, both in structure and technique. In Gaines' papers are several drawings and letters from middle school children attending Walnut Hill Elementary School in Baton Rouge who have interpreted *Miss Jane* in their own way. One of the drawings shows author Gaines in a car.

* * *

John O'Brien says Miss Jane is a "character who works harmoniously with time." She views time itself as change, and because of this man is able to order the present.

> Otherwise he becomes a slave to history and a stifling social order that blindly repeats the evils of the past. . . . Gaines, with some remorse about the loveliness of certain qualities of the past, reaches toward a future that can potentially shape the world in a more humane way. Death is not the ultimate enemy that man submits to out of despair and frustration, but is part of a natural process which in itself is good and in which man must take his place.[133]

Along a similar train of thought, Ronald G. Billingsley picked Ned as an example of someone who gave his all to what he thought was right, and because he needed a positive definition for himself, he was willing to give his life. He refused to live as a "nigger," as defined by the white community.[134] Another essayist points out the difference in Miss Jane's and Ned's standards and compares her passivity to his unrest. His death prompted progress because the community finished the school that he started and a usable past was thereby conserved on which

[133]O'Brien, *Interviews*, p. 80.

[134]Ronald G. Billingsley, "Forging New Definitions," 15-21.

to build a "viable future." Miss Jane travels toward salvation after "finding religion," and her psychological development has prepared her for the last act of self-assertion. Various characters in *Miss Jane* are seeking escape, each in a different way.[135]

A writer in *Phylon* rated *Miss Jane* as superior over other contemporary novels about blacks, commenting that the reader of *Miss Jane* gets "a sense of the continuity of a black spiritual assertion both in everyday life and in its struggles against oppression." Though he felt a lack of intensity in the passages when Miss Jane does not have center stage, he called the novel a "fine remaking and regrasping of the dense past deriving from secure grasp of black culture and its mixtures."[136]

In a critical essay, titled "Ernest J. Gaines—Change Growth and History," found in Gaines' papers without date or author named, the writer presented an in-depth study of *Miss Jane.*

> She's some 110 years old when she tells her story, time enough for her to have lost her edge of independence and pride. But those qualities echo from every word she speaks. . . . She's an attractive combination of the idealist and practicalist. Above all, Jane has a capacity for growth, for change. . . . She brings into Gaines' fictional world a new element, a new relationship between black men and women. Miss Jane seeks collaboration with her black men, not control of them.
>
> Jane's relationship with her men has an explicit political meaning. . . . To break the white man's control, some kind of political action is required to force change. . . . The political act, performed in courage, suggests Gaines, is the sign of growth, and implies both duration and satisfaction.

[135]William L. Andrews, "We Ain't Going Back There: The Idea of Progress in *The Autobiography of Miss Jane Pittman," Black American Literature Forum* (Winter, 1977), 146-149.

[136]George E. Kent, "Struggle for Image: Selected Books By or About Blacks During 1971," *Phylon,* XXXIII (1972), 308.

The depth and value of *Miss Jane*, however, is

> Gaines' understanding of what this political point means at the level of common life and its disruptive effects upon the lives and emotions of simple, apolitical people. . . . One of Gaines' real accomplishments [is] the matter-of-fact conveyance of true heroism, and the treatment of political subjects without ideological stridency or sociological apologetics.

Continuing on Gaines' skill, the writer finds one fault, one not present, however, in *Miss Jane*.

> His [Gaines'] self-consciousness about point of view reflects a common concern of many novelists, but it has produced in his writing some annoying mannerisms. Most irritating, he calls the reader's attention to the fact that the narrator can't know everything and therefore must rely on observers who were on the scene of the action to be reported. . . . *The Autobiography* transforms this weakness into one of the basic strengths of the novel. Not only does Miss Jane use eye-witness accounts of events that make up her narrative, some of the details that she describes as if her own come from someone else. . . . It's an impressively organized novel. . . . *The Autobiography* illustrates the way in which character not only permeates history but is the vehicle for its transmission.

Professor Alvin Aubert, longtime friend of Gaines, wrote that the mass graves in *Miss Jane* are an erasure of the past and a symbol of hope for the future. God created man as a free and responsible being, but man creates the situations that complicate his life. Things may usually be reunified with the help of a visionary leader, such as Ned or Jimmy in *Miss Jane*.[137]

[137]Aubert, "Ernest J. Gaines' Truly Tragic Mulatto," 72.

Barry Beckhman in an essay, "Jane Pittman and Oral Tradition," said that Gaines "had achieved a triumph of style" in this novel. His skill in story-telling techinques, largely oral testimony, has led to a larger appreciation of his accomplishments. His selection of a few of Miss Jane's words in her inimitable black dialect is impressive and amusing: fiyer (for you); Luzana (Louisiana); retrick (rhetoric); Fedjal Goviment (Federal Government); invessagator (investigator); bue (but); 'pending (depending); and lectwicity (electricity). He recognizes that Gaines not only wants to preserve the authenticity of speech but to cherish its special quality.

Other devices Gaines uses are past tenses of verbs (such as gived for gave); the ommision of the possessive form ("That's my girl name. . ."); deletion of definite articles; absence of verbs; redundancy; improper agreement of subject and verb; and a generalized use of tense. Gaines "possesses an ear (and transfers that sensitivity to his narrator, Jane) for oral utterances which may be said to vibrate with an inherently appealing verbal good." Spacing these passages of "pleasant orality" shows Gaines' narrative control.

Beckhman also points out unpleasant oralities, used to convey the bad person, or an undesirable quality in someone. Verbal abuse is another of Gaines' devices, used in some instances when Jane decides to tell someone off for misbehaving or being smart-alecky. Gaines uses "incidental directness . . . a larger technique of the art of narration or the art of ordering episodes into a coherent testimony," like a story within a story, or an aside. He creates narrative tension by announcing what will happen later (such as someone's death), and then inserting other events before fully relating the announced one. In this way Miss Jane has courted the listener, brought him into her own private theater, "kindled his interest and then satisfied him with an episode of romantic disaster."[138]

Albert Wertheim provides further insight. Jane's journey is not so much of miles as it is "spiritual and sociological,

[138]Barry Beckhman, "Jane Pittman and Oral Tradition," *Callaloo,* (May, 1978), 107-108.

played against the changing landscape of race relations in the deep South." The book ends, but the epic journey of black people does not, as the civil rights movement is imminent. Jane rather represents the motive of the black masses. Wertheim places the blacks in *Miss Jane* in three categories: those who assert themselves, knowing they may die for doing so; those who are silent and remain obscure as a means to survive (a "tragic pattern" pervading the book); and the group that Jane calls "niggers"—the ones "who have neither open nor suppressed definance but willingly, unquestioningly, accept a slave mentality and the idea of natural inferiority."

Wertheim compares Gaines' landscapes and the people who inhabit them to those of George Eliot. He says that Miss Jane's silent screams (when Cluveau tells her that he will kill Ned) symbolize the silent suffering of all blacks. Ned's efforts symbolize Gaines' moving and eloquent picture of the black man's role in America—that of making blacks Americans. He could have gone further by writing in a white horse rather than a black one, as Jim's killer, symbolizing the white man, as did the film of *Miss Jane*. Other symbolism might be read into Miss Jane's travels across the river, which give her a spiritual freedom, a rebirth not connected with religion.

In Gaines' chapter abstractly titled "Of Men and Rivers" a symbolic context is provided for Tee Bob's episode: man can control neither rivers nor human life by segregation, slavery, or unnatural restrictions. As Jules Raynard says, society's rules killed Tee Bob. "Increasingly in the novel the games and rules are no longer completely in the white man's hands and Jane's admiration for the emergent breed of black sports figures—Robinson, Louis, Liston—underscores the growing adeptness of blacks at white games." Wertheim calls Miss Jane's line at the end of the book, "Me and Robert looked at each other there a long time, then I went by him," a "line of triumph: one that marks a new beginning rather than an end."[139]

[139]Albert Wertheim, "A Journey to Freedom: Ernest Gaines' *The Autobiography of Miss Jane Pittman*," in Peter Bruck and Wolfgang Karrer, eds., *The Afro-American Novel*, pp. 220-224.

* * *

Gaines said in his speech for the Modern Language Association in 1981 that a young lady from Turkey who had read *Miss Jane* had told him he was still writing letters for the old people. "The language," she said, "the language. The rhythm of the sentence, the vocabulary, the dialogue, it's all about the old people. . . . That's all you're doing in your work, writing those letters. *Miss Jane Pittman* is just one long letter. Oh, I said, I didn't know that.'"

* * *

Reviews of *Miss Jane* are too numerous to include *in toto* here, even if they were all available, but suffice it to say that practically every book critic in America had comments about *The Autobiography of Miss Jane Pittman*. A representative list of reviews in American journals may be found in the *Book Review Digest*, 1971 and 1972. *Miss Jane* also received reviews in leading foreign journals and newspapers, particularly in Germany and Japan, after it had been translated into those languages.

One of the most thoughtful reviews came from Gaines' friend, author Alice Walker. In a letter to Gaines shortly after Walker's review in The *New York Times*, May 23, 1971, she apologized for her lack of clout with that particular paper. She called *Miss Jane* a

> grand, robust, most valuable novel that is impossible to put down. Gaines' handling of her [Miss Jane's] religious belief, her faith in God, is marked by humility before the reality of Miss Jane's spiritual experience of physical endurance, before the living result of her belief in God. For Miss Jane leaned on a god who, in turn, supported her; whether He was dead or had never existed was a question she did not need to raise.

Readers might say, Walker continues, that since politics are "strung throughout the rich and very big novel that it is about politics." But Gaines is too skilled a writer "to be stuck in so sordid, so small a category." His preoccupations with Southern politics as they relate to the Negro show in all his works, but they never "obscure the stoical dignity and worth of the people they have largely been used against. Nor must they be more than an underscoring of what is most obvious about the people they represent." Gaines presents the rednecks, despite their racism as people, nevertheless, as having a "haggard futility, a pale and shrieking dullness, a pained unsatisfiedness that makes them appear wounded and deficient and far less complete than the blacks they attempt to intimidate." The whites never quite get the best of the blacks, because Gaines' heroes are so strong and heroic. "They have seen the level to which mankind can sink and have managed to remain standing all these many years."

Walker places Gaines closer to Dickens, DuBois, Toomer, and Langston Hughes than to Richard Wright or Ralph Ellison.

> There is nothing in Gaines that is not open, to love or to interpretation. He also claims and revels in the rich heritage of Southern black people and their customs; the community he feels with them is unmistakable and goes deeper even than pride. . . . Gaines is mellow with historical reflection, supple with wit, relaxed and expansive, because he does not equate his people with failure.

Geoffrey Wolff's review from *Newsweek* was partially included on the jacket of *Miss Jane.* Comparing Miss Jane to Dilsey in Faulkner's *The Sound and the Fury* for her endurance, Wolff says,

> Gaines' novel brings to mind other great works: 'The Odyssey' for the way his heroine's travels manage to summarize the American history of her race, and 'Huckleberry Finn' for the clarity of her voice, for her

> rare capacity to sort through the mess of years and things to find the one true story in it all.

Josh Greenfeld in *Life*, May 10, 1971, said,

> Never mind that [the book] . . . offered up in the form of taped reminiscences is artifice. The effect is stunning. [It exudes a] refreshing mix of wit and wrath, imagination and indignation, misery and poetry. And I can recall no more memorable female character in Southern fiction since Lena of Faulkner's *Light in August* than Miss Jane Pittman herself.

Time, January 3, 1972, selected it as one of "The Year's Best Books for 1971." An undated review from *Teacher's Notes* found in Gaines papers scrutinized *Miss Jane* from a religious angle, saying that Jane always spoke on two levels: the surface level (one of philosophical matter-of-factness), and the under level, "always present to the discerning, [which] carries the burdens of a lifetime of sorrow and sadness, of terror and tragedy, of injustice and inhumanity." The critic compares this dual level to the structure of Negro spirituals: "The ostensible meaning conveys to the white masters what they want to hear. The underlying meaning contains the true import of the hymns—the essential knowledge that the blacks are circulating among themselves." He cites Jimmy as a Messiah figure, an often used literary device, who was chosen at birth as a leader of the plantation blacks. His Messiahship is comparable to that of the New Testament Christ, but very much related to present events in the black struggle for equality.

* * *

After *Miss Jane* was reprinted by Michael Joseph in London in January, 1973, a whole new set of reviews appeared. Writer James Baldwin, who was not particularly complimentary about *Of Love and Dust*, was quoted on a flyer which announced the book's coming: "I have waited for this book for a very long time, and so has everyone else in America, whether they know it or not. A great artist has begun the excavation of a bitter and healing truth."

The following, less accessible reviews from English and other United Kingdom newspapers, were collected in Gaines' papers. Many of them commented on the fact that Miss Jane was not a real person. Some are not dated; names or complete names are missing on others.

> She [Miss Jane] tells her own story of those hundred years of oppression in her own characteristic voice—vivid, touching, exciting and eye-opening, in a way no manifesto [could] be. But this is fiction. Technically and textually this is a staggering achievement. . . . Life on plantations and ranches comes sharply into focus. . . . A quite superb novel.[140]
>
> She [Miss Jane] is a representative of type, and therefore worthy of a place in United States Negro history. . . . This is not an angry book, so it won't be seized upon as a treatise by black extremists. It isn't a sell-out, either, to have to bear that saddest label of the whole civil rights dilemma, 'Uncle Tom.' Incidents are played out in the low key of genuine recall. The style is vernacular. Gaines has striven hard to produce a document of significance. He succeeds not because he says so, but because he stays out of sight.[141]
>
> Although it [*Miss Jane*] lacks the anger, and the dialectic of other more polemical efforts, it seems a useful contribution to the cause. . . . It is extremely simple. . . . Apart from a brief introduction, . . . [the] framework doesn't obtrude, and there is a real gain in the sharp, colloquial style in which the incidents are unfolded. . . . A very moving individual story which also provides an impressionistic history of the black

[140]*The Times* (London), February 1, 1973.

[141]*South Wales Echo*, n.d.

> American, the outstanding quality being the humour and lack of bitterness. . . . The book . . . has been much praised by no less a black apologist than James Baldwin, but one can't help wondering what militants like Angela Davis and Stokely Carmichael made of it. Presumably to them it would seem damagingly liberal, at best a disguised exercise in 'Uncle Tomism.' But if art of any kind can help to bring about political change, by influencing the way in which the great mass of non-activists feel, then this novel is surely a very good example.[142]

Nina Bawden of London's *Daily Telegraph*, compared *Miss Jane* to *Moll Flanders*, calling it "fiction masquerading as oral history. . . . Her [Miss Jane's] voice rings clear and true as a good bell." Though it is a story of more than just Jane,

> Mr. Gaines has not weakened his powerful tale with generalities. He has used the rhythms of Jane's speech, seen with her eyes, and through her courage and simplicity has shown us, as no factual account could ever do, the triumph of the human spirit. This is a beautiful and moving book.[143]

> Quietly written, with deep sincerity, by an author who worked on a Louisiana plantation when nine years old, the sad tale convinces.[144]

> And very good it is, a smooth-flowing account . . . a sort of traditional novel composed of action, characters, and moral conflicts.[145]

[142]*Glasgow Herald*, February 10, 1973

[143]*The* (London) *Daily Telegraph*, February 1, 1973.

[144]*Yorkshire Post*, n.d.

[145]*Birmingham Post*, February 17, 1973.

> [*Miss Jane* is] an interesting idea and provides some fine ironies of perspective, although it is hard to convey so briefly a real sense of time passing, and a few parts of Jane's life are much more memorable than others. Jane Pittman is a tough, realistic, Christian, superstitious, credulous, baseball-loving, convincing old woman, rendered by the author with love and without sentimentality. . . . This is a condensed history of black Americans written by one of them: it is repetitive and terrible. . . . It is an inspiring story of endurance and determination.[146]

Another critic called *Miss Jane*

> a pleasant hors d'oeuvre, combining personal and racial history into a rich amalgam, which manages to avoid the usual pitfalls of ethnic literature. . . . Her life . . . is unremarkably average, but for that reason all the more interesting. . . . in the way it mingles social documentation with personal history into an authentic whole. . . . [It is] an achievement [in] the sustained use of Southern idiom which . . . emerges as an immensely vital language with its roots planted firmly in [its] environment. . . . Miss Jane is a very deep character, warm, colourful, wise, honest and very conscious and finally optimistic for herself and her race. . . . not merely a catalogue of virtues—she is redeemed by her humour and her human ability, which saves her from being oppressively saintly.

Gaines has avoided the pitfall of being a "white nigger," or having too limited a view of white society by combining the "joint values of tolerance and radicalism in a work which stands secure on its own literary merit . . . enhanced by its social and political comment."[147]

[146]*Financial Times,* February 13, 1973.

[147]*Hibernia,* Febraury 16, 1973.

Denis Hatfield, in *The Cape Times*, February 3, 1973, calls *Miss Jane* "stirring and often poignant. . . . The style and the language are so simple, and the narrative has such convincing moments of hesitation and side-tracking, that one is almost entirely persuaded to accept this richly dimensioned book as a personal narrative, and forget that it is fiction. Mr. Gaines . . . has achieved a *tour de force* in this engrossing novel."

Another reviewer was not as enthusiastic.

> The ventriloquism—though full of circumstantial detail—is an artful but in the end not wholly achieved device. Miss Jane is certainly a memorable character, but she is endowed with such wise omniscience and goddess-like calm, that she doesn't quite ring true.[148]

> Despite its title, *The Autobiography of Miss Jane Pittman* is a novel . . . and the author—far from being Miss Jane Pittman—is a man, Ernest J. Gaines.[149]

> This is not an outstanding, or particularly original, novel. . . . But Gaines' rambling colloquial story has its moments of pathos and generally makes interesting reading.[150]

> Miss Jane's story is a bloody slice of life, a protracted blow-by-blow battle with the moonish ignorance of the plantation blacks and the quite unearthly greed and bestiality of the white Southerner. . . . It is true that, Lordy, nobody know the trouble she seen, but Jane is without self-regard and so the book is without sentimentality, which makes it all the more remarkable.[151]

---

[148]*The Observer* (London), February 4, 1973.

[149]*Smith's Trade News*, London, January, 1973.

[150]*Eastern Daily Press*, Norwich, Norfolk, February 8, 1973.

[151]*New Statesman*, February 9, 1973.

Speaking of *Miss Jane*'s being an oral biography, reviewer Robert Nye remarked in *The Guardian*:

> Mr. Gaines gets the voice right and tells a tale which cannot be read without anger, pity and respect. . . . One does not need to be a Marxist to see that the poor and the black have other experiences of American rats than the amatory ones dreamed up by Old Thingy.

As for resembling oral history, Nye continued, *Miss Jane*

> could well be a transcript from tape-recordings of an old woman reminiscing, in her own lively vernacular, about her 100 years of life. In the USA the book is being tipped as a Pulitzer Prize candidate, and critics are bracketing Gaines with Faulkner in the annals of Deep South literary masterpieces. . . . The book is full of the bogey-men of black people in American history—Klux Klan murderers, crooked sheriffs, corrupt officials. . . . As a statement on the sickness of American society, it takes some beating, because it has the force of fact.

Surprisingly, a critic for *The* (London) *Times Literary Supplement*,[152] found *Miss Jane*

> bitter beyond any doubt. . . . Cheerfully free of self-pity or dramatics, taking for granted unspeakable persecutions and endurances, faded into matter-of-factness by the suggestion of old age remembering, the record's implicit revelation of wickedness is nevertheless so hard that one would like to turn away from such truth. Of course the book is finely done—the detail as fresh as life, the rhythm of black Southern speech carrying the long chronicle easily, the characters

[152]*The Times Literary Supplement*, March 1, 1973.

> growing naturally out of detail and dialogue. But just to label it a *tour de force* is a dilution of the whole impact. . . . Critically it may be inadequate to say: it hurts to read it. But perhaps it is what the author would most like to hear said.

The Irish Press[153] said of *Miss Jane*:

> The device, and the story, are perfectly credible—as credible as the fine portrait of an ancient woman on the jacket of this book. The century of personal history is valuable as a human document and as an essay in the little known social history of part of the United States as seen through the eyes of the coloured people . . . its most indigenous inhabitants. The writing is succinct, vernacular and pithy. The effect on the mind is out of all proportion to this book's 250 pages. It could well have stretched to a bulky and baggy American epic, and it is a blessing that it was treated so much better.

Miss Jane even caught the attention of British critic Jack Cooke. Cooke viewed the post-Civil War reconstruction as a block to progress along political, legal or economic paths. The roles of blacks on the plantation changed very little until WW II inflicted its culture shock, and the ruralites began moving to the cities. Speaking of the evolution of jazz, Cooke likened the events that shaped jazz to the same ones that motivated and shaped Miss Jane's life. Poignancy, reconciliation, frustration, defeat, bitterness, anger, and fitting ends to means are often masked, but nevertheless present.

Cooke considered the book stylistically well constructed. Controlling events were dimly apprehended; for instance, Reconstruction's end was not a positive act or the beginning of something, but rather a void. The characters were skillfully thinned out by migration to the cities.[154]

[153]March 31, 1973.

[154]Jack Cooke, "Reviews in Print," *Jazz Monthly* (July, 1973), 18.

THE FILM OF THE AUTOBIOGRAPHY OF MISS JANE PITTMAN

When Dorothea Oppenheimer, Gaines' New York agent, told him that the Tomorrow Entertainment Company wanted the movie and television rights for the novel, Gaines quoted a figure four times the original asking price, and remained almost incommunicado until it was met. At first there was trouble getting financial backers. As Gaines said, "Nobody wanted to buy the story of an old Black woman talking into a tape recorder about her past life. . . . They felt it was too episodic; they had to cover 100 years in 110 minutes and couldn't concentrate on anything very long. I couldn't have written the screen version and I had my doubts that anybody could."[155]

Production of *Miss Jane* did not materialize with first-approached ABC television network, officials of which are reported to have said it was "drudging and that no one would watch it." Gaines received $50,000 from the CBS television network for the film rights when *Miss Jane* was accepted. He told a journalist for the *San Francisco Examiner*, June 20, 1978, "A lot of people think I made a lot of money. You don't with a TV film. I just wish I had made all the money people think I have."

Despite the lack of monetary fame, the film of *Miss Jane*, which Gaines has referred to as "that film thing," was considered to be a critical breakthrough for establishing his author's reputation. Book sales increased considerably after the film was aired. One impressed newsman remarked, "After Miss Jane Pittman, the excitement is down hill on TV this week."

Preceding the public television presentation Gaines was informed of a prestigious private event in a letter from Robert Christiansen and Rick Rosenberg, *Miss Jane*'s producers. The letter from Gaines' papers, dated December 11, 1973, reads in part:

[155]Carter, "Ernest Gaines," 52.

> We have just finished cutting the film, and it will run one hour and 49 minutes. . . . We are very pleased that Xerox is the sole sponsor since there will be fewer commercial interruptions than usual and they are also spending, we have heard, $150,000 to publicize the show.
>
> Furthermore, the picture will be screened in Washington, D. C. on January 23, for Congressmen and Senators and other VIP's. This does not happen often, and we are quite pleased with this honor.
>
> We will have an invitational screening here in Los Angeles on January 8, and if you have anyone here that you would like to see the picture at that time, please let us know and we will make sure that they get invitations. Of course, if you would like to come down for the screening, we would love to see you.

Gaines did attend. Cicely Tyson, the show's star, got a five-minute ovation from over fifty TV editors and newspeople, the "normally jaded press," before she was interviewed after this advanced screening. The press and the critics, as well as Gaines and the rest of the audience, wept without shame. In an undated item, Hal Crowther, a critic for the *Buffalo Evening News* said, "I hate to give CBS the satisfaction of knowing they made me cry."

Sponsored solely by the Xerox Corporation, the film has been acclaimed as the best drama ever to be shown on television. Its first public airing was on January 31, 1974, and estimates of the number of viewers have varied from fifty to eighty-five million, according to news items. Out of twelve nominations for Emmy Awards, it won in nine categories: outstanding comedy or drama special for the year; Cicely Tyson for best actress of the year; Tyson for best actress in a television dramatic special; Bruce Walkup and Sandy Stewart for outstanding achievement in costume design; Stan Winston and Rick Baker for outstanding achievement in make-up; Fred Karlin for best music composition for a series or a single program of a series (special program); Lynda Gurasich for hair stylist; John Korty for best directing in drama (a single program), comedy or drama; and Tracy Keenan Wynn for best writing in drama or comedy (a single program).

Of the gala Emmy Awards evening, June 7, 1974, *The Sun Reporter* said,

> Also on hand in Miss Tyson's party in the theatre were Assemblyman Willie L. Brown and Ernest J. Gaines, the latter being the author of the book, *The Autobiography of Miss Jane Pittman*, the best-selling novel on which the TV drama was based. Gaines was elated, of course, over the honors amassed from his book . . . but he was understandably disappointed that the Bay Area's own John Korty did not win as Director of the Year.

Jet, June 13, 1974, quoted a part of Tyson's Emmy acceptance speech:

> Of course I have to thank Ernest Gaines, the author of the novel, my producer, and director and hair stylist. . . But I owe a load of thanks to all the Jane Pittmans throughout our history. Thank you all.

An undated, untitled news item found in Gaines' papers reported:

> While his terrific *Autobiography of Miss Jane Pittman* was winning all those Emmys last week, San Francisco author Ernest Gaines was modestly serving as foreman of a jury hearing a pimping-pandering case in the court of Superior Judge William Mullins. Short recess for congratulations.

* * *

A discussion guide of the film was prepared by Lynn M. Mills under the auspices of the Learning Corporation of America, providing an outline for an in-depth study and comparison of the book and the film. It is a thought provoking pamphlet for a student of any level.[156] Supposedly for a 1977 issue of *Reader's Digest* Tracy Keenan Wynn, the screenplay writer, adapted a short five-scene drama of *Miss Jane* for school use, with questions following for comprehensive purposes.[157]

A few months after the film's release a well-received rebroadcast was presented in five segments through station KCBS in San Francisco, according to an undated item in a September, 1974, Palo Alto *Black Times*. Another undated, untitled item said that CBS received one of the 1974 Sidney Hillman Foundation prizes ($750) for the movie. This money was given to the National Scholarship Service and Fund for Negro Students. The Hillman family foundations are particularly interested in culture and the arts.

* * *

Though it may have had the look of a low budget film, *Miss Jane* cost approximately $1,000,000, as opposed to an early projected fee of $250,000, to make and produce, several times more than most two-hour TV films, according to the *Cincinnati Enquirer*, January 27, 1974. It was hoped that this deficit would be made up from showings of the film in theaters abroad. At first the movie was three hours in duration, with twenty minutes allowed for commercials. CBS paid $650,000 for two showings, the *Enquirer* said. The Memphis *Commercial Appeal*, January 27, 1974, said, "The sponsor is to be commended for taking only nine minutes of commercials and taking them quietly."

Originally scheduled to be filmed in the spring of 1973, the venture was postponed until the following September. The film was shot in thirty days, at Magnolia Mound off Nicholson Drive in Baton Rouge, at Belle Helene Plantation on the River Road south of Baton Rouge, and at Evergreen Plantation, in St. John

[156]Pamphlet found in Gaines' papers, undated.

[157]The specific issue of *Reader's Digest* was not given in the source found in Gaines' papers. A search in 1977 issues of the *Digest* did not confirm its publication.

the Baptist Parish. Most of the movie props, including the slave quarters and the overseer's house, came from Louisiana State University's rural-life collection. The tools and buggies were borrowed from the grounds of the Burden Research Plantation Museum. The youthful scenes were shot first, then for ten days the aging scenes were shot in sequence.

Twenty professional actors, plus several non-professionals from the filming area, were chosen for approximately seventy speaking parts and group scenes. Artists' Representatives of New Orleans screened persons in Baton Rouge and New Orleans, about sixty percent of the cast, to be used as "extras." An ad in Baton Rouge's *Morning Advocate*, September 15, 1973, offered "transportation and meals on the set in addition to a fee paid for participation" by the production company.

Having been told that Louisiana was a difficult place to work, due to racial conflict, the movie crew contacted the state capitol in Baton Rouge. "They were shocked to see blacks and whites working together and eating together on a crew. One day a red neck guy on the next plantation kept revving up his motorcycle and ruining our sound." A parish sheriff intervened and took care of the motorcyclist.[158]

Gaines and *Gris-Gris* reporter Charlie East took an unexpected detour the first time they tried to locate the filming site. East described the Sahara Bar and Lounge in Pride, Louisiana, where they stopped for directions, as a "place filled with black men drinking beer, just sitting around friendly like and passing away the morning hours. 'This is a neighborhood bar for everybody—blacks and whites,' the old guy in the cowboy hat said. 'Come here any time, and bring a gang of women with you, too.' He was 73. Gaines bought a round of beer for everyone and played a few tunes on the jukebox. Then it was back on the road." East related not only humorous events which occurred during the filming, but commented on the nuisances of heat, humidity, mosquitoes, and the buzz of a Delta Airlines plane.[159]

[158]*The Hollywood Reporter*, October 16, 1973.

[159]Charlie East, "On the Movie Set with Cicely and Friends," *Gris-Gris*, October 10-13, 1973.

Gaines, as non-interfering film consultant, came to the set each day for three weeks, accumulating mixed feelings as the movie progressed. He gave no unasked-for advice, saying that he did not come to the set to spy, that he was not really officially involved with the filming. He spoke about his anxiety in attending the first filming session to a North Carolina journalist, and frankly admitted to stage fright. On his first visit to the plantation house site, arranged by Tomorrow Entertainment, Inc., he met producers Bob Christiansen and Rick Rosenberg and director of the film John Korty. Gaines was in awe of Korty's patience, gentleness, and total cooperation. Script writer Tracy Keenan Wynn's scene of the temporarily housed homeless children on the old-timey pallets was staged just as Gaines had envisioned it.

Gaines was showered with favorable comments by the local people, many of whom believed Miss Jane had been a real person. He loved receiving pats from elderly women, but took a dim view of their mention of nice daughters. One high point occurred during lunch on the film site, as he talked to an elderly white man. The man was familiar with Gaines' part of the country, and had even hunted and fished there. He was pleased that at this time blacks and whites could sit together, eating or chatting peaceably, an improvement over black/white relations of two decades earlier.[160]

The modest Director John Korty had some interesting comments following the production. He has been described as a quiet man, doing quieter films than the usual Hollywood run. "What I took home for *Pittman* was the same as what San Francisco streetsweepers get paid. I know about the big money scene now, and I'm not sure I want it," he said. "It affects the way you think of yourself . . . . I would like to make successful films without becoming successful too fast."[161] Gaines thinks highly of Korty, saying of him, "He worked like a mad man. I mean this guy worked his ass off out there."[162]

[160]Greenville, N. C., *Reflector,* January 27, 1974.

[161]*San Francisco,* (February 1974), 54-60.

[162]Mill Valley, Calif., *Pacific Sun,* November 7, 1974.

When asked if he objected to having been bypassed as writer of the TV script, Gaines replied, "Never. I have never written a movie or TV script, and would not even have attempted this one. That requires a special skill, a special craft. But when I read Tracy's script, I thought he had done a tremendous job."[163]

Gaines thought that Wynn did a creditable job with the script, realizing that communication from the written word of a book and from the screen must be handled differently. Though he had omitted the water fountain scene in the book, he agreed that it was a powerful one in the movie. He said,

> I heard Tracy was adamant—the march to the fountain *had* to be there. That's what people remember more than anything, and that's what I didn't write! But you know, it doesn't matter to me one way or the other. . . . Once I've finished a book, you can say or do anything you want; my book is there. I hope people will credit me or damn me for the book, *not* for the film.[164]

Gaines was "startled" to see the white narrator, Michael Murphy, who was Wynn's idea, rather than following the book in this respect. His words were:

> One day I was on the set and I saw this tall, handsome blond there. I thought at first that he was an assistant director. But then he was reading the script and I found out it was Michael Murphy. The film was one of the first ones to deal with a 'controversial' topic, so the narrator was added for sympathy.[165]

He had told the *Alameda Times Star*, February 22, 1980, that this substitution may have been made because white viewers would

[163]Quoted from a flyer for the movie found in Gaines' papers.

[164]Carter, "Ernest Gaines," 52.

[165]Lafayette, La., *Daily Advertiser,* September 25, 1983.

not have watched a serious, almost all-black movie. (Actually, Murphy's hair was darkened for the movie.)

When Gaines asked Wynn why he thought a white man could write about Southern blacks, Wynn replied that it was not a matter of color, but of humanity. Nevertheless, Gaines felt that being in Louisiana was a culture shock for Wynn. He proffered the thought that Wynn, by changing the novel's black female school teacher as interviewer to a white male reporter from New York, saw himself as Quentin, the white reporter, perhaps a way of conditioning himself to the *Miss Jane* story.[166]

Michael Murphy who played Quentin found it a most rewarding role and felt, "an almost physical wrench when the filming ended," according to the *Modesto Bee*, January 27, 1974.

* * *

Cicely Tyson in the role of *Miss Jane* was as much the real Miss Jane as anyone could have been. Gaines had made it a point to meet her during the filming of *Sounder* and discuss the *Miss Jane* script. During the filming of *Miss Jane* Gaines showed her where his relatives lived. In Gaines' papers are over a hundred news clippings, film reviews, photos, and biographical articles from newspapers and periodicals concerning Tyson and her performance, with which he was well pleased. Tyson, smitten with the idea from the onset, totally got into the role, researching as avidly for the film in a concentrated period as Gaines had for the novel. She visited several very old black women, listening to them talk and observing their gestures and posture. One of them was 108 and the other, considerably deaf, was 105. She also trained for physical stamina by running each day and dieting on healthful foods. Actor Rod Perry, who played Joe Pittman, took a crash course in horseback riding at a dude ranch to prepare for his part.

Tyson was thirty-four when *Miss Jane* was filmed. One actress on the set did not know for days that she was not really old. Her make-up befitting Miss Jane's maturing age was a

[166]*San Francisco Examiner,* December 31, 1973.

masterpiece, meticulously designed by Stan Winston and Rick Baker. They spent two months developing three faces for her, first making a plaster cast of her face and of other aged faces of their own design. This was combined with a pliable, thin foam rubber overlay. The mask was put onto her face and neck in pieces. Similar coverings were fashioned for her hands. Tyson was on the set each morning by 4:00. Before each shooting, from six to seven hours were required to get the mask on properly, though it could be removed in approximately forty-five minutes. During this time she could not eat, but was allowed to drink through a straw. Almost as taxing for Tyson was speaking in the old voice of Miss Jane, since she had to affect a hoarseness. Wigs, as well as tooth structure/color were also considerations of the make-up team.

Co-starring with Tyson were Richard A. Dysart (Master Bryant), Katherine Helmond (Lady at House), Michael Murphy (Quentin, the journalist), Roy Poole (Mister Robert), Josephine Premice (Mme Gautier), Thalmus Rasulala (Ned, age forty-two), Collin Wilcox-Horne (Mistress Bryant), and Beatrice Winde (Lena, Jimmy's mother).

Minor roles were taken by Eric Brown (Jimmy at age seven), Barbara Chaney (Amma Dean), Joel Fluellen (Unc Isom), Will Hare (Cluveau), David Hooks (Colonel Dye), Elinora B. Johnson (Mary), Warren Kenner (Job), Dudley Knight (Trooper Brown), Derrick Mills (Little Ned), Valerie O'Dell (Ticey), Odetta Felius (Big Laura), Rod Perry (Joe Pittman), Al Scott (Ferry Captain), Dan Smith (Ned, age eighteen), Carol Sutton (Vivian), Wilbur Swartz (Confederate colonel), Bill Walker (Elder Banks), and Arnold Wilkerson (Jimmy).

Overall, the myriad reviews of the film gave it high praise. Most critics agreed that Tyson's superb acting completely absorbed the audience's attention. (She was awarded an honorary Doctorate of Letters from Loyola University in May of 1974 for "promoting understanding between the races.") Pauline Kael said of Tyson's performance,

> She's an actress all right, and as tough-minded and

> honorable in her methods as any we've got. . . . I'm comparing Tyson to the highest, because that's the comparison she invites and she has earned. . . . [*Miss Jane* is] probably the finest movie ever made for television."[167]

"Cicely Tyson makes you proud and sad to be a member of the human race."[168]

* * *

Gaines, somewhat resigned about the distortions of the film, nevertheless, continued to feel strongly about them in the years following. In 1976 Gaines said of the film:

> I liked what they did with the two hours that they had. . . . . The film could not depict the book as it was. No film ever can, and this one definitely did not. But I think the two hours did give us an idea of what the book was about. . . . Even when we were shooting the film here around Baton Rouge, the aim was toward shooting a better film, more than a two-hour film. I wish the viewers could see all the good footage that was done which had to be edited out in Hollywood. So what you have now in the film is peaks—a lot of peaks. But you don't have the valleys and slopes as you would have had, had the film been longer. But the film as it is . . . is quite good. . . . For example, in the film after the Cajun Albert Cluveau kills the professor [Ned], you never see Cluveau ever again. In my book, after Cluveau has killed the son of his closest friend [Miss Jane] he gradually goes mad. In the film, before it was edited, you see him going mad after he had killed the professor. The actor, Will Hare does his best acting in the mad scene. . . . When the

[167]*Ebony* (August, 1977), 136.

[168]John Carmody, *Washington Post,* n.d.

> footage went back to Hollywood all this was edited out. So what we get is the assassination and nothing about Cluveau's madness. The assassination is a peak, but the gradual madness is a slope and a valley. And that is what I think is missing in the film. . . . The slopes and valleys are missing.[169]

In an undated item from the Baton Rouge *State-Times* found among Gaines' papers, Gaines said:

> Of course there was a lot of stuff left out. Cecil B. DeMille didn't do a damn thing to improve the Bible. And neither has anyone done anything to improve Moby Dick or War and Peace. The Bible will be there when DeMille is already rotten in the ground or whatever. . . . I'm pretty sure the old man upstairs didn't like the stuff DeMille was pulling, but he let him go and do it anyway. It'll take care of itself. That's the way I feel about my book. It didn't perturb me. I know its's a different medium. And I think the people who criticized it most were people who just wanted to say something.

He reflected that many small details were wrong, such as showing Miss Jane in bed with no mosquito netting, or a clothesline pulled taut instead of slack. He was offered the position of technical advisor on the film but turned it down, just as he has turned down offers of scriptwriting since the making of *Miss Jane*. He has said that one positive result of his *Miss Jane* and Alex Haley's *Roots*, both televised, has been that young black writers were given a new approach, and young black people were given a chance to identify with writers as role models. Though Gaines felt that *Roots* deserved to be televised, he thought that the panorama was thin. Too, he has referred to the "quite bad" script, the "atrocious dialogue," and miscasting in some instances.

An undated speech found in Gaines' papers gave a fuller

[169]Rowell, "This Louisiana Thing," 48-49.

critique of the film and its deletions. Of Cluveau's deleted mad scene Gaines says, "When he is going mad it is so convincing that it is chilling." Viewers in southern Louisiana parishes told Gaines that Will Hare's Cajun accent was the "most atrocious that has ever been put on film." Gaines mentions another example where the "valley" was edited out, those scenes between the time Miss Jane visits the voodoo woman until the actual scene of the horse dragging Joe Pittman to his death. "What we don't see, and what was filmed, and a scene I think is as important as any other in the entire movie, a warm, loving, tender scene, is the one where Joe Pittman tells Jane why he must ride the horse."

Continuing about Joe Pittman Gaines says,

> He wanted to challenge nature because Whites would not let him be the kind of farmer he wanted to be. Well, Nature would not submit to his wishes. But in the film, the horse no longer represents nature, but something evil—according to some people. John Korty told me that he wanted a white horse because he wanted to shoot the scene at night, and the white horse would show up better than a black horse would. . . . (I should add here that the horse was one of the best actors in the film. There was no need for a second take on his leaving the corral, or returning, dragging the dummy which represented the body of Joe Pittman. A good whack on the hanch, and he did exactly what he was supposed to do.)

Speaking of putting the scenes together he says, "It had to be a patched job . . . molded into one. Parts from several different speeches had to be molded into one. Sometimes that one molded speech was shorter than any of its original parts." He speaks of Miss Jane's being the focus of nearly every scene as a "distortion," especially in instances where Ned or another character should have more attention. Gaines analytically cites other faults of the film, but makes it clear that as author of the book he understands why what happened in the film, happened in the way that it did. "I hope that what I'm saying here doesn't seem to you that I feel that the editors in Hollywood destroyed what might have been a great film. Nothing is farther from the truth. I think the film is very good."

Gaines' disappointment at the omission of Cluveau's mad scene may have been due to the fact that his killing of Ned was based on a true incident which occurred in 1904 on False River. That year a Frenchman actually killed a black man who was trying to build a school.

Gaines visited several elementary schools in Louisiana after the filming of *Miss Jane*. "Everywhere I went kids would come up to me and talk about the film. For the first time, they could come up to a black writer and say 'I know that person.'"[170]

* * *

The excellent photography, script adaptation, creative make-up, and direction got their share of compliments. Minor negative comments criticized the film as being too episodic; as lacking depth of character in some instances; as too condensed for the 110-year time period; for presenting only the good side of the blacks and the bad side of the whites; for slowness of pacing, however appropriate for its time; as lacking in humor on the whole; for vagueness of relationships; for disruption of continuity, due to editing of the novel, producing "unneeded roughness;" for the occasional inaudibility of Tyson's raspy voice; for the belittling of Miss Jane's accomplishments other than achieving longevity; for "arid stretches;" and for oppressive solemnity. A few of them rightfully thought that Gaines should have gotten more attention as a result of the film's success.

A critic for the *Berkeley Gazette*, January 26, 1974, faulted the white caricatures of the "beefy sheriff who lovingly caresses a club during a civil rights demonstration; a senile plantation owner; a sweet, kindly Union army corporal; a contemporary plantation owner who walks softly but carries a big stick; and others drawn in similar vein."

[170]Baton Rouge *Sunday Advocate*, April 17, 1977.

John Callahan, in summing up his essay "Image-Making: Tradition and the Two Versions of *The Autobiography of Miss Jane Pittman,*" compares basic differences in the novel and the film. After a detailed discussion of necessary changes from the novel to make the image a visual one (such as condensed conversation), some of the violence, many of the unspoken feelings, and the actual long years of racial struggle are missing. "Unlike the novel the film allows us to guess at nothing. Everything is supplied."

Impressive as the film's ending was, Callahan doubted that Miss Jane's brave drinking from the white folks' fountain would change anything soon for the black race. He liked the scene, which was indeed a heroic tear-jerker. He pointed out instances in the film of looking versus seeing, which the film's imagery presented simply, demanding no commitment from the viewer to judge as a witness. Gaines' book, on the other hand, catches up the reader in its more powerful imagery, calling for his sympathy through a revelation of common truths.[171]

* * *

Excerpts from reviews by leading critics and from prominent newspapers follow.

Rex Reed said in the *Daily News*, January 18, 1974, that *Miss Jane* was

> One of the most profound and deeply-moving experiences in the history of film. . . a fantastic experience, not only the best film about black pride I have ever seen but one of the best films about human dignity ever made. . . . It is an ending that rips the heart out, a piece of history so well-written and perfectly photographed and sublimely acted that I predict it will make

[171]John Callahan, "Image-Making: Tradition and the Two Versions of *The Autobiography of Miss Jane Pittman,*" *Chicago Review*, XXIX (Autumn, 1977), 61, 62.

motion picture history.

Pauline Kael, longtime eminent movie critic wrote in *The New Yorker*, January 28, 1974:

> A Cajun character certainly doesn't help; no Cajun on the screen ever does. Yet none of this does serious damage. There's one unfortunate change. In the novel Jane dreads a black stallion that she thinks will kill Joe Pittman. . . . An albino [stallion] was used instead; the eerie white horse, with a ghastly pink look around the eyes is mystically effective, but the color switch suggests a racial symbolism that doesn't quite fit the situation. The clumsiest addition is the device of using Michael Murphy as a journalist interviewing the ancient Miss Pittman to link the episodes; toward the end, we feel the shift to amateurishness each time he appears. . . . John Korty tells the story at a satisfyingly leisurely pace, befitting a woman who accumulates a hundred and ten years. . . . The movie is still so much cleaner and simpler than just about any other movie made for TV that the fictional Jane Pittman has the singularity and dignity of a person in a documentary, [though] there never was a Jane Pittman. . . . The exteriors and the closeups of Jane show the sane affection of an artist with no fakery about him. John Korty has no show business in his soul. . . . 'Miss Jane Pittman' isn't a great movie, though with more directorial freedom and a better script it might have been. But it's the finest movie ever made for American television.

Another movie maven, Judith Crist, called Tyson "that always exquisite actress" and the movie "near-epic in scope."

> Ms. Tyson . . . is the actress who goes beyond appearance so that every fiber of her body seems attuned to a time and age, and every gesture and intonation changes with such subtlety that we are drawn deeper and

> deeper into the sense of shared experience. Ms. Tyson's accomplishment is sheer perfection and it is complemented by the remarkable balance of the screenplay and the gentle pacing of the direction, despite the constant flow of events and the taut drama of the story, we can pause and penetrate the very heart and soul of Miss Jane.[172]

The *New York Times* carried at least four reviews of the film. One by Charlayne Hunter simply related the story and was non-critical and unopinionated. John O'Connor wrote that "the puffery is entirely justified." He called *Miss Jane* a major TV special that the network had every right to be proud of. The story was "treated intelligently on all levels." Korty's direction was "cool and restrained, never underlining and always avoiding what could easily be mawkish." Scenes of "stunning beauty" were created by James Crabe, director of photography. Speaking of the switch from the black school teacher in the novel to the white reporter in the film O'Connor took issue with the "presence of do-good mentality." He termed the use of the white horse an "obvious and superfluous racial metaphor." He had high praise for Tyson and the other actors who were "satellites spinning around her."[173]

Another reviewer for the *Times,* Stephanie Harrington, who had not read the book, wrote a resentful, bitter review showing no understanding of either Gaines' or the film's aim. "I saw nothing, not even the flesh and blood of drama. . . . Was I crazy or were the apostles Kael, Reed and Crist (not to mention John O'Connor and Richard Shickel)?" she wrote. She said the film tried to make up for a former neglect of black history. "But did it? . . . . I doubt that [it] offered a million dollars worth of education for anyone." The events were "stuffed into the narrative like meat into a sausage." The script was "generally

[172]Pauline Kael, "Cicely Tyson Goes to the Fountain," *The New Yorker,* January 28, 1974, p. 74. From REELING (Atlantic-Little Brown). © 1974 Pauline Kael. Originally in *The New Yorker.*

[173]*New York Times,* January 31, 1974.

hokey." Harrington proceeded to make fun of everything, calling Ned and Jimmy in their roles as "Messiahs" not real men, and Tyson merely "a symbol and a stereotype . . . imprisoned in the crust of her make up." She allows the favorable reviewers their own opinions, but "only as a moral decision to reward a politically well-meant gesture by excusing it from any test of redeeming artistic value." She wondered how the sheriff could stand silent while Miss Jane walked to the drinking fountain, since he was supposed to restrain her, or at least say something in protest.[174]

Curiously, reviewer Nikki Giovanni in her critique lamented Harrington's complete misunderstanding of the story and the fact that she had not read the novel.

> I hope Mrs. Harrington explains slavery to her children better than she explained drama to me. . . . I'm afraid [she] doesn't know the history of blacks in America or she would have been more accurate in her criticism of certain plantation scenes. The sheriff did not touch Jane Pittman because she refused to be less than the majesty that she was. . . . *Miss Jane Pittman* fulfilled my deepest expectations. That the show will spawn another film depicting other blacks in other experiences is unquestioned. That it was a triumph of and for the enduring strength of black people is also beyond doubt. . . . I am appalled and disappointed that Stephanie Harrington did not see the same Cicely Tyson I did.[175]

* * *

Most viewers who had previously read the novel preferred it to the film. Despite what any of the critics thought or wrote Gaines must have been most gratified by two particular congratulatory letters, out of the dozens he received. His friend,

[174] *Ibid.*, February 10, 1974.

[175] *Ibid.*, March 3, 1974.

editor William Decker, wrote:

> I just wanted you to know that Anne and I watched *Miss Jane* last night and enjoyed it very much. We felt that they almost did her justice. From all the rave reviews the critics gave the show I thought that it was going to be as good as the book. It wasn't. Not anywhere near. I'm saddened by the fact that millions of people who saw the film will never really get to know Miss Jane, your Miss Jane. They will never read the book and that's their loss.[176]

Another letter found in Gaines' papers, undated, is from his godchild, a young lady in perhaps the eighth grade in San Jose. Its sentiment by far outweighs its misspellings.

> Dear Paran,
>
> Miss Jane Pittman was so fantastic I was in tears at the end. I thought it was the most fantastic thing I ever saw, thats no lie. I am so proud to have you for a godfather. I told 86 people in my school to watch it. I hope you will get lots of awards for it. If you go to the emmy awards you can take me with you Ha Ha. If you know Cissalie Tyson well tell her that I don't think anyone in the *world* could have acted better. And sense I am studing to be a great actress I would like to be that good. I will be going to High School next year or rather this September and I would like to see you as soon as possible.
> I love you always,
>
> Keli
>
> P. S. for your next picture I'm avalable. I'm in the San Jose Junior Theater and San Jose Jr. Reppitura, Repitory.

[176]Letter from Decker found in Gaines' papers, dated February 1, 1974.

IN MY FATHER'S HOUSE

In My Father's House was first published in 1978 by Alfred Knopf, and reprinted in paperback by W. W. Norton in 1983. Its dedication reads: "To the memory of George and Mamie Williams and Octavia McVay—they gave you whatever they had; they asked you for nothing in return." The Williamses were likely River Lake plantation inhabitants, though they have not been identified at this time of writing. Octavia McVay is presumed to be a relative of Gaines, since the McVay name is that of his grandmother. Inquiries to the owner of River Lake Plantation and to the McVay family, however, revealed no information on these persons.

Gaines has said repeatedly that *In My Father's House* was perhaps the most difficult of all his novels to write. It took a good six years and underwent many revisions, confirmed by correspondence and editing suggestions from Dorothea Oppenheimer found in Gaines' papers. "I keep sending it to my editors (at Knopf) and they keep sending it back, saying 'It ain't ready yet,'" Gaines told journalist Ruth Laney. "They're right. Each time I just send it to get it out of the house for a while, but I know it still needs work."[177] An item in *Essence*, July, 1975, suggested that Gaines had not met the deadline by some two years. "I hate to sound like I'm complaining, because I hate for anybody to complain to me. . . . But it is giving me more hell than anything I've ever written. 'But it doesn't do any good to talk about it,'" he quoted Hemingway as saying.[178] At the time of its publication it was the shortest of Gaines' books by some thirty pages.

In My Father's House was named one of the fifty "Notable Books of the Year" in 1978 by the American Library Association.

[177]Baton Rouge *Sunday Advocate*, April 17, 1977.

[178]Carter, "Ernest Gaines," 72.

Gaines told an interviewer for the *San Francisco Examiner*, June 20, 1978, that he had been accused of developing a psychological block after finishing *Miss Jane,* a situation accounting for the slowness of *In My Father's House.* Gaines has not agreed, but admits that this was his most difficult book to write from a technical standpoint. In retrospect he has said *In My Father's House* resembles a play in prose form, and though it is dramatic, he never felt that it had the poetry or panorama of *Miss Jane.*

In My Father's House deals with the alienation of a black father and a black son. "My philosophy is that [they] have been separated since slavery days and have not caught up yet. The black father is never in a position to help his son. That is the theme I try to deal with," Gaines said.

In an interview with Ruth Laney, he described the book as a "tale of conflict between father and son, old and young, Christianity and atheism, the [Martin Luther] King philosophy and the philosophy of the younger generation."[179] And in another interview he explained further: "The son has been away for twenty years and when he returns to the South he finds his father has found religion, become a minister, gotten involved in civil rights. The son doesn't believe in *anything* that's going on, and that's the cause of the conflict that the story is based on."[180]

Washington Post critic Julian Moynahan, a novelist himself, combined narrative with the Gainesian insight in his critique in the *Post*'s *Book World* column, June 18, 1978. Moynahan, well aware of the novel's dramatic elements, compares its central character, Phillip Martin, to a character which Ibsen might have drawn. Martin, a minister, community leader, and father, is the focus of the piece, set in St. Adrienne, Mississippi, near the Louisiana border. He has become entwined with both personal problems and timely public issues.

[179]Baton Rouge *Sunday Advocate,* April 17, 1977.

[180]Mill Valley, Calif., *Pacific Sun,* November 7, 1974.

The novel, set in 1969, explores relations between male generations, particularly black fathers and sons, situations rooted in slavery which have been distorted, now hoping to find proper perspective with the advent of the Civil Rights cause. Phillip's prestige in St. Adrienne has stemmed in large part from his efforts of the past decade for this cause. But he has not always been a respected model nor a paragon of virtue. Before a religious conversion, his past was one of unsteady employment, drinking, gambling, and sexual pleasure. With Johanna, a lover whom he never married, he fathered three children, whose whereabouts are unknown.

Phillip is now married, has more children, and is waging a campaign against an unjust white store owner. He even aspires to a congressional career. Suddenly a mysterious young man who calls himself "Robert X" appears in St. Adrienne. Phillip feels threatened by the unknown, shaken, and puzzled, especially when he learns that Robert is his first son by Johanna. Robert's purpose is vague, and as the story unravels, Phillip is overcome with fear and self-doubt. Robert could have come either to avenge his father's negligence by killing him, or to kill himself, thereby placing further guilt and grief upon his father. Robert's sister has been raped and her other brother sent to prison for killing the rapist. Robert is a tortured young man.

In the black district of Baton Rouge, Phillip seeks out his longtime friend, Chippie, who is said to have information on Johanna, now deceased. Here Gaines' description of shotgun houses and corner bars is vivid, and as Phillip walks among them he senses longing for the love he failed to cherish, and remorse for the lack of self esteem to follow his own feelings. Success has come to him only at a great price. Before the novel's end, Robert dies.

Moynahan was impressed with Gaines' description of the St. Adrienne milieu, which incorporated mixed rural neighborhoods, various religious cultures, and with his keen understanding of Civil Rights' undercurrents. He suggests that the characters of Phillip and Robert are drawn to represent historical generations.

Again Gaines uses the technique of suspense by introducing

extra characters for whom he creates situations which engross and detract from the story's main thread. His idea of a character on a road, going somewhere, is evident. And again he uses the contrast in dynamics at which he is so skilled—a violent scene, such as the unleashing of Phillip's anger and bitterness in the bar, followed by his wife Alma's calming influence. Phillip is verbal; Alma is a woman of few words whose understanding and heart stream run deep.

As in "A Long Day in November" and *Of Love and Dust* Gaines makes good use of the sounds of bed springs. When Chippo is telling Phillip about visiting Johanna's house he had thought that she was there alone, but learned differently.

> That's when I heard the noise—the bed. I had thought all the time it wasn't nobody in the house but me and her. I know the storekeeper had told me about a 'him' who stayed there with her, but I hadn't see 'him.' I didn't see him or hear him that first day, and didn't hear him that second time either, till I mentioned where you was preaching. That' when I heard the bed. Like somebody had been laying in one place a long, long time—and when he heard what I said he turned over. No sound from him himself, just the screeching of the bed when he turned over.[181]

Just as Robert's lying on the bed could well signify his physical and emotional depletion, Phillip's wife Alma was similarly debilitated with despair. When Chippo returns with Phillip to his home, after their talk, Gaines makes another reference to bed springs. "Both of them could hear the springs as Alma turned over on the bed in the other room."[182] Alma chose to stay in the bedroom until Chippo had gone, not wishing to interfere. She would comfort Phillip in her own calming way.

Like *Catherine Carmier*, *In My Father's House* is told from

[181]Ernest Gaines, *In My Father's House* (1978, reprint ed., New York, 1983), p. 191.

[182]*Ibid.*, p. 213.

the omniscient point of view.

> You cannot tell that story from the minister's point of view because the minister keeps too much inside him. He does not reveal it—he won't reveal it to anybody. It would be totally impossible to tell this story from anyone else's point of view—or should I say, have anyone else tell the story. . . . That is, I, the author, must tell the story rather than let a character tell it for me,

Gaines said.[183] As he said about the creation of *Miss Jane*, he writes of people's successes and their failures as well. He draws the picture of an individual who must stand alone before he can stand with the crowd in the character of Phillip Martin. But he is doubtful that Martin will survive as Miss Jane did, for his situations give him too many doubts.

* * *

Found in Gaines' papers were two undated pages titled PLANS FOR WORK, obviously plans for *In My Father's House* from their content.

> The title of the novel, as of this writing, is *Revenge*. It is the story of a son who wants revenge against his father. The boy, Robert, his brother and sister were taken North because the father refuses to marry the mother. Since Robert is the oldest child, he looks after his younger brother and sister while his mother is at work. When he is old enough to work he helps his mother raise the other two children.
>
> When at fifteen the girl is raped by one of her mother's lovers, Robert is too cowardly to seek revenge. His younger brother finds the man, kills him with a knife, and as a result the brother is sent to prison. When this happens both he and his sister turn against the

[183]Rowell, "This Louisiana Thing," 41-42.

> mother because they blame her for bringing the man into the house. The mother dies after so many years of worrying over her two children. Robert feels guilty about her death because he being the oldest son felt that it was his duty to revenge his sister. He would not have turned against his mother as his other brother did, and he would not have let his sister do so either. This feeling of guilt becomes an obsession with him, and to expiate his guilt he must go back South and get revenge on the other man, his father, who was responsible for their going North in the first place.
>
> When he returns to the South twenty-one years after he had left, he finds that his father is a minister, very influential in the community and married to a woman half his age. She is about Robert's age—both about twenty-five. Robert will get revenge by seducing his father's young wife and then revealing himself to his father. But the father is no longer the sinner he was twenty-one years ago. He is a man of God now—just the opposite from Robert who, because his family has been destroyed, does not believe in God. And instead of destroying his father he destroys himself and his father's innocent young wife.

Gaines evidently wrote this prospectus for some kind of fellowship, though it is not named. Continuing, he says,

> I have written about a third of the novel, but I need time to write the rest of it. This fellowship will solve my financial problem and give me time to work. The novel, which is to be very short (65,000 words) very direct, powerful (I hope) will require a lot of re-writing. It is not a realistic or naturalistic novel. It is a drama, a tragedy—a tragedy caused by slavery in this country.

Basically Gaines followed through with this overview of the story, though not in the same sequence. Alma, Phillip Martin's wife, was not raped by Robert, who was arrested on a flimsy charge of having no identification papers, in order for the white sheriff to get back at Phillip for his participation in civil rights matters. Robert, however, possessed a gun, so there is the strong possibility that he came to St. Adrienne intending to kill his father in order to get revenge, and then kill himself.

Less complete notes made by Gaines for the novel indicate that he periodically questioned himself on *why* a certain character would do such and such an act, or *why* he would say such and such a thing. For instance, he had a note about Phillip: he could have done it "as easily as flicking off a fly. Wouldn't that have been the thing to do?" Another one said, "Do I know what my story is about?" Such examples prove that he knows that his characters must be convincing, thereby leaving no holes in his actions, good or bad. Too, there were some phrases, jotted at random, perhaps to be incorporated into the novel, such as "Jumpy as a nigger on Election Day," "Jumpy as a whore in Sunday School," and "Hoppy as a sissy in a CC Camp."

Revision upon revision was made, especially of the opening chapter, some on Gaines' own part and others at the suggestion of Oppenheimer. One draft of the first chapter began with Chippo, Phillip's friend who in the final version was not introduced until much later, telling the story in first person. In another opening Virginia Colar, the woman who houses Robert, is telling the story. And still another beginning has Robert getting off the bus, before Virginia Colar ever sees him. At some point in Gaines writing Robert was to have a brief love affair with a character named Frances, who might have been Beverly in the finished draft.

One of Gaines' concerns was how to reconcile the switch from the gentler, early personality of Etienne (Robert's real name) and Robert as an angry, revenge-obsessed enigma. After Gaines had titled the novel *Revenge* he later changed it to *Revenge in St. Adrienne*, (the fictitious town where the story takes place), and then to *In My Father's Land*. One tentative ending was that Robert should die in the arms of his stepmother, Alma.

* * *

Oppenheimer insisted on certain revisions because she wanted the novel to be "right," seeming to know that at her persuasion Gaines would not give up until it was "right." As Gaines' agent her involvement with *In My Father's House* went on for the entire six years of its preparation. Letters concerning it, some accompanied by copious notes for revising sentences, etc., were found in Gaines' papers. An early one, dated August 16, 1971, read:

> Dear Old Ee,
>
> Here are all those notes on IN MY FATHER'S HOUSE. I'm not satisfied with what I did. But I worked very hard, and I hope at least some of it will be helpful.
>
> Was at the Strauses yesterday, and Roger Straus asked me again to show him your new novel and I told him that since they rejected OF LOVE AND DUST, you didn't feel we should offer them this book. I hope it was all right to say *you*.
>
> Haven't got the formal release or the ms. back from Dial, but it doesn't matter. . . . I'll call you when all the terms are settled. One thing I like much better about the Knopf contract is that you can get your subsidiary rights money (paperback, reprint, etc. etc.) right away instead of waiting for the next royalty statement which can take up to 11 months. Never could get that on any Dial contract.
>
> I'm going to send the ms. parcel post air mail tomorrow. pp-air mail always takes a bit longer anyway.
>
> Can't think of anything else. If you don't like anything I say in my notes I hope you won't want to fire me.
>
> Take care old E.

Another letter, dated February 21, 1975 reads:

E—

Here are my notes. You know by now that I always write about the things that could still be better and not about the ones that are already good. I was not lying when I said I love the book (though I hated the scene between Philip and Shep). I love it and I couldn't put it down. But when I read it the second time I looked hard for all the faults. I had to because I'm trying to do a job. Now you can take these notes or leave them.

I was exaggerating a bit about Robert. He did have my sympathy this time. And I hated for him to die. But I also think you can still do more.

Big L. Hug,
DO

Two years later the novel had jelled into what was to be its final form. A letter from Oppenheimer dated September 20, 1977, included some of her last suggestions.

E—

That novel is beautiful. You put soul in it this time. I guess it was worth all that suffering.

The things I've listed are all little bitty things the copy editor would catch. Except for a couple or so paragraphs that could stand a bit better phrasing.

About use of "the new tenant." This worked fine at first but then it didn't seem to fit so well any more. Perhaps you could call him [Robert X] Virginia's tenant? I don't know, I don't know. Perhaps Bob or someone at Knopf will have some comments on that.

Possible titles:

I WANT MY SON

A MEETING IN ST. ADRIENNE

THE FATHER (I think that's been used before)

IN DETTIE'S DINETTE

I like the last one best.

Talk to you Thurs.

Big hug,
Dee O

* * *

Gaines expanded on the novel in an interview for *The Southwestern Review* in 1979. Rather than going to Dial Press, who published but did not adequately promote *Miss Jane*, Gaines and Oppenheimer turned to Alfred A. Knopf, Inc. He said, "This book was not the kind of book they are ready to push. But it was the only thing I could write after *Miss Jane Pittman*. Maybe five years from now I could have written it better, but as of right now it was what I could do. And they are doing nothing to promote it."

The interview continues:

> SR: I know it is not being well promoted. . . . It's a good length; it's not over-priced, and it's certainly a timely book. Where is and what is the black leadership after the death of Malcolm and of Martin Luther King? To pick up a figure like Rev. Martin in his dilemma—which way he should go, what he should do—I don't think you could find a more timely subject. . . . I like the way you leave it at the end. We don't know what's going to happen.
>
> GAINES: I've been criticized a lot in bars for that. I

go to a couple of my bars in San Francisco. We play dominos together or shoot dice together. They read my books, you know, and they complain. 'Now what the hell am I supposed to do? "You stopped the book half way. It took you seven years to write. Don't you think you could have written another chapter?' That's the kind of thing I've run into, but I felt it was complete once he [Martin] went back into the room, when she [his wife] tells him, 'We just have to start again, that's all.' To me it's complete.

SR: I think you stopped it at a very good place. You gave the whole problem but not the whole solution.

GAINES: The problem is: here are two men, and neither able to stand at a particular moment in his life, neither father nor son. The father hears the son knocking at the door, but he is unable to say, 'I love my children, my wife, and I'm going to be responsible to them.' And the son blames himself for not being able to commit a murder, when his sister is raped. The novel is based on two moments in life. If the first man had done what he felt later he *should* have done, there would have been no problem.

SR: There would have been no Rev. Martin.

GAINES: There would not have been a Rev. Martin; there would never have been any reason for them to go to California, so there would never have been the reason for the rape. Other tragedies could have followed, but it would never have been that. So this is what the story is. . . . There is a moment in everyone's life when you become paralyzed to do the thing that you *should* do. You have regrets later on. It can be a moment that can cause a complete change in one's life, a moment that you should have taken to throw on the lipstick properly or put some perfume behind your ear. You know, that's what Chekov would deal with, the little thing you didn't do exactly right at the right moment, and you have to pay for it later on. You can make that moment as important to one's life as you want to, and I've tried to use it in this case, to make it a point that would just *change* a man's life, completely change it and lead to tragedy. I was writing it as a *play* in prose form. And, we have some people who are interested in trying to do it.

SR: As a play?

GAINES: Yes, as a play. Interested. Not that we have signed a contract or that we are sure there *will* be anything. But there are people interested. . . .

SR: I have a sense as I read it [*In My Father's House*] that it is the most depressing of your books. . . . It doesn't have those moments of lightness, of humor, of the ridiculousness of existence. I thought it was going to, because I loved that woman. . . .

GAINES: Virginia Colar.

SR: Yes, I liked her. She is one of those women of yours. And you come close to the humor I'm talking about in the opening chapter when she makes excuses for taking Robert X into her home. She knows it's a dumb thing to do, but her heart is so big that she feeds him, with the excuse that she had made a mistake and cooked too much soup. There it is. But before that book was over I found myself terribly depressed. It seems as if the options are running out. If the Civil Rights Movement, the Martin Luther King movement, *didn't* really change very many things, if he is dead, and the movement has petered out, and Robert X seems to be just a destructive, self-destructive . . .

GAINES: No, no. I don't think I was saying that Martin Luther King didn't really *change* things. That's the *last* thing I would ever say. . . . because he *did*. Billy [the guerilla fighter] is the one who says those things. And Billy says things out of complete anger, the little fellow from the war. . . . What I'm saying and what Martin is saying, what the story is saying, is all the things we've done—we fought to drink together, ride on the bus together, eat in the same places, but we have only recently realized that we are strangers. Martin and his son are strangers. We're not close. No, there's no way that I am criticizing Martin Luther King. Not me. Because King is probably one of three men of his century that I'll call heroic. A fantastic man as far as I'm concerned, for all that he did. But the movement was not aimed at fathers and sons. It was aimed at breaking down social conditions.

SR: In writing this book, did you have Turgenev's *Fathers and Sons* in the back of your mind?

GAINES: Yes, oh yea. That was not the original title, but that was what I always had in mind, the conflicts between fathers and sons, the strangeness and strength of those relationships, the distance between fathers and sons.

SR: An estrangement?

GAINES: Yes, I would say so.

The interview closed with more about *In My Father's House*.

GAINES: I wrote the book as honestly as I possibly could. I've gotten really high praises from some reviewers. *Newsweek* and the *New York Times* gave it a very good rating, both the daily and the Sunday *Times*. The *Washington Post* gave me a very, very good review. . . . The Baton Rouge paper gave me a very good review. Others have put it down. Jim Baldwin thinks it's a farce. He cannot support it. . . . Baldwin said, "You must be the one [as a black writer] to keep it up, keep it going. You can't fail." That's what he tells me. "We have all failed, but you can't. You've still got the potential to *not* fail."

SR: But it's not right for him to put that on you.

GAINES: I know it's not. But that's what he wants. Just like anything else, you might write a book that's not up to what the others were, not up to the expectation of what people wanted after *Miss Jane Pittman*.

SR: What people want is *The Return of Miss Jane Pittman*.

GAINES: Right, right.[184]

Having dealt in his own life with the absence of a father and its effects on children, the theme of father and son relationships had long been in Gaines' mind to write. It was a question of "bringing it off" in the right technique.

* * *

In My Father's House was widely reviewed with mostly favorable comments. (Some of the following reviews found in Gaines' papers are undated.) Larry McMurtry said that "the variety and richness of its minor characters" are portrayed "with Flaubertian economy but equally Flaubertian vividness. . . . It is the force of Mr. Gaines's character and intelligence, operating through this deceptively quiet style, that makes his fiction compelling." The novel is characterized by "its quiet force." The characters raise their voices, but the author does not. They cry out to each other or to Heaven: "Their pain, struggle, bewilderment, joys and agonies are registered with precision and sympathy, but the strong prose that carries their stories is not affected by the fevers or the biases of those it describes." Gaines' is a "serene, considered and unexcited" prose. He takes his own good time, which results in a "mature and muscular" novel. The book's tone is set in the "miserable, frigid, sunless Louisiana winter. The sun never shines on this story," and metaphors of chill describe Robert's doom.[185]

Another review in the *New York Times*, July 20, 1978, presented a second analysis, calling the book a "finely textured narrative." Because the character of Robert X is so radical, the novel seems like a "striking departure" for Gaines. Robert X "controls the tempo" of the first half of the book and acts as a "catalyst that shakes the traditional assumptions and tentative

[184] "An Interview with Ernest J. Gaines, " 43-44, 45, 46, 49, 50.

[185] *New York Times Book Review,* June 11, 1978.

equilibrium of the St. Adrienne blacks . . . Reverend Martin, and even the white power structure." The minister is forced into a "painful odyssey." Gaines' transition from the mystique of Robert's ambiguity to the sudden focus on Martin, his father, is not convincing to this *Times* reviewer. Robert's character is not nearly as well explored as is Martin's. "The shift from an objective, factual rendering . . . to a more subjective, nearly stream-of-consciousness narrative is jarring," the review said, but the novel is still "powerful, deeply probing, . . . a deeply layered, resonant tale."

A review by Mel Watkins, also for the *New York Times*, was included on the book jacket of the Norton edition of *In My Father's House*. Watkins called it

> a powerful, deeply probing novel . . . . The Rev. Mr. Martin emerges as a complex, memorable character. . . . [A] resonant tale. . . . Mr. Gaines' ability to portray the rhythm and cadences of Southern mannerisms is unerring. . . . This is a solid contribution to the impressive *oeuvre* of one of America's finest Southern writers."

Comments by Ishmael Reed, writer and longtime friend of Gaines, were also included on the book jacket. "The dialogue is mesmerizing. The characterization comes right off the page. . . . No one writes about mainstream, ordinary black life as well as he [Gaines] does."

Robert Bone in a critique titled "Black Writing in the 1970s" calls Gaines a regionalist, saying that in this book he is reconciling the differences between generations. "Exploring these concerns through a father-son relationship, both in its psycho-cultural and theological dimensions, Gaines has broken new ground."[186]

A reviewer for the *San Jose Mercury*, June 11, 1978, saw the novel as being in the same tradition as Ellison's *Invisible Man* and Toni Morrison's *Song of Solomon*. It "exposes the

[186]*The Nation*, December 16, 1978, 678.

superficiality of black relationships as each person struggles to be a self in an alien world." Phillip Martin is suggestive of Martin Luther King, for he is "physically and politically charismatic" with his "strong following and agressive enemies." Nevertheless, he must start at the beginning in sharing his unburdening with compassion for another. "The other characters . . . seem thin in comparison." Robert's feelings "seem a thin thread on which to hang a murder."

The Houston Chronicle, August 6, 1978 called it a "moving and eloquent . . . novel," made even more powerful and meaningful because the "characters never shout." They "speak with intelligence and eloquence," trying to understand. "In the end Gaines . . . gives the reader a poignant and revealing picture of the effects of sin, on both those sinned against and the sinner."

The Boston Globe, August 9, 1978, said that the book, a bigger challenge for Gaines than *Miss Jane*, "has a spare, vivid eloquence." Instead of a "good" main character, he deals with a "flawed hero." The basic theme is not Martin's reassessment of himself but about fathers and sons. Robert X, who says little, is "delineated through gesture and context." Most of the events are viewed through the father's eye, but this is no blemish. Gaines captures the "fogbound emotional atmosphere. . . . As always, the author's ear for varying levels of Southern speech is impeccable. . . . [It] never falls into the falsely melodramatic: it is an exceedingly sensitive achievement."

Francis Mignon, reviewer for the Nachitoches, Louisiana, *Times*, hoped that *In My Father's House* would become a film, as had *Miss Jane*. Mignon was "struck forcibly by the power of this novel, played out on memory's screen of lush green, storied plantation homes and vanishing cabins." He called the book "a masterpiece in prose. . . in which we are offered his [Gaines'] own memory of habitations."[187]

An undated, unnamed news item in Gaines' papers called him a "master storyteller . . . a master of dialogue who captures the speech of his characters exactly [with] never a false word in

[187]Undated review found in Gaines' papers.

the compact, tightly-plotted story." Another not so complimentary unnamed piece, dated March 27, 1978, said, "The title gives it all away . . . while Gaines poignantly reflects the conditions of black life in the South, a thin plot line and unconvincing character delineation defeat his efforts to build suspense and establish significance." Phillip's "suffering and redemption never become real to the reader, a serious flaw."

Newsweek's reviewer commented: "Gaines' best writing is marked by what Ralph Ellison, describing the blues, called 'near-tragic, near-comic lyricism.' . . . Gaines writes eloquently of the frustrated love between fathers and sons—an old, powerful theme he treats with dignity and honesty."[188]

The Pacific Sun called the novel "a search . . . and strictly male." Regarding Phillip's falling to the floor when he recognized that Robert might be his son the reviewer said,

> This may be dramatic but Rev. Martin is no Victorian character needing smelling salts when his son appears out of the past. At this point Gaines starts to lose hold on the story. . . . The intensity of the first half of Gaines' book is not sustained. The ending is a masquerade of suffering and forgiveness.[189]

Gaines' friend Alvin Aubert wrote "Ernest Gaines is at his best in a meditative mode, in which there is a certain brooding over experience," as in *Miss Jane*.

> *In My Father's House* . . . might have been strengthened by a more meditative mode of narrative presentation, since Gaines seems to achieve his greatest narrative power in that mode. In compensation, however, stand the superb architectonic features of the work, involving the use of such elements as imagery, allusion, and temporal and spatial juxtaposition.[190]

[188]*Newsweek,* May 29, 1978, 85-86.

[189]Mill Valley, Calif., *Pacific Sun,* June 2-8, 1978.

[190]Alvin Aubert, "Self-Reintegration Through Self-Confrontation," *Callaloo #3,* I

* * *

The *San Francisco Examiner*, June 20, 1978, said that Gaines had begun three other books before *In My Father's House*, but that he had set them aside. He even began a ghost story, set in his own flat, but decided it was not right just at this time, that maybe he might come back to it if he lived to be eighty. Then he began a story titled "The Death of an Old Woman," but realized that it was too much like *Miss Jane*. In Gaines' papers an undated hand-written note, possibly a scheme for the overall structure of this story, read: "The opening scene of every part must definitely point toward the closing scene of that part and each part must point to the closing scene of the book—and that is her death."

* * *

A GATHERING OF OLD MEN

Gaines sixth published book, *A Gathering of Old Men,* is his third work to have been adapted as a movie. After the first edition by Knopf in 1983, others by Thorndike Press (1984), Random House (Vintage paperback, 1984), and a large print edition by Knopf (1984) followed. In October of 1983 for the Thorndike large-type print edition Gaines received $3,750, "payable on signing," with a promise of 10 pecent royalties for the next five years when the hardcover edition came out in February of 1984.

Gathering, frequently recommended for literature and social studies classes, was voted by the Young Adult Services Division of the American Association of Libraries as one of the "Best Books for Young Adults in 1983," selected from over 150 titles, confirmed by a letter from the executive director of YASD, May 1, 1984, which read:

(May, 1978), 132, 134-135.

> We congratulate you on this well-deserved honor, and would like to encourage you to continue to write books that will appeal to teenage readers—a group often neglected by authors and publishers. By highlighting books such as *A Gathering of Old Men*, we feel we are focusing attention on quality material of interest to teenagers.

A quite prestigious honor came to Gaines from the Commonwealth Club of California, which selected *Gathering* as the best work of fiction for 1983, the same honor he had received in 1971 for *Miss Jane*. He was asked by Michael Brassington, executive director of the Commonwealth Club to make an address when the award was presented. The entire speech/reading was printed in *The Commonwealth*, club bulletin, June 18, 1984. At this time *The Commonwealth* had worldwide circulation to over 200 libraries, and the Commonwealth Club had 14,000 members. It also gave weekly broadcasts and frequent programs on National Public Radio.

Gaines prefaced his reading from *Gathering* with a short introduction of appreciation, one initially longer, according to the draft of a speech found in his papers. It read:

> It is an honor, indeed, to be here today to stand where writers like John Steinbeck, William Saroyan, Wallace Stegner, C. S. Forester, and others whose names are as familiar stood long before I did—writers whose work I had to study in college. And one in particular, Wallace Stegner, who helped develop my craft as a writer while I was a student of his at Stanford.

* * *

Though not as arduous to complete as *In My Father's House* Gaines did rewrite *Gathering* at least three times. As early as November of 1978 he had planned for it to be told by one narrator, as opposed to the fifteen of the final version. He told an interviewer for *The Southwestern Review* :

> The narrator of the story is a Cajun. He's going to be the hero of the book. Now you know I'm saying something now that maybe I should't say, because I don't know how the book is going to turn out. I've written now about 20-30 pages of it. But he's the narrator. I'm going to have him say somewhere that he's a Cajun. He is the most *decent* person in the entire book, as of right now. I don't know what's going to happen later. . . . At the same time, there is going to be a Cajun and Black conflict. He is going to be the one to tell the story exactly as he saw it . . . a newspaper man from Baton Rouge. He is going to visit both black and white and try to see just what the problem is. It involves a murder in which a white man gets killed and the blacks are held responsible, a whole village, a whole quarters. He is engaged to the girl who owns or is one of the owners of the plantation. When this thing happens, she calls him on the telephone and says, 'Get over here right away. I'm going to need you. All hell's going to bust loose.' So he is going to tell the story of exactly what goes on. . . . I'm not trying to do that to pacify anybody. I try to write a novel as I feel a novel, and I could not have written this book . . . which I entitle *The Revenge of Old Men*, two or three years ago because I was not ready to write it. It was something that I thought about after I finished *In My Father's House*.[191]

* * *

In another interview ten years later regarding *Gathering* Gaines talked about the relative security of black women as opposed to black men. As mentioned in Part I, he had admitted to feeling more comfortable with the women who visited his Aunt Augusteen than with the men. He believed that black women themselves were probably more secure,

[191]"An Interview with Ernest J. Gaines," 37-38.

> because the women in their work did not come in conflict with the outer world as much as the men did in their work. The men competed with the white man and there could be conflicts there. The black man competed with the white man as sharecropper and when he went into town, whereas the black woman seldom competed. She was just a worker there . . . in the big house. . . in the field. She did not have to—as I have in *A Gathering of Old Men*—compete with racing to the derrick to unload the sugar cane or go into the cotton gin to unload the cotton. . . . I don't know how secure her position was. I guess she had to suffer and work.

He continues about the attitude of the men in *Gathering*:

> They've reached a point in old age at seventy years where it doesn't make any difference anymore. . . . So at seventy, seventy-five and eighty, they say, 'Well, what the hell am I going to live for? So I die today, what of that?' But they would not say that at fifty, not as a group. As one, yes, maybe, but they would never have come together like that.[192]

* * *

Dorothea Oppenheimer's correspondence to Gaines, as well as Gaines' notes to himself, indicate that *Gathering* was somewhat hardborn. Its earlier title was *Revenge of Old Men*. Gaines' notes to himself in his papers read: "Rewriting: There must be more dialogue between Candy and Chuck (Charles?). And between Miss Merle and Mathu. Much much much more here. Because Miss Merle knows Mathu—as a man —as Mapes sees him as a man. Remedy that."

Oppenheimer had questions and suggestions in great detail for Gaines' early drafts of *Gathering*. She was as critically constructive and gently patient as she had been with *In My*

[192]Wooton and Gaudet, "Talking with Ernest J. Gaines," 232-233.

Father's House. But, again, the slightest things had to be "right" in her own mind. The editing comments from her to Gaines found in his papers read in part: "Is it really necessary for . . ."; "Here are some things that bother me"; "What were you trying to say?"; "Perhaps you could . . . "; "You could make it a shorter novel. Especially the first 100 pages or so move too slowly after the exciting beginning"; "This ranges from superb to so-so"; "Something is wrong here"; "This is not a play. It has an unusual form. It is both a who-done-it and a sort of tragi-comedy-folk opera sort of thing combined. Quite unique. Keep it that way all the way through. Never mind if it's different. . . . This is yours. Don't change the character of the book two-thirds through"; "Re-section where Possum narrates"; "tends to kill tension . . . . gets too talky and stagey."

After the title became *A Gathering of Old Men*, Oppenheimer said, "I do think it needs to be a bit fuller and even longer. I'm afraid it can't be done quickly. It is so lovely, it deserves great care. You need to let it grow a bit more until you have it exactly or almost exactly the way you want it."

* * *

Mary T. Harper's essay "From Sons to Fathers: Ernest Gaines' *A Gathering of Old Men*" beautifully clarifies the action. It is quoted here with permission of the author and the *College Language Association Journal*. (Harper's page numbers are from the 1983 Knopf edition of the novel).

> As the novel [set in the 1970s] opens, Beau Boutan, a Cajun farmer and boss of leased Marshall Plantation land, has been killed in the Quarters in front of Mathu's cabin. Determined to protect Mathu, the eighty-plus-year-old black man who helped rear her, Candy Marshall, the plantation's young white owner, persistently declares that she has shot Beau and summons Mathu's peers so that together they can form a united front against both Sheriff Mapes and the expected retaliation from Fix Boutan, the Cajun family

patriarch.

Beau's death and Candy's summons set the stage for Gaines to present complex aspects of rural Louisiana life using a multiple first-person point of view. That is, the voices of eleven blacks and four whites reveal the ever-present social stratification and attitudes, especially the difficult acceptance of change. Certainly, these voices capture the richness—the humor and pathos—of folk life, centered on the introspection and actions of fifteen or more old men who answer Candy's summons, each bearing a twelve-gauge shotgun containing an empty number-five shell.

Candy Marshall's directive regarding the shotguns has several implications. First and most obviously, since Mathu has allegedly used such a weapon to kill Beau, pinpointing the actual killer will be difficult if everyone is similarly armed and admits guilt. Second but most important, an empty shotgun is a useless weapon just as the men possessing such weapons are harmless; hence, Candy becomes the protector. Regardless of her assertion that all black families have at sometime suffered Fix Boutan's wrath and that they now have an opportunity to confront both Fix and Mapes, this situation can be viewed as an example of the child-protector syndrome, with the thirty-year-old plantation mistress paternalistically and benevolently caring for her seventy-plus-year-old menchildren. Adamantly, Candy tells Myrtle Bouchard (Miss Merle), the white neighbor and family friend who also helped rear her: 'I will not let Mapes nor Fix harm my people. . . . I will protect my people. My daddy and all them before him did. . . .' Third, an empty gun is analogous to the lives these men have lived. Unlike the elderly Howard Mills of Gaines' *In My Father's House* who rejects his assigned social 'place,' or Ned Douglass, Jimmy Aaron, and Joe Pittman of *The Autobiography of Miss Jane Pittman* who face life fearlessly, realizing that they must risk death in order to live fully, these men—with the exception of Mathu—have faced life fearfully, refusing to take risks. Instead, they have become empty shells of men, regarded by whites such as Miss Merle as bedbugs—hidden, infesting insects—hidden in the tall weeds which presently mar the landscape of the Quarters.

Further, having seen how past fears have immobilized their elders, even the young blacks do not expect them to be other than elusive bedbugs. Gaines presents this negative image through the remarks of Fue, a somewhat effiminate but perceptive youth. After delivering Candy's message to seventy-two-year-old Robert L. Stevenson Banks (Chimley) and seventy-one-year-old Matthew Lincoln Brown (Mat), Fue sardonically reminds them of their alternatives: to act or 'go home, lock y'all doors and crawl under the bed like y'all used to.' (p. 28)

These words, demeaning in their implication of men crawling and hiding, serve as a catalyst, moving Mat and Chimley from idle reflection on their past to an assessment of their present and future. In spite of their visible but unspoken fears—for they know this is the first time a black man has actually killed a white man in their parish—they renew their dormant spiritual strength and rise to Fue's challenge. Gaines shows the beginning of this transformation in the men's conversation:

Mat: He works in mysterious ways, don't He?
Chimley: That's what they say. (p. 29)

Mat: 'Bout that bed. . . . I'm too old to go crawling under that bed. I just don't have the strength for it no more. It's too low, Chimley.
Chimley: Mine ain't no higher. (p. 31)

Mat: I have to go, Chimley. . . . This can be my last

chance.

Chimley: I'm going, too. (p. 32)

Determined, Mat returns home to prepare both himself and his wife Ella for this new action, an exchange Gaines again succinctly captures:

Ella: You old fool. Y'all gone crazy?

Mat: That's right. . . . Anytime we say we go'n stand up for something, they say we crazy. You right, we all crazy. (p. 36)

He describes feeling as if he'd 'been running up a . . . steep hill, and now . . . had reached the top.' (p. 36) With this description Gaines' images change from negative to positive—from crawling to running to ascending.

Reminding his wife of his years of unrewarding toil, of having cursed God and the world, of turning in frustration against her, of their son's death for lack of medical care because of his color, Mat restates his realization: 'He works in mysterious ways. . . . Give a old nigger like me one more chance to do something with his life.' (p. 38) Similarly, such introspection and reassessment seemingly characterize all the elders to whom Candy's summons has been directed, for Fue's comment to Mat and Chimley has symbolically echoed throughout the parish challenging the men to act, as Mathu had bid them do in years past.

One of these men, Cyril Robillard (Clatoo) becomes a leader, tending men's spirits rather than crops. Instead of peddling his produce, the gardener Clatoo now uses his truck to transport this aged, scared, but proud group. In effect, he nurtures a rebirth of spirit as he picks up elders throughout the parish. Perceiving their need for unity, their need for sustenance, he directs them to assemble in the black graveyard so that together they may walk to Mathu's cabin.

Clatoo intuitively understands the significance of

this gathering spot, for here past, present, and future merge. Each man searches among the unmarked graves for his family plot as if to draw strength from the ancestors, to recall how many of them had lived and suffered. This unkept burial ground, covered with weeds and grass like the landscape of the Quarters, also parallels the fear which stifles their lives. But among the weed-covered graves is life, for just as the abundant fruit from the nearby pecan tree covers the ground about them, providing actual physical nourishment, so too are their spirits nourished, even as they realize that their actions may result in their deaths. They are then ready to heed Clatoo's command as he tells them: 'Heads up and backs straight. We going in like soldiers, not like tramps.' (p. 49)

This transition from tramps to soldiers is a new experience, for much of their lives they have been trampled. Throughout the novel Gaines most poignantly allows the various voices to reiterate the many ills they have endured. He shows how their displacement, ill-treatment, and non-recognition have resulted in a loss of pride, moving them towards invisibility, with little regard for their past efforts and creativity. Corrine, for example, one of the elderly women gathered to lend support to the men, bemoans their losses as she speaks of the St. Charles River which they have been prohibited from using freely:

> 'That river . . . . Where the people went all these years. Where they fished, where they washed they clothes, where they was baptized. St. Charles River. Done gived us food, done cleaned us clothes, done cleaned us souls. St. Charles River—no more though. No more. They took it.' (p. 107)

Their restricted use of the river with its nurturing, renewing, life-sustaining powers then becomes symbolic of all they have lost—physically, spiritually, and psychologically.

Gaines' voices make it clear that until the elders accept the challenge to unite at Mathu's cabin, they have mainly been old people recalling past years, looking down the empty Quarters deserted by the young for greener fields, looking at the weeds wondering what has happened to the roses, the four-o'clocks—the flowers of nature and the flowers of humanity that once kept the community vibrant. Gaines depicts this resurging vibrancy as Clatoo's 'army' joins Mathu, Candy, and other men, women, and children already gathered. And though they at first have empty shotguns, like the soldiers Clatoo has commanded them to become, they indeed ready themselves for battle as they one by one load their guns with shells hidden behind Mathu's cabin.

Sheriff Mapes, however, remains unsuspecting. While he initially regards these elders as mere extensions of the Quarters' overgrown weeds, he does respect Mathu. He comments, '. . . I admire the nigger. He's a better man than most I've met, black or white.' (p. 74) Mathu, still tall and straight, described by Gaines as 'built like . . . [an] old post in the ground,' the only black ever to stand up to Fix Boutan, does not deny killing Beau. Looking Mapes directly in the eye, he tells him: 'A man got to do what he thinks is right, Sheriff. . . . That's what part him from a boy.' (p. 85)

"The actions of the men reflect Mathu's words, for in spite of the tactics Mapes and his deputy employ, the men remain united, each steadily admitting guilt, with the exception of Rev. Jamison. Like the preacher in the dentist's office in 'The Sky is Gray,' he prefers passive acceptance to direct action. Philosophically outside the group, he is willing to surrender Mathu, afraid of their taking a stand primarily because he fears his personal loss, his own further displacement. He and Lou Dimes, Candy's fiance, refer to the 'wall of old black men with shotguns' (p. 59) as fools. But unlike the others, Rev. Jamison cannot withstand the physical abuse and falls to the ground. Just as Rev. Phillip Martin of *In My Father's House* falls to the floor when confronted by his illegitimate son, so too is Jamison felled, not only by physical pain but also by fear and spiritual weakness.

Mapes' respect for the men grows, however, and as he converses with them, we see his awareness of changes wrought by time. The Lifesavers he continually sucks come to represent what he stands for—a saver of lives—for he, too, realizes that the vigilante tactics of Fix and his friends are outmoded. Accordingly, he disperses a deputy to dissuade the Boutan family from retaliating.

As the who-killed-Beau mystery unfolds, we learn that Charlie, the godson of Mathu, is the actual killer. Constantly humiliated by Beau's curses and threats to beat him no matter how diligently he works, he finally can take no more, and he and Beau fight in the canefield. Thinking he has killed Beau, he runs to his parrain or godfather, Mathu, who gives him a gun as Beau approaches on a tractor. Then fearing for his own life, he shoots Beau; and as Candy approaches, he asks Mathu to take the blame while he runs.

His running, however, takes a new turn. Just as the cemetery renews the elders' spirits, so does Charlie experience a spiritual conversion as he hides among the cane and in the swamps. It is as if the spirits of those before him stop his running away from life. Returning just before Mathu surrenders to the sheriff, he recounts his experience: '. . . I heard a voice calling my name. I laid there listening, listening, listening, but I didn't hear it no more. But I knowed that voice was calling me back here.'" (pp. 192-93) (Harper's footnote here reads in part: "Communing with ancestral and spiritual voices frequently recurs in black literature.") "No longer does he see himself as 'Big Charlie, nigger boy' (p. 189); after fifty years of running he becomes Mr. Biggs and demands that Mapes address him accordingly. In effect, Charlie's process of unnaming and renaming signifies his self-liberation, his re-creation and reformation.

Gaines also shows the effect of change on others in this Louisiana setting. Just as skin color and personal motivation have separated the black community in the past, so do the social codes separate the whites. For example, Gil Boutan, Beau's brother, tells Candy of her attitude toward Cajuns:

> 'You never liked any of us. Looking at us as if we're a breed below you. But we're not, Candy. We're all made of the same bone, the same blood, the same skin.
> Your father had a break, mine didn't, that's all.' (p. 122)

Ironically, these words also mirror black feelings.

Then there is Candy's Uncle Jack, aloof and nihilistic, uninterested in the present, one who closes his eyes to the controversy about him. Gaines allows Jacques Thibeaux, the white owner of the combination grocery and liquor store, to describe Jack Marshall:

> '. . . he live on the land 'cause they left it there, but he don't give a damn for it. . . . Get up and drink. Take a little nap, wake up and drink somemore. . . . don't give a damn for nothing. Women or nothing. . . . Politics or nothing. Nigger or nothing. . . . Things just too complicated. I reckon for people like him they have always been complicated—protecting name and land. . . . Feeling guilty about this, guilty about that. It wasn't his doing.He came here and found it, and they died and left it on him.' (p. 154)

Marshall finds his refuge in drink, and though he curses the system that forces him to uphold its tradition, ironically, he still does not fully perceive of blacks as people; to him they are still possessions. To Luke Will's statement that Beau had been killed by 'one of your niggers . . .' (p. 159), Jack replies: 'I have no niggers. . . . Never will have any niggers. They belong to her [Candy].' (p. 159)

Unlike her uncle, who abhors such possessions, Candy sees these blacks as extensions of the plantation's property and has difficulty understanding that she no longer owns them. Although Merle and Mathu have cooperatively reared her—'one to raise her as a lady, the other to make her understand the people who live on her place' (p. 197)—she fails to understand the changes that are continually occurring. For example, she becomes irate when the men exclude her from their conference inside Mathu's house, not understanding that their excluding, their refusal of her paternalistic protection, is another meaningful step towards their manhood.

Gaines also used Candy to illustrate the theme of racial interdependence when she tells Mathu that having known all of the Marshalls, he is the essence of the plantation's life. Recalling her forefathers' words, she tells him: 'They said if you went, it went, because we could not—it could not—not without you, Mathu' (p. 177). But Lou, her fiance, does not understand both the changes that have occurred and the transformation the men are presently undergoing. He tells Candy that Mathu doesn't need her protection, that he must live his life 'his own way.' (p. 184)

The author again illustrates the same interdependence theme with Gil 'Salt' Boutan, the Cajun LSU fullback, and Cal 'Pepper' Harrison, the black LSU halfback. Together, they are a formidable team, a pair on whom both blacks and whites are depending if LSU is to defeat 'Ole Miss' in the football game scheduled for the next day.

Although distraught over his brother's death, Gil tells his father that he refuses to participate in the vigilante acts for which his family is known and further tries to explain how such acts will invalidate his chances to become an all-American and how he and Cal work together on the football field. Hurt and unable to understand Gil's point about black-white cooperation nor his refusal to protect family honor, Fix concedes—but not Luke Will, a fellow Cajun determined to avenge Beau's death and to control blacks. Fix, however, now as old as the blacks awaiting his arrival, refuses to support Luke, asserting: 'I have no other cause to fight for. I'm too old for causes. Let Luke Will fight for causes. This is family' (p. 147). With such scenes, Gaines develops another dimension of Cajun life—their differing values and rationales for their actions, the conflicts they, too, experience as a result of change.

Thus, the confrontation between Cajun father and son culminates with Gil planning to play in the forthcoming game—a symbolic gesture to beat Luke Will and also symbolic of a changing South and hope for the future. Deputy Russell tells Gil: 'Sometimes you got to hurt something to help something. Sometimes you have to plow under one thing in order for something else to grow. . . . You can help this country tomorrow. You can help yourself' (p. 151).

However, when Mapes informs the elders that Fix is not coming, they believe him to be lying. But he is happy that violence has been avoided, and drawing an analogy using Gil and Cal, he reminds them of the effects of change:

> 'No, y'all wanted them to play together. . . . Y'all the one—you cut your own throats. You told God you wanted Salt and Pepper to get together and God did it for you. At the same time, you wanted God to keep Fix the way Fix was thirty years ago so one day you could get a chance to shoot him. Well, God couldn't do both.' (p. 171)

Mapes' joy is short-lived, for Luke Will and his friends, strengthened by liquor, arrive to avenge Beau's death.

> Once children but now men, the elders bravely confront the enemy, led by Charlie and Antoine Christophe (Dirty Red)—all having been reborn in the plantation's swamps, canefields, and the graveyard; having been infused with the spirit of their ancestors, a spirit that lives on just as the pecan tree continually bears fruit. Just before he stands and moves toward Luke, Charlie tells his friend Antoine that 'life's so sweet when you know you ain't no more coward.' (p. 208)
>
> Once again, Gaines effectively depicts the trauma of change. Both Luke and Charlie kill each other—one dying trying to prevent change, the other having been changed. Charlie's act then culminates the transformation of 'men-children' to fathers, symbolizes a recognition by all that thwarted dreams can become present realities, that resignation can be replaced by renewed involvement and commitment, and that one's mortality need not preclude one's becoming a 'new soldier' in the quest for manhood and dignity."[193]

* * *

Gaines is quoted as saying: "I know someone like Candy, and I know someone like Miss Merle who would fuss and cuss you out and then turn around and feed you." And as the book progressed, he said, "I can hear them [the old men] saying 'I hope the Lord give me a chance to stand up before I die.'" Then he said, "If the Lord doesn't do it, then I'm going to give you that chance when I write it."[194] The character of Mathu was obviously modeled after Walter Zeno ("Pete") to whom the book is dedicated.

[193]Harper's essay was published in the March, 1988 issue of *The College Language Association Journal*, Vol. 31, No. 3, pp. 299-308. Mary T. Harper is professor of Afro-American Literature at the University of North Carolina in Charlotte, N.C.

[194]*Peninsula Times Tribune*, January 24, 1984.

* * *

Gaines was at B. Dalton bookstore in Lafayette for an autographing on October 15, 1983, and in Palo Alto for the same on January 17, 1984, according to unnamed news items found in his papers.

A Gathering of Old Men has been aptly described by one critic as "an intricate tapestry being unraveled in an effort to show how it was woven in the first place." Reviews of the book have been plentiful and varied.

A part of the review in *The New Yorker*, October 24, 1983, which called it an "eloquent novel," was printed on the back cover of the Vintage Press edition, concerning itself mainly with the story rather than critiquing it. An excerpt of another review on the jacket read: "Gaines writes with humor, a strong sense of drama and a compassionate understanding of people who find themselves in opposing positions. . . . Not least, he knows how to tell a story, and *A Gathering of Old Men* is a good one."[195]

A review by Reynolds Price in *The New York Times Book Review*, October 30, 1983, said: "In a crucial way the . . . novel is distinctly different from the earlier work and not so immediately attractive," for the reader must adjust to its innovative method and conclusion or else be disappointed. Gaines' "narrative method has largely dictated his achievement. . . . Since the majority of Mr. Gaines' characters are oral narrators who, because of their rural Southern heritage, have adopted some elements of the entertainer's arsenal, they selectively exaggerate certain aspects of the larger story or omit others," particularly the landscape (plantation house, red-neck tavern, the Cajun home). Gaines must sacrifice these in order to shape the book as he chose to do.

> In *A Gathering of Old Men* Gaines has built, with large and single-minded skills, a dignified and calamitous and perhaps finally comic pageant to summarize the history of an enormous, long waste in

[195]*Los Angeles Herald Examiner,* nd.

> our past—the mindless, mutual hatred of white and black, which, he implies, may be slowly healing. . . . Mr. Gaines' unflagging commitment is to a breadth, even grandeur, of grasp and comprehensiveness.

Inevitably a few critics compared *Gathering* to works of Faulkner. *The London Observer*, February 5, 1984, said its style is "so Faulkneresque as to read almost like pastiche. . . . It's soft and simple where Faulkner, on the same subjects, is fierce and difficult." *The Christian Science Monitor*, December 2, 1983, said that Gaines transcended Faulkner and his own *Miss Jane* by depicting "stubborn men who create, in their twilight years, a sense of community." *In These Times*, February 15-21, 1984, called Gaines "something of a William Faulkner of the black South. . . . The Faulknerian voices that narrate his novels ring with the rhythms, humor and history of this rural area." Some of the speeches in the book were "of near-operatic power. . . . a riveting book, . . . powerful portrait" with "vivid fictional history . . . a superb example of realistic 'regional' writing."

Another reference to Faulkner was made by a critic for *The London Times Literary Supplement*, April 6, 1984, who pointed out that by reintroducing doubt as to the killer halfway through the story, an extra dramatic component is added. Gaines' historical examination and "choric self expression" sets him apart from Marquez [*Chronicle of a Death Foretold*] and Faulkner. Gaines is probably the most distinctive of Southern black novelists, having broken from the Faulknerian tradition. "For all the poignancy and horror of the situation *A Gathering of Old Men* is a fine comic novel." This critic said the final shoot-out scene is "too obviously parodic."

The London Daily Telegraph, February 10, 1984, considered its story "so tense, fresh and penetrating that we are kept on edge from beginning to end. . . . The tension is admirably maintained and in-depth characterization achieved by using various people as mouthpieces."

A somewhat sour reviewer in Dublin's *Irish Times*, February 18, 1984 said:

> His old men are so ennobled, so stately, they slow down the story until it has the pace of a Spanish pavane. He allows his ending to resemble one of those earnest liberal movies of the early Fifties when everyone was right except the villain. . . . Nevertheless, *A Gathering of Old Men* is worthy and colourful, giving a vivid idea of this patch of the Old South which is bayou country in Louisiana—I think.

The reviews continue.

> For anyone who finds irresistible the long shadow of the American deep South. . . Ernest J. Gaines, who sets his *A Gathering of Old Men* in contemporary, backwoods Louisiana is your man. . . . Concerned with old men, old scores, it is remarkably balanced, warm and living; place is as potent as it can be, the atmosphere crackles, the gathering is as astonishing as it is deadly serious.[196]

The New Republic reviewer called it an "eloquent new novel." Its setting in rural Louisiana is

> the profound stage for a remarkably original gathering of voices. Change is Gaines' obsessive theme. . . . As the novelist Alice Walker noted more than a decade ago, one of Gaines' strengths is that he knows his world and loves it so well he cannot bear to reduce even the ugliest, cruelest, and most loathsome redneck to a stereotype. . . . The novel . . . gathers voices, stories, and actions into a rhetorical whole that re-creates a vanished world of living people, horses, trees, flowers, and a river. Gaines' novel affirms the power of human voices to keep the past alive.[197]

[196]*The New Statesman,* February 10, 1984.

[197]*The New Republic,* December 26, 1983, 38.

A reviewer for *Saturday Review* saw Gaines as not only sympathetic to the old black men, but that he even made patriarch Boutan and Sheriff Mapes worthy of pity. "The story moves beyond sentimentality and becomes a celebration of old age" wherein "the black men find the strength to act and produce equality." Gaines "eloquently describes the strata of our supposedly classless society."[198]

The *Fort Worth Star-Telegram*, November 27, 1983, called *Gathering* a "meritorious work whose intensity never falters." Gaines' rich, quick-moving yarn, with carefully shaped dialect and phrasing, is filled with imagery. He is artist enough to know that effectiveness depends on an ironic and numerous handling of the theme. The book more resembles "a finely tuned murder mystery than a novel predicated on bigotry."

Sheriff Mapes is

> weary, confused and merely a shell of the man who once posed such a formidable threat to the black community's independent thinkers. Mapes has a bad stomach and can't rid himself of the thought that it is caused by guilt and not by gas. . . . Gaines' novel is a diamond rising from the bayou rough.

Louisiana Life, predicting that Gaines might be best remembered for this book, called it a finer work than *Miss Jane* for "the capturing of human motivations in fiction." Gaines does not try to make any of his characters 100 percent perfect, an "honesty that few novelists assume. . . . The results are warmth, humor, taut drama and good reading."[199]

The Scotsman, March 10, 1984, called it "a well-paced and fairly gripping drama, rich in the bayou atmosphere." However, Gaines' sympathies are "divided too obviously between meanest whites and noblest blacks, and he offers very

[198]*Saturday Review* (November/December, 1983), 61.

[199]*Louisiana Life* (January/February, 1984), 102-103.

little that's new. . . . Mapes and the Boutans are almost soap-figures and too many of the blacks are sentimentalised by their own eloquence."

The reviewer for *The Newcastle Herald*, October 16, 1983, wrote: "At first I felt that I'd begun reading this novel in its middle instead of at the beginning. But that's often the way with violence: it erupts suddenly and everyone's confused. . . . [It is] a hopeful novel."

An undated review from the Cleveland *Plain Dealer* said: "Not only nobility, not only friendship, motivate the old men, but also awareness of their shared guilt in their own subjection. . . . Each shame remembered strengthens an old man to claim responsibility for Boutan's death." Gaines carefully portrays the Cajuns' indecision as to which code to serve—family honor or family fame and business success? "The style is as spare as the furnishings in old Mathu's home."

The Chicago Tribune, October 30, 1983, called *Gathering* "a fine and elegant novel not to be missed. . . . In simple words, without preaching or moralizing, Gaines says it all." An undated item in *The Village Voice* called it "the best-written novel on Southern race relations in over a decade." *The Library Journal*, August, 1983 commented:

> After the first two pages this new novel . . . moves along as briskly as any reader would wish. . . . The narrative is passed like a baton from character to character as each successive chapter is related by a different person. Although the tone occasionally becomes a trifle exalted, the fictional world created in this book is mesmerizing.

Two reviews mentioned Gaines' structure in comparison to the oriental drama. *The Washington Post*, September 21, 1983, perceived it to be about a "weak, downtrodden people who seize upon the opportunity to stand up for themselves. Gaines was praised for skillfully combining humor, dramatic intensity, and a sincere understanding of people holding opposite views. He was clever enough to not make Mapes a stereotype of the white Southern sheriff. Rather, Mapes is sympathetic and wants to keep the peace. Gaines has made the most of melodrama. An unbiased frankness in drawing his characters rules out any dishonesty or posturing which might have been given them. Candy's depiction is especially subtle and amusing. Gaines' clever mixture of bravado and genuine bravery, as seen in the characters of the old black man, is but another example of his superb storytelling. (This same review was carried in the Los Angeles *Herald Examiner*, November 13, 1983.)

The second comparison, in the Chicago *Sunday Sun-Times*, September 11, 1983, said the title suggests a "ceremonial quality." Gaines uses the *Rashomon* technique wherein the same events are related by several characters, each with his own perspective. Gaines is concerned with the "nature of solidarity—how multiple acts of individual courage, linked by a common goal, are at the root of true liberation." He never "sacrifices the sheer art of story telling." Essentially *Gathering* is a fable, with the moral that manhood to both blacks and whites is denied in a racist society, and "rites of passage beyond that condition are harsh and perilous—but achievable."

The San Francisco Chronicle, October 23, 1983, called the book "a riveting, intricate and tension-filled novel that takes off like a shot and keeps your heart pounding right through the final climax." Originally Lou Dimes was to tell the story, but Gaines apparently decided it was everybody's story as the action progressed. Just as one character's thoughts are bursting, Gaines goes to another one—a technique he uses well because of his ear for rhythmic flow of language and his eye for authentic detail. "There are flaws—some voices don't work as well as others, a few characters are weighted in stereotype, the story bogs down in the middle—but it is definitely one of Gaines' best books to date, well worth careful attention of serious readers everywhere."

The Baton Rouge *Sunday Magazine*, October 30, 1983, carried a lengthy review of *Gathering* by Phil Ward, who recommended the book for general public reading. "Gaines' method is part oral history, part roving narration. . . . It is a murder mystery . . . a social commentary on racial relations. . . . The old times fade under the tractor and the land developers who have taken away all the good fishing holes." As each character is revealed so are his "private thoughts of the heart. The reader soon realizes that no one would tell this to Sheriff Mapes. Not before, not after. Are we, then, the authorities?" Gaines has used a blend of wisdom and art to achieve

> a force that takes the reader out of the ordinary world into a moment where the old black men, the young white woman, the racists, all become us, the reader. . . . It is refreshing to read a novel that is so well-written without resorting to gross violence, sex, or superficial 'modern' issues. . . .

Though *Freedomways* said the book had "a compelling pace that keeps one turning the pages," it was deemed unsatisfactory on two counts. Its theme was not adequately resolved because its conclusion does not "measure up to the tragi-comic predicament of the main characters—the old men." Too, the method of using first person from several viewpoints confines the story. Gaines' vision of the back-country characters is limited; depth and dramatic power are lacking. "I found myself yearning for more than a superficial rehash of black victimization at the familiar hands of racists." But it is "a delightful, very amusing novel that will leave the reader smiling and yet thoughtful . . . a refreshing departure from the gloomy, pessimistic, embittered moralizing of some recent novels." Gaines has depicted the blacks' ordeal "without sinking into despair."[200]

The reviews of *Gathering* have been endless. The more critical reviewers, however, have all seen it as a worthy book, despite saying Gaines' characters are stereotypes and that the first person technique of telling of the story is a bit cumbersome or confusing. The *Providence Sunday Journal* for November 20, 1983, called some of the chapters "as intimate as news passed between two pick-up trucks meeting on a back road," and the book "an American classic."

[200]Loyle Hairston, review in *Freedomways,* XXIV (Summer, 1984), 57-60.

David Bradley, New Orleans journalist, wrote:

> The plot of *A Gathering of Old Men* is difficult to summarize, not because the action is complicated—in fact, it is achingly simple—but because what is essentially a tightly constructed drama with a few minimal sets—with action confined, in classic style, to a single day—is based on a web of relationships between characters, tradition, the land and the changing Southern society, on a background as fecund, fetid and jungly as the Louisiana bayous themselves.

Bradley said that *Gathering* could have been written for the screen, but the depth of its vision "can be achieved only in a fine novel. Gaines has achieved it. And the novel is indeed fine."[201]

Another critic suggested that *Gathering* would "make a first-rate movie. . . . Gaines is particularly fine at getting inside the minds of little old ladies and red necks." The book is a "major dramatic achievement, buttressed by all the trappings of a first-rate thriller."[202]

* * *

A Gathering of Old Men was made into a first-rate movie, as mentioned in Part I. Again, Gaines was a non-interfering, unofficial consultant. The movie was filmed at Melodia Plantation, six miles south of Thibodaux, Louisiana, chosen particularly because there was not enough cane growing at the time in Gaines' native Pointe Coupée Parish, where the novel was set. Filmed as a two-hour CBS television dramatic special, it was aired on May 10, 1987. Curiously, it won no Emmys.

Most of the cast, was selected by the film's director, Volker Schlondorff, who gathered the "old men" from auditions in New York City, Los Angeles and New Orleans. Schlondorff,

[201]*Times-Picayune*, October 30, 1983.

[202]Undated item found in Gaines' papers; critic and publication unnamed.

described by journalist Ruth Laney as "a short, balding man with a cigar clenched in his teeth," had just finished directing the award-winning TV version of "Death of a Salesman." *Gathering*'s producer was Britisher Gower Frost, who had no problem identifying with Gaines' story. He told Laney:

> Someone gave me the book one weekend. I read it straight through on Sunday and phoned Gaines' agent on Monday. It came across very strongly as a film. Sometimes you read something you can just visualize as a film. I've read it a half-dozen times, and each time I see more in it. I like the way the story is told with overlaps through other people's eyes.[203]

Playwright Charles Fuller was commissioned to write the script. Fuller said to Laney, "Initially I wasn't sure if we could come up with a screenplay to do justice to Gaines' unique style of writing. But I think we've done that."

Most of the film's male actors were over fifty. In the starring roles were semi-retired Richard Widmark as Sheriff Mapes and Lou Gossett, Jr. as Mathu. Gossett is best known for his role in "An Officer and a Gentleman." Other of the film's "old men" were Joe Seneca, script and song writer; Sandman Sims, a professional tap dancer; Danny Barker, guitarist, songwriter and autobiographer; New York actors Julius Harris and Tiger Haynes; and Papa John Creach, a jazz/pop violinist. Actress Holly Hunter as Candy said to Laney, "I really feel close to this character."

Laney, an avid Gaines interviewer, gives a colorful report of happenings on the movie set, directions to which were marked by a

> hand-lettered cardboard sign stuck on a fence post which read 'Gathering.' . . . The center of activity when

[203]Ruth Laney, "*A Gathering of Old Men:* Another Ernest Gaines Work Converted to Film," Baton Rouge *Sunday Advocate Sunday Magazine,* April 26, 1987, p. 5.

> Gaines arrived on the set was a weatherbeaten shack with double front doors. An old car seat rested on the front porch alongside a wooden bench. Ancient shutters hung crookedly from the doors and windows. A brick chimney rose from the tin roof.
>
> Inside, the two-room shack contained torn linoleum, ripped wallpaper, an unmade iron bed, a battered chiffarobe and two ancient oscillating fans. A welter of cameras and lights filled every inch of available space. Crew members greeted Gaines with silent smiles as they squeezed around corners and tiptoed over wires. The climactic scene being shot was the gathering of old men inside Mathu's house.
>
> Gossett, hair and beard whitened for the role, wore beat-up pants and a faded pink longjohn shirt. Just moments before, he had greeted Gaines with a joke, laughing and talking easily. Then, with cameras rolling he exuded a quiet intensity as he addressed the old men. Clad in battered clothes, each holding a shotgun, the men listened to him solemnly. . . . Their eyes were fixed on Mathu as he told them that, because they had stood up to the white sheriff, 'This is the proudest day of my life.'

This was Gossett's big scene, which left some of the crew members misty-eyed.[204]

As stated in Part I, Gaines was honored in Lafayette at the film's premiere with an elegant reception. Despite his pleasure of the filming of three of his works, he still wished to continue writing novels rather than screen plays, grateful that television might possibly make *Gathering* as well known as *Miss Jane*.

* * *

[204]*Ibid.*

GAINES' NOVEL IN PROGRESS

Gaines has said several times that he hopes to write a panoramic novel someday—one requiring extensive research in the countries which have a large black population and one covering a longer period than did *Miss Jane*.

A Lesson Before Dying, now in progress, will not be that panoramic novel, however. Possibly forthcoming in 1990 it confines itself to an event in the 1940s. The story is of a convicted black man, age twenty-one, who is not guilty of the murder of which he has been accused. He is not an idiot, neither is he quite of average intelligence. As Gaines describes him, "This boy has no idea what size his clothes are. He doesn't know Christmas from Fourth of July. He doesn't know a thing about Keats . . . Byron . . . the Bill of rights." He certainly is not capable of planning a murder. He hardly realizes what has happened to him, and is in no way able to verbalize his feelings. An older lady, his grandmother or aunt, asks the local black male school teacher to talk with the young man while he is in jail before he goes to the electric chair.

In 1987 Gaines revealed something of the book's progress and problems to USL English professors Carl Wooton and Marcia Gaudet, authors of *Porch Talk*. The school teacher is reluctant to get involved.

> He says my job is to keep other kids from going that way. I want nothing to do with any of this. The crime is there. So this is what the story is about. I've reached the point now, chapter six, that he's deciding whether or not he will go to the courthouse and visit this guy. I have no idea what the guard's going to say. I know he [the teacher] has a little car, a '46 Ford he drives around. I don't know where he's going to get gas from, where he's going to fill the tank. I've no idea of anything, nothing. But the thing will move along, it will come out. These are the problems I'm having with this. And this is what I wanted to see, what a jail looks like, how does this guy sleep. Those are small details. I have a twofold problem

> here. Number one, I can create the jail. . . . But to get that character to tell that damned story in a way that makes it flow smoothly . . . I don't know what the teacher wants, you see. I know the teacher doesn't want to be there, but I know damned well he's going to be there. This is the kind of conflict I'm having there. I have to get that personality together and make him do what I want him to do without controlling him. . . . I've got him to a certain point where he's doing some of the things. . . . What is a man? This is one of the things that the teacher must find out. And another conflict is in the question, Why should we make this man a man if he's going to die tomorrow? The old lady says I want it done. . . . [To the sheriff] Your wife owes me something. I don't know what she has on the guy's wife. These are the little tricks. . . . I must find some reason to convince that sheriff through this old lady and the sheriff's wife that the teacher will come to the jail twice a week. . . . You pull all these little deals and you throw them all in there. It's just like making gumbo. If you mix it well, you don't notice the tricks.

At the time of this interview Gaines did not know whether his young man would actually be executed or not. But, he said, "I'm going to have him give a very good speech before it happens, if it happens. He has to stand up as a strong man and give this talk." Urged by another character of Gaines' invention, perhaps a newsman or the young man's defense attorney, the young man will eventually talk.

> He's going to stand up real tall—and tell him what he thinks manliness is and citizenship and what life is about and then he's just going to say, okay, let them do what they want. . . . The teacher is cynical—I mean he hates teaching—but hearing what he has done for this man who was condemned will bring something out of him. And he will go back to these small kids he has around him, and he will realize he has a duty to perform.

> And that duty is not to run away to the north as he wanted to, to get the hell away from all of these things. But, okay, I'll just give my life here and this is it. But this other person, this condemned man must be the one to convert him to this, to give his life. That's what the whole thing is about. He in one way makes the condemned boy, who is like an animal, a man, and the condemned one makes him a man so that he can go back to develop something. That's what this is about. If I ever get it done.[205]

* * *

He will "get it done." The University of Southwestern Louisiana is extremely proud that author Ernest J. Gaines is a member of its faculty. Using his writing and speaking talents with diligence, modesty and sincerity, without pretense, has made him an asset to the university and business communities and to the entire literary public. Within Gaines, the man, is a wealth of creativity and warmth which hopefully he will continue to share.

[205]Wooton and Gaudet, "Talking with Ernest J. Gaines," 241-243.

APPENDIX

1. The series of fourteen photos, taken between 1963-69, also includes "The Quarters" of River Lake Plantation; the "Miss Jane Pittman tree" in Lakeland; the church-school; Gaines with a group on the cabin porch; two elderly ladies whom Gaines talked with for help on *The Autobiography of Miss Jane Pittman*; the plantation store where the family bought everything; the road to town (New Roads); a night club "where we drank, danced, fought and died;" the plantation cemetery where Gaines' people are buried; and a squatting black man, Walter Zeno, drinking from a glass. Gaines says Zeno was also known as "Salute, Rider, Pete, and a few other names." Zeno, who lived to be ninety, had known five generations of Gaines' family and "everything that had happened on that plantation for the last sixty years." *A Gathering of Old Men* was dedicated to him.

These photos, titled "Home," were published as a photo-essay, along with additional essays solicited by *Callaloo #3,* I (May, 1978).

2. Chris (John Christopher) Brookhouse (b. 1938) is an English professor at the University of North Carolina in Chapel Hill. It was he who suggested to Joe Ritok that Gaines might speak for the above mentioned engagement in 1969, which Gaines claimed to be his second of such nature. In 1968 Brookhouse re-edited, in meticulous scholarly fashion, *Sir Amadace* and *The Avowing of Arthur*, two romances from the Ireland manuscript. In 1977, with Howard Harper, he co-authored an English text, *An Introduction to Film Criticism*, and the following year his bizarre novel, *Wintermute*, was published. It deals with the reunion of a college class of 1950. The group meets at Wintermute, estate of the most successful class member. A review in *Publishers Weekly* for January 16, 1978, said: "There is enough variety in this book to appeal to most any reader—murder, drugs, miscegenation and a broad spectrum of sex, yet it is all presented as necessary to the story, not as gimmickry."

Ken Kesey may be remembered not only for his novel *One Flew Over the Cuckoo's Nest* but for his unusual lifestyle. One Kesey biographer said that as a Hippie he "assumed the role of a religious leader to a growing cult." In the 1960s Kesey volunteered at Veterans Hospital in Menlo Park, California, as a guinea pig for experimental drugs, and consequently got hooked on them. He spawned several misbegotten children and escaped to Mexico after numerous scrapes with the law. He continues to write.

Quite the opposite personality, Kentuckian Wendell Berry has been called a "guru" of the environmental movement. Berry is a widely published and prolific poet, novelist, essayist and agriculturalist, best known for *The Unsettling of America*, *The Country of Marriage*, and *Sayings and Doings*. Berry has kept in touch with Gaines from his Kentucky acreage, according to letters found in Gaines' papers.

Chilean born Luis Harss, novelist, journalist, lecturer, and translator, received a Master's degree from Stanford in 1959. He was a Senior Fellow at St. Anthony's College in Oxford, England, and a lecturer in Spanish at West Virginia University. Two of his novels, *The Blind* and *The Little Men*, published in the mid-1960s, were followed by several works in Spanish, and another novel, *Sor Juana's Dream* (English translation), in 1987.

Though Russian-born Jewish Tillie Olsen (b. 1913) preceded Gaines by two years as a creative writing fellow at Stanford, they were professionally acquainted from the late 1950s. Due to family commitments with four daughters, Olsen was a late bloomer, remaining unpublished until she reached her late forties. She has been described as a feminist and a "working class" writer. Before her marriage to Jack Olsen in 1936, she held many odd jobs, always with a sympathetic ear for injustice to her fellow workers. She was twice jailed for her political activism.

It would appear that Gaines and Olsen are opposites. Gaines had no immediate family to consider. He always chose to put his writing first. Olsen could not allow herself a choice. Her family came first. But they both write clearly and explicitly about what they know best, their families—whether black or

Jewish—in various situations.

Olsen's story, "Tell Me a Riddle," which won the O. Henry Award for the best short story of 1961, was first published in *Stanford Short Stories, 1960*, along with Gaines' "Mary Louise" and Berry's "Harvest" in the same issue. In the preface co-editor Scowcroft of this Stanford series spoke of Berry and Olsen as "Egyptian slaves lashed into subjection to a concept: one wrong stone and they find themselves with a cube instead of a pyramid."

A rather poignant letter from Olsen, dated October 15, 1968, from Laguna Street in San Francisco, was found in Gaines' papers. In part it read: "Ernie please won't you call and tell me about your book; I think you went east, for the phone rings into unyieldingness. Painful where and how we did our time when we did see each other. . . . I will probably go away again after the first of the year for solitude for work; let's meet before. Late night or dawn risings, I look up those few blocks to where you have worked on, all these years—and it helps." The "book" Olsen asked about could have been either *Bloodline* or *Miss Jane Pittman*.

Olsen is a fascinating writer, whose emphasis is on the "literary tragedy of silenced writers," those either not paid attention to, or those involved with family or other responsibilities, who must put their writing careers second. She has received grants and fellowships from Radcliffe Institute; the National Endowment for the Arts (in 1968, one year after Gaines received the same); and the MacDowell Colony. She has taught at Amherst, the University of Massachusetts and Stanford. In 1973 she was writer in residence at MIT.

"Tell Me a Riddle" was included in Olsen's volume of four short stories by that title (1961) which had seen thirteen reprintings by 1981. Also to her credit are her edited compilations of selected poetry and essays *Silences* (1978) and *Mother to Daughter, Daughter to Mother* (1984). A novel, *Yonnondio: From the Thirties* (1974) was reprinted in 1979. In May of 1987 an essay by Olsen and her daughter, Julie, was published along with a photographic exploration of mother-daughter relationships, titled "Mothers and Daughters: That Special Quality." The piece, showing the work of many photographers, was exhibited at the Burden Gallery in New York City in May, 1987.

3. Fuller's letter to Gaines, November 8, 1967:

> I do not feel I can find words adequate to state my recommendation of Ernest J. Gaines for a Guggenheim grant. It is my opinion that this young novelist is one of the most promising writers of this generation—of any race or color—a fact (or, rather, opinion) which I have stated in print in the enclosed review of his new novel, *Of Love and Dust*.
>
> I have followed very closely Mr. Gaines' literary career since the publication in the magazine I edit (NEGRO DIGEST) of one of his early short stories, "The Sky is Gray." I felt that his first novel, *Catherine Carmier* was deserving of far more attention than it received in the literary world.
>
> It seems to me that Mr. Gaines is eminently qualified to undertake the research and the subsequent literary task described in his 'project' statement. The author possesses that rare and necessary quality in the serious and significant writer which compels him to seek out the *humanity* and the *truth* about the people about whom he writes; he does not settle for the facile and the surface.
>
> Also, it seems to me that the particular areas and period which Mr. Gaines wishes to investigate are rich in literary possibilities. A skillful and honest writer can make a valuable contribution to the nation's literature and to its understanding of itself by exploring with fresh vision the history of the post-Revolutionary period in the Louisiana Territory.
>
> I would like to add that, in sticking to the area of his own beginnings, in exploring his own past, that life and world which are closest to him, Mr. Gaines is following the very wise advice of William Faulkner who thought a writer could not do better than to deal in depth with the 'postage stamp' of land that the writer knew best.

> It is with enthusiasm that I recommend Ernest J. Gaines. I feel the Guggenheim Memorial Foundation would have reason, in the future, to be pleased that it aided this young writer.

4. King's success came gradually. For some years he and his style took a back seat to rock and roll, until the late 60s when the blues-and-rhythm style was again in demand. Since then he has become internationally famous. He has received the Grammy Award twice, and honorary doctorates from Yale and the University of California in Berkeley. He and "Lucille," his beloved guitar, play lowdown, irresistibly earthy, solid beat blues, "the only kind of music Lucille can play," King says. King has been called "The Chairman of the Board of the Blues," "The Man," "King of the Blues," and "Blues Boy," from which he adopted the initials "B. B."

Lester "Prez" Young, the son of a band leader, was born in 1909 in Woodville, Mississippi. He received early musical training, first playing drums, then alto sax with his fathers' band. He soon switched to tenor sax and made a name for himself, travelling with such high cotton groups as Count Basie, Fletcher Henderson, and King Oliver. After WW II he made Los Angeles his home, but continued to tour with bands.

As early as 1937 Young recorded with Holiday (1915-59), albums which won for her international recognition. Young's laid-back, slightly breathy interpretations provided perfect background and ensemble for Holiday's ballad styling. His swinging style, which strongly influenced contemporary tenor sax players, was reserved, though lyrical and tender. It was, however, considered controversial by some jazz analysts, as having derived more from the styles of two white saxophonists, Jimmy Dorsey and Frankie Trumbauer, than from Colman Hawkins' rich, muscular jazz.

"Prez," a light black and a pacifist, was taunted and miserable during his stint in the US military service, from which he was dishonorably discharged for abusing alcohol and drugs. His death, attributed to heart failure, was actually caused by internal bleeding and malnutrition brought on by alcoholism. "Prez" and "Lady Day" first met in 1934, and by

1937 a strong friendship had developed. During a few lean months Prez of necessity moved in with her and her mother. Their recordings were under auspices of Norman Grantz' "Jazz at the Philharmonic" enterprise in Los Angeles in the 40s and 50s. Grantz always provided top backup groups for Holiday.

Holiday's father, Clarence Holiday, was a professional jazzman, whose death, precipitated by racial violence, deeply affected the young Billie for the remainder of her life. She began singing in Harlem night spots at age fifteen. A tall, slender beauty, she exuded an inimitable mystique while singing her best tunes, "Good Morning Heartache," "Strange Fruit," "Fine and Mellow," and "Lover Man." Though she rose to fame touring with not only her own band, "Billie Holiday and Her Orchestra," but with many of the other bigger bands of the 40s and 50s, her personal life was ravaged both physically and emotionally by drug dependency and unfortunate love affairs. She died, exhausted from the pressure of these burdens, at age forty-four in 1959, the same year of Young's death. She attended Young's funeral just a few months before her own demise.

Despite the envious Ethel Waters' barb, "She [Holiday] sang as if her shoes were too tight," Holiday's unique talent still commands respect. Scholar Eileen Southern has written: "Holiday was regarded as the finest jazz singer of her time; her voice was small but deeply expressive, whether projecting despair, bitterness, or humor. She consciously used her voice as if it were a horn, phrasing and improvising with delicate nuance."[1]

5. Alice Walker (b. 1944) was one of several children of a Georgia sharecropper. Her early world, like Gaines', was one of neck bones and fatback, though her talent was discovered earlier and more actively promoted than was Gaines'. Walker's brother accidentally shot her in the eye with a BB gun when she was four years old. In 1961, of college age, she entered Spelman College in Atlanta on a scholarship for disabled students. In 1964 she accepted a scholarship to Sarah Lawrence,

[1]*Biographical Dictionary of Afro-American and African Musicians,* p. 186.

traveled to Africa, and began to write. Other study grants were given her by Radcliffe Institute and Harvard University. In the mid-60s she became interested in civil rights issues, married civil rights lawyer Melvyn Leventhal, and had a daughter.

She and Leventhal divorced in 1978 and she has since moved from New York back to San Francisco. *The Color Purple*, Pulitzer Prize winner for 1983, is evidence enough that she writes about what she knows best. Walker was the third black Pulitzer Prize winner, preceded by Gwendolyn Brooks (a collection, *Annie Allen* 1950) and James McPherson (a short story, *Elbow-Room*, 1978).

BIBLIOGRAPHY

Most of the material in this book has been compiled from Gaines' file of personal papers and manuscipts which he donated to Dupré Library at the University of Southwestern Louisiana in Lafayette. Newspaper items, Gaines' speeches, manuscripts and correspondence cited in the text are not included as a part of this bibliography, and neither are general reference works, brochures and other publicity materials which supplied peripheral information.

Books

Botkin, B. A., ed. *Lay My Burden Down*. Chicago: University of Chicago Press, 1945.

Bruck, Peter, and Karrer, Wolfgang, eds. *The Afro-American Novel Since 1960*. Amsterdam: B. R. Gruner Publishing Co., 1982.

Bruck, Peter, ed. *The Black American Short Story in the 20th Century*. Amsterdam: B. R. Gruner Publishing Co., 1977.

Colby, Vineta, ed. *World Authors 1975-1980*. New York: H. H. Wilson Co., 1985.

Durham, Frank. *Studies in Cane*. Columbus, Ohio: Charles E. Merrill Publishing Co., 1971.

Emanuel, James A., and Gross, Theodore L., eds. *Dark Symphony*. New York: The Free Press, 1968.

Ellison, Ralph. *The Invisible Man*. New York: Random House, 1952.

Fletcher, Mary Dell, ed. *A Century of the Short Story in Louisiana*. Lafayette, La.: Center for Louisiana Studies, USL, 1985.

Gaines, Ernest J. *The Autobiography of Miss Jane Pittman*. 1971, reprint edition, New York: Bantam Books, 1972.

______. *Bloodline.* 1968, reprint edition, New York: W. W. Norton & Company, Inc., 1976.

______. *Catherine Carmier.* 1964, reprint edition, San Francisco: North Point Press, 1981.

______. *A Gathering of Old Men.* 1983, reprint edition, New York: Vintage Books, 1984.

______. *In My Father's House.* 1978, reprint edition, New York: W. W. Norton & Company, 1983.

______. *Of Love and Dust.* 1967, reprint edition, New York: W. W. Norton & Company, 1979.

Littlejohn, David. *Black on White: A Critical Survey of Writing by American Negroes.* New York: Viking, 1966.

O'Brien, John, ed. *Interviews with Black Writers.* New York: Liveright, 1973.

Olsen, Tillie. *Tell Me a Riddle.* New York: Dell Publishing Co., Inc., 1981.

______. *Yonnondio, From the Thirties.* New York: Dell Publishing Co., Inc., 1979.

Porter, Lewis. *Lester Young.* Boston: Twayne Publishers, 1985.

Rowell, Charles H., ed. *Ernest J. Gaines: A Special Issue.* Lexington: University of Kentucky Press, 1978.

Schrafnagel, Noel. *From Apology to Protest: The Black American Novel.* Deland, Fla.: Everett/Edwards, Inc., 1973.

Southern, Eileen. *The Biographical Dictionary of Afro-American and African Musicians.* Westport, Conn.: Greenwood Press, 1982.

Stegner, Wallace, and Scowcroft, Richard, eds. *Stanford Short*

Stories, 1960. Stanford, Calif.: Stanford University Press, 1960.

Tooker, Dan, and Hofheins, Roger. *Fiction! Interviews with Northern California Novelists.* New York: Harcourt Brace Jovanovich, Inc./William Kaufman, Inc., 1976.

Toomer, Jean. *Cane.* New York: W. W. Norton & Company, Inc., 1975 (reprint from 1923 edition by Liveright).

Vinson, James, ed. *Contemporary Novelists.* New York: St. Martin's Press, 1972.

Walker, Alice. *The Color Purple.* New York: Harcourt Brace Jovanovich, 1982.

Journals and Periodicals

Andrews, William L. "We Ain't Going Back There: The Idea of Progress in *The Autobiography of Miss Jane Pittman.*" *Black American Literature Forum*, XI (1977), 146-149.

Aubert, Alvin. "Ernest J. Gaines' Truly Tragic Mulatto." *Callaloo*, I (1978), 68-75.

Beauford, Fred. "A Conversation with Ernest J. Gaines." *Black Creation*, IV (1972), 16-18.

Beckhman, Barry. "Jane Pittman and Oral Tradition." *Ernest J. Gaines: A Special Issue.* Lexington: University of Kentucky Press, 1978, 102-109.

Berry, Jason. "Jazz Literature." *Southern Exposure*, VI (1978), 40-49.

Billingsley, Ronald G. "Forging New Definitions: The Burden of the Hero in Modern American Literature." *Obsidian*, I (1975), 5-21.

"Books Noted." *Negro Digest*, XIV (1965), 78-79.

Bright, Daniel. "An Emmy Award for Cicely?" *Sepia*, (April, 1974), 16-20.

Bryant, Jerry H. "From Death to Life: the Fiction of Ernest J. Gaines." *The Iowa Review*, III (1972), 106-120.

Burke, William. "*Bloodline*: A Man's Black South." *College Language Association Journal*, XIX (1976), 545-558.

Callahan, John. "Image-Making: Tradition and the Two Versions of *The Autobiography of Miss Jane Pittman*." *The Chicago Review*, XXIX (Autumn, 1977), 50-62.

Carter, Tom. "Ernest Gaines." *Essence,* (July, 1975), 52-53, 71-72.

Chronicle (Louisiana Endowment for the Humanities), XI (1989), 1-7.

Chronicle (Louisiana Endowment for the Humanities), XI (1990), 1.

"Cicely Tyson: A Versatile Actress," *Ebony,* (August, 1977), 136.

"CLA Journal Receives One of Five Awards from Black Academy of Arts and Letters." *College Language Association Journal*, XVI (1972), 256-259.

Cooke, Jack. "Reviews in Print." *Jazz Monthly,* (July, 1973), 18.

Crist, Judith. "To Set the Tube Aglow." *New York*, January 28, 1974, n. p.

Davis, Thadious M. "Headlands and Quarters: Louisiana in *Catherine Carmier*." *Callaloo*, XXI (1984), 1-13.

Desruisseaux, Paul. "The Making of Ernest Gaines." *Black Times,* IV (September, 1974), 10.

Duncan, Todd. "Scene and Life Cycle in Ernest Gaines'

Bloodline." *Callaloo*, I (1978), 88-100.

Fabre, Michel. "Bayonne or the Yoknapatawpha of Ernest Gaines" (trans. from French by Melvin Dixon and Didier Malaquin). *Ernest Gaines: A Special Issue*. Lexington: University of Kentucky, 1978, 111-112.

Fitzgerald, Gregory. "An Interview: Ernest J. Gaines." *New Orleans Review*, I (1969), 331-335.

Fuller, Hoyt W. "Contemporary Negro Fiction." *Southwest Review*, L (1965), 321-335.

______. "Black Writers' Views on Literary Lions and Values." *Negro Digest*, XVII (1968), 27.

Gaines, Ernest J. "The Autobiography of Mister Ernest Gaines." *Cultural Vistas*, I (Spring, 1990), 4-6, 15-16.

______. "The Boy in the Double-Breasted Suit." *Transfer*, 1957 (San Francisco State College literary journal), 2-9.

______. "Chapter One of *The House and the Field*. *The Iowa Review*, III (1972), 121-125.

______. "The Hunter." *Black World,* (February, 1971), 53-57.

______. "Mary Louise." *Stanford Short Stories, 1960*. Stanford, Calif.: Stanford University Press, 1960, 29-42.

______. "My Grandpa and the Haint." *New Mexico Quarterly*, XXXVI (1966), 149-160.

______. "The Turtles." *Transfer,* 1956 (San Francisco State College literary journal), 1-9.

Gayle, Addison, Jr. "Strangers in a Strange Land." *Southern Exposure*, III (1975), 4-7.

Harper, Mary T. "From Sons to Fathers: Ernest Gaines' *A Gathering of Old Men*. *The College Language Association Journal*, XXXI (1988), 299-308.

Hicks, Jack. "To Make These Bones Live: History and Community in Ernest Gaines's Fiction." *Black American Literature Forum*, XI (1977), 9-19.

Ingram, Forrest, and Steinberg, Barbara. "On the Verge, An Interview with Ernest J. Gaines." *New Orleans Review*, III (1973), 339-344.

"An Interview with Ernest J. Gaines, September 22, 1978." *The Southwestern Review*, IV (1979), 33-50.

Kael, Pauline. "The Current Cinema: Cicely Tyson Goes to the Fountain." *The New Yorker*, January 28, 1974, 73-75.

Karman, Mal. "Why John Korty Doesn't Have Stars in His Eyes." *San Francisco,* (February, 1977), 54-60.

Kent, George E. "Struggle for Image: Selected Books by or About Blacks During 1971." *Phylon*, XXXII (1972), 307-308.

Knopf-Williams, Leigh. "Author Ernest Gaines Selected 1989 Humanist of the Year." *Chronicle* (Louisiana Endowment for the Humanities), XI (1989), 1, 7.

Laney, Ruth. "A Conversation with Ernest Gaines." *The Southern Review*, X (1974), 1-14.

_____. "Echoes of a Southern Childhood." *50 Plus,* (July, 1985), 69-71.

Peden, William. "The Black Explosion." *Studies in Short Fiction*, XII (1975), 231-241.

Reid, David, and Contis, Alexander. "Searching for Miss Jane." *New Wings*, I (1980), 11, 20.

Rowell, Charles H. "This Louisina thing That Drives Me." *Callaloo #3.* Lexington: University of Kentucky Press, 1978, 39-51.

Shelton, Frank W. "Ambiguous Manhood in Ernest J. Gaines'

Bloodline." *College Language Association Journal*, XIX (1975), 200-209.

Stoelting, Winifred L. "Human Dignity and Pride in the Novels of Ernest Gaines." *College Language Association Journal*, XIV (1971), 340-358.

Turner, Darwin T. "Black Fiction: History and Myth." *Studies in American Fiction*. Boston: Northeastern University, V (1977), 120-128.

Wideman, John. "*Of Love and Dust:* A Reconsideration." *Ernest J. Gaines: A Special Issue*. Lexington: University of Kentucky Press, 1978, 76-84.

Wooton, Carl, and Gaudet, Marcia. "Talking With Ernest J. Gaines." *Callaloo*, XI (1988), 229-243.

Newspaper Articles

Arkansas Gazette, Little Rock, April 24, 1977.

Baton Rouge, La., *Gris-Gris*, October 10-13, 1973.

Baton Rouge, La., *Sunday Advocate*, April 17, 1977.

Baton Rouge, La., *Sunday Magazine*, April 26, 1987.

Birmingham, England, *Post,* February 17, 1973.

Dublin *Hibernia*, February 16, 1973.

London *Financial Times*, February 13, 1973.

Los Angeles Times, February 9, 1975.

Glasgow Herald, February, 10, 1973.

The Greenville, N. C., *Reflector*, January 27, 1974.

Hollywood Reporter, October 16, 1963.

Indianapolis News, February 27, 1982.

Lafayette, La., *Daily Advertiser*, September 25, 1983.

Lafayette, La., *Times of Acadiana*, March 25, 1982.

The London *Observer*, February 4, 1973.

London Times Book Review, February 10, 1973.

Mill Valley, Calif., *Pacific Sun*, November 7, 1974.

Morning Advocate, Baton Rouge, February 2, 1974; February 22, 1974; September 22, 1981; December 4, 1988.

Morning Advocate Magazine, Baton Rouge, October 30, 1983.

The London *New Statesman*, February 9, 1973.

New York Times, June ll, 1978.

Norwich, Norfolk, England, *Eastern Daily Press*, n. d.

Palo Alto, Calif., *Peninsula Times Tribune*, January 24, 1984.

San Francisco Chronicle, April 29, 1976.

San Francisco Examiner, December 31, 1973.

San Jose Mercury, September 1, 1968.

Smith's Trade News, London, January, 1973.

South Wales Echo, n.d.

Washington Post, n. d.

Yorkshire Post, n. d.

Book Reviews

Best Sellers, August 5, 1968.

Boston Sunday Globe, November 3, 1968.

The Charlotte, N. C., *Observer*, September 8, 1968.

Freedomways, Third Quarter, 1968, 262-264; Summer, 1984, 57-60.

The Journal, Winston-Salem, N. C., October 6, 1968.

Kannapolis, N. C., *Daily Independent*, September 8, 1968.

The Kirkus Service, July, 1968.

The Liberator, London, December, 1969.

Library Journal, July, 1968.

Los Angeles Herald Examiner, n. d.

Louisiana Life, January/February, 1984, 102-103.

Mill Valley, Calif., *Pacific Sun*, June 2-8, 1978.

The Natchitoches, La., *Times*, n. d.

The Nation, December 16, 1978, 678.

The New Orleans Review, incomplete date for 1968.

New Orleans, La., *Times-Picayune*, October 30, 1983.

The New Republic, December 26, 1983, 38.

The New Statesman, London, February 10, 1984.

New York, January 28, 1974, n. p.

New York Times, January 31, 1974.

New York Times Book Review, August 10, 1975; June 11, 1978.

Newsweek, May 29, 1978, 85-86.

The Nickel Review, October 23, 1968.

Publisher's Weekly, June 3, 1968.

St. Louis Dispatch, August 11, 1968.

St. Paul Sun, October 13, 1968.

Saturday Review, November/December, 1983, 61.

Citations from Gaines' Papers

"Ernest J. Gaines—Change, Growth and History," an anonymous essay.

Gaines' speech at Southern University, Baton Rouge, La., 1971.

Interview with Ed Levitt of the *Oakland Tribune*, n. d. except for 1977.

Item from *The Guardian*, undated except for 1975.

Letter from Robert Chrisman to Gaines, October 3, 1974.

Letter from William Decker to Gaines, February 1, 1974.

Mills, Lynn M., Discussion guide of film *Miss Jane Pittman*, n. d.

White, Doris. "A Stain in the Blood: the Ominous Presence in the Society of *Catherine Carmier*." Manuscript in Dupré Library, Louisiana Room, University of Southwestern Louisiana.

Correspondence

Berry, Jason, to Anne K. Simpson, November 24, 1989.

Decker, William, to Anne K. Simpson, April 3, 1990.

Packer, Nancy, to Anne K. Simpson, January 21, 1990.

San Francisco Public Library, Newspaper Department to Anne K. Simpson, January 26, 1990.

Tenney, Thomas A., to Anne K. Simpson, February 9, 1990.

Index

OTHER CENTER PUBLICATIONS OF INTEREST

Mary Dell Fletcher, ed., *A Century of the Short Story in Louisiana.* 1985, 371 pp. Cloth, $10.00.

Charles Edwards O'Neill, *Viel: Louisiana's Firstborn Author with* Evandre, *the First Literary Creation of a Native of the Mississippi Valley.* 1991, 92 pp. Cloth, $10.00.

Sidonie de la Houssaye, *Pouponne and Balthazar/Pouponne et Balthazar.* Translated by J. John Perret. Critical (French) edition by May Waggoner. 1983, 2 vols. Cloth, $10.00.

Bernardine B. Proctor, *Black Art in Louisiana.* 1989, 259 pp. Paper, $25.00.

Anne Butler and C. Murray Henderson, *Angola: Louisiana State Penitentiary: A Half-Century of Rage and Reform.* 1990, 180 pp. Cloth, $19.95.

Barry Jean Ancelet. *Cajun Music: Its Origins and Development.* 1989, 58 pp. Paper, $5.00.

Ron Bodin, *Voodoo, Past and Present.* 1990, 101 pp. $5.00.

Thomas J. Carruth, *Tales of Old Louisiana.* Reprint, 1990, 161 pp. Paper, $10.00.

Austin Sonnier, Jr., *Second Linin': Jazzmen of SOuthwest Louisiana, 1900-1950.* 1989, 62 pp. Paper, $5.00.

Ethelyn Orso, *The St. Joseph Altar Traditions of South Louisiana.* 1990, 55 pp. Paper, $5.00.

Prices include shipping and postage by U.S. postal system
mail orders to:
The Center for Louisiana Studies
P.O. Box 40831
University of Southwestern Louisiana
Lafayette, LA 70504-0831